CANNABIS capital

HOW TO GET YOUR BUSINESS FUNDED IN THE CANNABIS ECONOMY

ROSS O'BRIEN
FOUNDER OF BONAVENTURE EQUITY, LLC

Entrepreneur Press®

Entrepreneur Press, Publisher
Cover Design: Andrew Welyczko
Production and Composition: Eliot House Productions

Library of Congress Cataloging-in-Publication Data
LCCN link: https://lccn.loc.gov/2019041063

Printed in the United States of America

24 23 22 21 20 10 9 8 7 6 5 4 3 2 1

CONTENTS

ACKNOWLEDGMENTS

There are countless people who have influenced me over my career and have been instrumental as I pursued a very nontraditional career path. I have been fortunate to receive mentorship and guidance, be challenged by, and receive help from an extraordinary group of friends, family, and contacts since I entered the workforce at 14 and started my first business at 19. I have also discovered the hard way that not everyone has good intentions. But what has become clear is that you simply cannot be successful without a support system of great people who will be instrumental in shepherding you through the difficult times, of which there will be many if you also choose to be an entrepreneur.

No one in my life bas been more important and supportive on this journey than my parents. They are not entrepreneurs per se and certainly don't share my tolerance for risk and uncertainty. Time after time, I found myself going to the "Bank of Mum and Dad" to make a withdrawal for my next pursuit. This book would not be possible without their unwavering support. Without them, none of this would be possible. Many times during the sleepless nights of writing this book and building a successful business I would use them as my compass to ensure that I was always trying to be the best I can be and bring value to others.

This book started as a finance book. But it really became about entrepreneurship and how starting and running a private company intersects with finance. I consider myself fortunate to have years upon years of failures, all of which have contributed to the experiences that this book is founded on. And without the unwavering support of my Mum and Dad, none of this would have been possible.

I launched Bonaventure Equity as the next chapter in my personal lifelong ambition to be a leading financier of best-in-class entrepreneurs. When we embraced cannabis as our core investment thesis, it became clear that by working with fellow entrepreneurs as true financial partners, we could have a massive impact with what we do. Our mission is to create $1 billion in value and to positively impact 1 billion lives. This means that we need to be global in our scope. We are grateful to President Vicente Fox for anchoring our advisory board to help us realize this mission and for his considerate and inspiring forward.

This book is part of the foundation we are building to deliver on our ambitious plan. I am committed to personally helping create no less than 100 millionaires (or 10 percent of our value creation goal) from the entrepreneurs and business partners we work with every day in support of. This book may be the catalyst for you to be one of those people.

I have intentionally used the term "we" a lot in this book, as everything I do is empowered by my wonderful family, friends, colleagues, advisors and mentors. I cannot possibly thank everyone who has had an impact on me, but the following people truly stand out in my life and this project:

My best friends, Todd and Tracey Walters and Jarrett and Kristina Bostwick: Your belief in me and support of our mission humbles me every day and although we may not technically be family, you are the extended family that I fight for every day. Our wonderful core team at BVE: Tara Waglow, Bill Kehoe, Mike Elion, Ryan Michaels, and Cody Hughes. To Bryson Nobles, Mike McKenna and Mark Sluiter for friendship and always pointing out when I could use a little humility! Thanks to our partners and friends Hal, Shirley & Jason Eis, Nick Leibham (everyone needs a super lawyer as a friend) and Diane Newburg. And thanks to advisors Greg Shugar, Peter Sheptak, and Ricky Williams.

Many thanks to all the contributors: Joe Mimran, Brett Finklestein, Tyler Beuerlien, Mitch Baruchowitz, Troy Dayton, Jon Traubin, Tahira Rematullah, Emily Paxhia, Scott Greiper, Giadha Aguierre de Carcer, David Mangone, Lori Ferrara, Ryan Ansin, Sara Presler, and Michael Schwamm. And to all friends and colleagues I owe a thank you to: Sahpira Galoob, Skyler Baab, George J Von Burgh, Jon Barden, Bimal Kapoor, Brian Dooley, Jim Dullum, Ralph Manaker, Jay Lopez, Juan Garcia, Darcy Gramm, Paul Lambert, Greg Whelan, Paul Kasnetz, David Wesner, Ray Hennessey, Maggie Kelly, Scott Cantini, Jennifer Dorsey and Vanessa Campos, Randall Harper, Patty Schreiber, Michael Hilf, Adam and Dawn Weil, Evan and Rachel Dash, Michael Swackhamer, Colin Conway, Ian McCormack, Dan Klein, and my godparents Len and Avis Bruton and the whole Bruton family, my Bulldog family Bob Paganelli and Brian "VH" Van Horn. Finally, I owe a huge thank you to Congressman Earl Blumenauer and Congressman Ed Perlmutter, Ted Chueng, Jim Baudino, Keith Bonnici, and the incomparable Cheech Marin for being early icons and contributing to establishing this Cannabis Economy.

—Ross O'Brien, Parksville British Columbia July 2019

FOREWORD

by Vicente Fox Quesada

former President of Mexico

A phrase I use often is that the path to happiness is simple; all you have to do is give back to others. This lifetime focus of service to the people of my country and to the citizens of the world brought me directly to the issue of decriminalizing marijuana and the establishment of the legal cannabis economy. When I left office, my wife, Martha, and I spent considerable time thinking about how we wanted to use our influence for good through our philanthropies, CentroFox (my presidential library), and our global connections with leading business experts and fellow former heads of state. Most important to us was identifying opportunities for the next generation of entrepreneurs and the youth of our communities.

If you are picking up this book, you likely already know that my family and I are cannabis advocates. I have been speaking at conferences around the world on this topic yet still get asked most frequently, "Why are you pro-cannabis?" The answer to this is simple: When Martha and I had that first discussion after I retired from public office, we knew we wanted to focus on how we could provide the most opportunity to the youth of Mexico and around the globe. There was no sector with more potential benefit than cannabis. The once-in-a-lifetime opportunity to get on board with this life-changing movement is immense, so we put all of our efforts behind accelerating the momentum of de-criminalization and legalization of cannabis.

In Mexico, the illegal drug traffic paradigm has led to few alternative job prospects for the youth in disadvantaged communities. It was clear that through legalization of cannabis, new and highly accessible career opportunities had the potential to launch a generation of entrepreneurial pursuits and innovations. It is in service of these children and helping build a future or their families that we saw an opportunity to be on the forefront the cultural wave of post- prohibition era cannabis reform.

Now at CentroFox, we host the largest cannabis business conference in South America, CannaMexico, as well as many other business conferences at our hotel and conference space. We are establishing research and educational cannabis agricultural programs. I think that I am the only former modern president to plant marijuana crops at my presidential library! I also sit on the boards of Kharion, Helix, and other leading global cannabis companies. All of these companies are led by dynamic entrepreneurs who all started somewhere and needed to find financing in the ways that Ross describes in this book. The experiences of going through building a private company are invaluable. While each experience is different, you will learn from some of the best who have done it successfully in this book.

Cannabis is finally being normalized as a viable medical, wellness, and recreational product. The model for legalization is working, and with the continuing momentum of positive relegation, legal cannabis businesses will be one of the most significant economic drivers for the foreseeable future. With this increase in entrepreneurship, however, there remains a major need for sophisticated resources, business tools, and access to the kinds of thought leadership and best practices that are available in other sectors. This book represents the most thorough alignment of cannabis, entrepreneurs, and financing available. Believe me when I tell you it is mandatory reading for anyone who is starting, building, expanding, or growing a cannabis company.

In my business career and in public life, I have learned that what it takes to be successful in entrepreneurship (a clear plan for growth and scale along with a strong financial plan) is what attracted us to working with Ross as an advisory to his investment fund Bonaventure Equity, and to participate in this book. His experience in financing and building companies from the ground up sets him apart from other investors in the space and makes him a great teacher in this respect.

We work with Ross because he and his team are committed to funding ethical, legal cannabis entrepreneurs on a global scale.

I know what it takes to build a company and this book represents one of the finest resources I have seen for entrepreneurs. The global perspective in identifying the Cannabis Economy, highlighting the opportunities and challenges in entrepreneurship, and identifying the unique outlook of cannabis entrepreneurs all impact the ability to secure the funding you will need to launch and grow your business.

I congratulate you for taking the first step in reading this book and invite you to join us as we change the direction of the world, one company at a time.

Sincerely,

Vicente Fox Quesada

INTRODUCTION

A fundamental change is underway across the globe. Cannabis is rapidly becoming a legal and accepted element of mainstream society. Once viewed as a dangerous and illegal contraband narcotic, today cannabis is seen as a valuable natural resource with multifaceted economic and scientific benefits. Although there remains a long way to go moving past prohibitionary restrictions and the need to repair the resulting mass incarcerations and legacy societal impact, this change is driving the rapid development of a marketplace that was once in the shadows. Countries like Canada and Uruguay have legalized nationally, and medical and recreational use is rapidly being accepted at the state level in the U.S. This is giving way to an explosion of new companies and a wave of entrepreneurship. Investors are seeking fortunes in all sectors of cannabis, yet raising capital remains the greatest challenge for entrepreneurs. Despite the hype and constant headlines about investing in cannabis, early-stage companies that rely on angel investment and venture capital still find it difficult to identify and reach investors for the capital they need. Many investors still fear regulatory uncertainty and historical stigmatism, and many established funds have internal restrictions that won't allow them to invest even though they are active in other established markets.

Despite a lot of media attention around cannabis investing, there will be a limited number of cannabis venture capitalists available to finance the growth of cannabis businesses for the foreseeable future. Raising capital for a cannabis company is very difficult. In established markets, less than one in 300 submitted business plans secure funding, yet each of those companies believes they are worthy of investment. Why is there such a small percentage of companies that receive funding? What common characteristics do the successful companies have in common?

Cannabis Capital aims to demystify the core concepts and best practices for successfully raising capital in the cannabis business. Understanding the keys to successfully raising capital are critically important for entrepreneurs who are innovating and creating the future industries impacted by cannabis.

This book will take you through some fundamental concepts you should know to secure the financing you need:

1. Understanding the cannabis economy and emerging cannabis venture capital industry
2. Essential business financial planning as a foundation for a company that warrants investment
3. The process, materials, and strategies for successfully raising capital
4. Creating pitches and exit strategies that drive investor interest and secure the funds to grow your cannabis business

By identifying the intersection of successful investing and operating through the lens of the cannabis economy, this book is laid out as a resource for entrepreneurs and their management teams. Through the foundation of financial and operational discipline, refined for the nuances and factors unique to the cannabis industry, *Cannabis Capital* aims to offer key guidance for building and extracting value in a privately held cannabis business.

In my business, we conduct a lot of primary research. We are always surveying our investor relationships and trying to learn from the industry at our ongoing events series, so much of the data you will see in this book is based on our own proprietary research and industry knowledge. We use this to inform our business decisions, and much of this will be published for the first time in this book and made available to you to help inform your own business decisions. For example, we ask the following question in all our surveys: "How would you assess the quality of management teams in the cannabis investments you've vetted?" As you can see in Figure I.1, only 8.33 percent of respondents graded the management teams they reviewed as "highly professional." Hopefully, after you read and apply the principles outlined here, you will be one of the management teams that are given this highest quality rating.

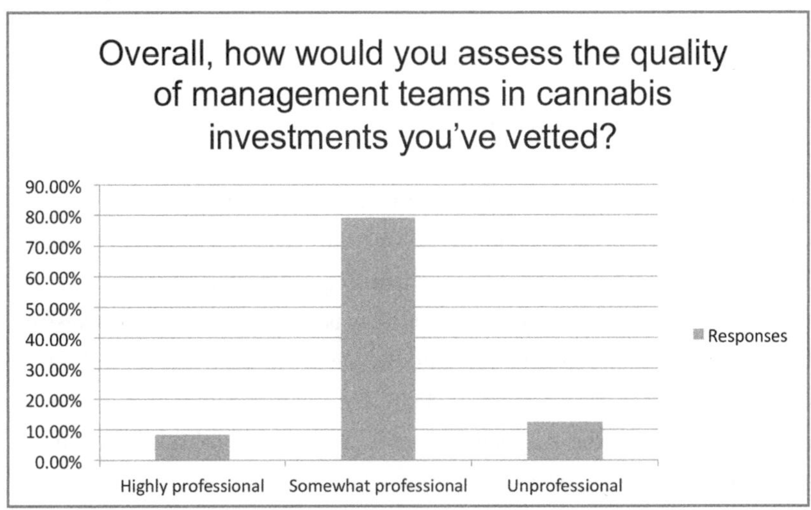

FIGURE I.1—Management Quality Survey Results
Source: Bonaventure Equity, LLC, Investor Surveys

CANNABIS IS A DYNAMIC MARKET

Cannabis is here to stay, and the industry is growing at a healthy rate. The global legal cannabis market was valued at $14.3 billion in 2016 and is projected to sustain a minimum 21.1 percent compound annual growth rate (CAGR) through 2024. Grand View Research predicts that the global legal marijuana market will reach $146.4 billion by 2025.

The rising demand for medical and recreational cannabis and related products and services is only predicted to continue to grow at a record pace. There were an estimated 30,000 or more new cannabis startups in the U.S. alone in 2018. At the state and federal level, support for legal cannabis continues to gain momentum along with support from regulators and their constituents. Investors are flocking to the public markets seeking outsized returns, yet access to private companies remains opaque and lacking in traditional institutional investment funds and professionals. In established markets, venture capital funds commit billions of dollars to the companies that meet their criteria for projected success.

Cannabis venture capital (CVC) is a nascent industry. Many cannabis entrepreneurs are not well-versed in raising CVC and likely have a hard time trying to find other sources of capital from angel investors and private individuals—groups that are extremely difficult to access even for the best operators.

That is why access to capital remains the greatest obstacle for entrepreneurs. Many investors continue to remain concerned about the lack of continuity in federal and state laws along with differing regulations within each state. Many existing venture capital funds are not yet able to invest in the industry, and many operators are unable to open bank accounts, let alone secure lending or working capital facilities.

The investment fund we manage today is fully committed to investing in private cannabis companies, and as we meet with more and more management teams, it becomes clear that many of the best practices, and indeed simply the language of venture capital, is inhibiting cannabis entrepreneurs from successfully raising capital, hence the impetus for writing this book. It is my personal mission to create $1 billion in value and positively impact a billion people through our efforts in cannabis investing. This book is one avenue to achieving that goal. Let me tell you a bit about how I got here.

ORIGINS OF *CANNABIS CAPITAL*

I was stricken by the affliction that is referred to as "entrepreneurship." I wish I could say otherwise, but I am wired to take significant risk, at times fool myself into thinking that I have all the answers, and I am enamored with unlimited opportunity. This cocktail of entrepreneurial tendencies has resulted in two decades of failures and a set of unique experiences and successes that I wish I had the benefit of understanding earlier in my career. But now, I see that these experiences informed my views on business in several areas:

1. I do not believe that formalized education prepares students for entrepreneurial success.
2. Entrepreneurship is a combination of nature and nurture; you either have the "bug" or you don't.
3. If success is an equation, it would be made up of nine parts execution and one part idea, like this:

$$\text{Success} = (\text{Execution} \times 9) + 1 \text{ Idea}$$

So as a young man, I embarked on a series of disastrous business ventures, each time believing with absolute certainty that it would be a success. None of them were. Yet each time I failed, I learned something. I certainly learned the hard way that a good idea is nothing without the ability to execute. Like many young entrepreneurs, I was full of opinions and confidence and was more interested in doing than listening and learning. This works for some people but is a recipe for failure for most.

As my career developed, I found myself teaching entrepreneurship and venture capital on nights and weekends after I was done with my day job investing in private companies. It was an enlightening experience to see a room full of neophyte entrepreneurs with endless questions, ideas, and desire. It was like looking into a mirror! When the class assessments came back, I was told the students gave my class the highest scores with the majority of the feedback highlighting that I tended to use real experiences to demonstrate the points I was trying to get across. It was in these moments when it became clear to me that because entrepreneurship is a somewhat nebulous concept, and so much of the disciplines I utilize today are either not taught or need to be learned through trial and error, what I thought were a series of failures can actually provide valuable insights for other entrepreneurs.

What became clear from the start is that in any industry the one challenge all entrepreneurs face is raising capital. Everything I am doing in my career stems from my decision to help entrepreneurs solve for successfully securing financing.

As my career transitioned to investing in other entrepreneurs, I made a commitment to one day capture the critical learnings and systems I was forced to develop for my own use in the hope that one day I could share them with others. This book is the combination of years of investing in companies, starting companies, running companies, raising money, managing mergers and acquisitions, sitting on boards, selling companies, and winding down companies. Through those experiences, some common threads have emerged, and I applied those concepts to cannabis entrepreneurship to form the basis for *Cannabis Capital.*

Being an entrepreneur in any industry is difficult at best. As a cannabis entrepreneur, you have the added dynamic of being a pioneer in a changing and complicated industry. The successful cannabis entrepreneur needs to be proficient in finance, technology, sales, marketing, operations, human resources, planning and forecasting, negotiations, leadership, and state and federal regulations to name a few. By definition, entrepreneurial ventures are starved of resources, so decisions need to be made without adequate time, the tools needed, and imperfect information. When presenting a compelling story to investors, it is not always about having the "right" answers, but rather transmitting the businesses decisions you have made given this dynamic.

As an investor, I am always looking for an entrepreneur to demonstrate they have made decisions that represent the basis of critical thinking and business acumen they have applied to running their venture. The ability to defend decisions in a thoughtful approach is almost more important that the correctness of the decision itself.

In an effort to help expedite the success in your business today, this book is laid out with concepts and systems that are all adaptable and reusable. As you go through each chapter, I encourage you to follow the templates and systems, which are designed to be adaptable for your specific needs. No two companies or situations are alike, but with the right foundation of knowledge combined with insights from the leading investors and practitioners in the industry, I hope you will revisit this book and build in your own best practices as your story of success advances along the way.

BRIDGING THE GAP TO CANNABIS VENTURE CAPITAL

Having identified the widening gap between what investors are looking for and how entrepreneurs are approaching the emerging CVC marketplace, I wrote this book specifically to address the core factors contributing to this widening disconnect. Investor interest continues to grow, and after the 2016 election in the U.S., we saw the largest investment activity ever and subsequent expansion in the legal cannabis markers, at that time only legal in four states. Regulatory momentum continued with the 2018 midterm elections. As of this writing, there are 10 states that have legalized marijuana for recreational and medical uses, and 22 other states that have legalized it for medical purposes. In 2018, Canada became the first G7 country to fully legalize marijuana for both medical and recreational use. According to a recent Pew Research Center survey, about six in ten Americans (approximately 62 percent) say the use of marijuana should be legalized. However, early financing remains difficult to access for entrepreneurs who may struggle with the dynamics of how to succeed in the widening legal cannabis industry. Your ability to identify and reach emerging CVC investors will be critical to your success.

Many of the technical aspects of venture capital, private equity, or investment banking have historically been the secrets of Wall Street firms and the mysterious "dark arts," like how to value a private company that brings the kind of paydays these masters of the universe harvested along the way. Today with access to information, a simple Google search can provide much of the technical explanations that otherwise would have only been made available in business school or working at a "white shoe" (professional Wall Street) firm. This information certainly would not have been presented in ways in which entrepreneurs could have applied to their business in a practical way.

It is, however, still evident that many cannabis entrepreneurs are not adequately experienced in working with investors. Although many are creating a level of success in their businesses, they are unable to properly capitalize and manage for rapid growth with financing that is even more difficult to secure than in most traditional industries.

To successfully raise capital, the entrepreneur needs to have a broad set of competencies and understandings. With a mastery of the tools presented in this book, you can go forward with confidence to seek CVC for your company. Ultimately, learning these methods will allow you to understand the investors' point of view and communicate with it in mind. From experience, I can say a lack of fidelity in the investment discussion is the leading contributor to the disconnect between investors and entrepreneurs, preventing them from consummating a deal together. But by identifying the intersection of successful investing and operating your business through the lens of the cannabis industry, you will be better equipped to build and extract value in your cannabis businesses.

HOW TO USE THIS BOOK

This book is meant to be an introductory course for you, the cannabis entrepreneur, to the world of CVC. As you follow the narrative from macroeconomic trends and concepts, you will dig deeper into the nuances of CVC by learning about its core foundational concepts. Before you raise capital, you will need to familiarize yourself with what it takes to create a business plan, set up operational best practices, master technical financial concepts, and lay the groundwork required to build an investible company. You will also read about the investment process, how to prepare your pitch, present to investors, set deal terms and exit strategies that appeal to investors, and manage a company after you have secured investment.

Focused on the current best practices (not to be confused with trends) and practical tools, *Cannabis Capital* uses proprietary information and data collected through surveys and primary research that I have done in my own company. Each chapter will feature anecdotes, quotes, real-world examples, and research providing a multidimensional approach to the core topics. The mission of this book is to inform cannabis entrepreneurs about the discussion of securing financing for a private company. The objective is to mitigate the disconnect between investors and business owners. As you read, whether in a linear fashion or by jumping from chapter to chapter, take ample notes and think about how the concepts can apply to your own cannabis venture. Let's take a quick look at the three major parts of this book.

Part I: The Cannabis Economy Landscape

Part I addresses the concept of identifying cannabis as an *economy* and not an industry and why that is important. Through the cannabis economy lens, entrepreneurs and investors can share the same core foundational elements of what it means to be operating a legal cannabis business. Only then can you add the specific identification of the sectors and industries within the cannabis economy. This will help you illuminate the core operational elements that are critical to success within your related industry and specific to your venture.

All this needs to be understood in the context of a dynamic and changing regulatory environment. Policy changes are largely driving the expansion of cannabis markets, so you will also learn about the current state of regulation and banking—an issue that is important for all cannabis entrepreneurs to understand and manage. The chapters in Part I will help you best position your business as a part of this vast, ever-changing, always-growing economy that encompasses multiple sectors, including health care, industrial and production technology, banking and finance, agricultural and farming, and retail and consumer products.

In this part, you will also read about CVC, how it works, and what you need to help develop your business plans and go about raising capital while tempering baseless enthusiasm to help you design a realistic approach to your venture and getting it funded.

Part II: Entrepreneurship and Planning

A key disconnect between investors and operators centers around the identification of first principles of operating a successful business. These are the elements that experienced investors look for in order to justify an investment. It is the entrepreneur's job when raising capital to demonstrate the operational discipline as indicators of future success for building a great company. Well-run companies and strong management teams attract investment. Venture funding is a symptom of building a great company. "Part II: Entrepreneurship and Planning" will highlight best practices that you can implement in your day-to-day operations to significantly impact your ability to successfully raise capital.

Investors want to invest in great companies, so this section will take you through how to identify if you fit investor criteria and will go into more detail on how to use self-assessment tools and brutal honesty about your business to achieve a clear and unbiased view of the inherit risks in your venture. As with any business endeavor, the results are largely dependent on the planning and preparation involved when creating your business plan and financial documents. This section will take you through models and proven strategies for predicting the financial outcomes specific to your company, developing a defensible rationale for what your business' financial needs are, and predicting the outcomes with relative certainty so you can secure funding.

Part III: Raising Capital

It's easy to imagine that because your business is innovative, exciting, or otherwise destined to succeed all you need to do is talk to a few investors who will wholeheartedly embrace your business plan and provide you with all the funding you could possibly require. But remember what I said earlier: Less than 1 in 300 businesses get funding in established industries. Raising capital, like any other core business function, requires strategy, a managed process, strong execution, and an ability to handle a lot of rejection.

The chapters in Part III will walk you through the materials and models you need to prepare to pass through an investor's due diligence process and create a successful investor presentation complete with exit strategies. This will lead you through cannabis-specific tax and accounting considerations and what terms you will expect to negotiate to close an investment.

Finally, many books on raising capital omit any discussion about what happens after the investment closes. By developing a deeper understanding of what will be expected of you in managing a company that has investors and what your duties and responsibilities are, you can start to explore the impact of the terms and business planning you do up front in your capital raising process.

Takeaways and Action Items

At the end of each chapter, you'll find the concepts from that chapter summarized as key takeaways along with action items. If you use these takeaway topics and their related action items as the baseline for how to approach your funding journey, you will have a head start over the competition. You can also use the takeaways as jumping off point to go back into the text and revisit these concepts for a deeper dive.

These sections are meant to be used over and over again as you grow your business.

It is my firm belief that entrepreneurs who raise capital and build successful businesses have a deep understanding and operational foundation in what it takes to first build a great company. Raising capital is a highly complicated and nuanced process, and it needs to be managed as such. Your opportunity to differentiate yourself from all the other entrepreneurs seeking capital comes when you show investors that you have a clear understanding of what it will take to succeed and you have a plan to do that. And—perhaps most importantly—it comes when you can speak the language investors understand and ultimately give them comfort that you will be a good shepherd of their investment. I am pleased to be your guide through the cannabis economy and what it takes to secure the equity you need to succeed. Let's get started on your *Cannabis Capital* journey!

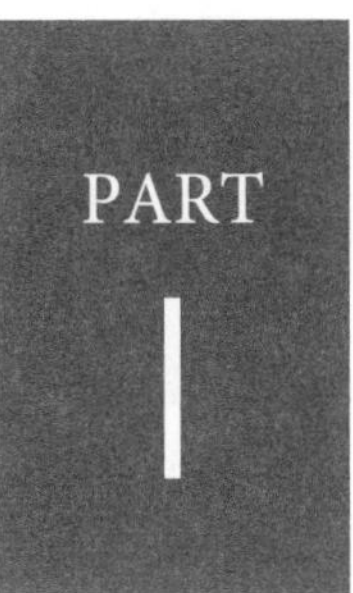

PART I

THE CANNABIS ECONOMY LANDSCAPE

THE CANNABIS ECONOMY

Defining the markets in which a cannabis business operates begins with the foundational concept that cannabis is an economy (in which multiple sectors operate and are impacted) and not an industry that is solely focused on a few related verticals. This concept was touched on in the introduction and may be considered controversial. But there are a number of important reasons to adopt this view for entrepreneurs and investors that have a profound impact when raising capital. Restrictions and prohibitionary laws and regulations have prevented commercial access to cannabis until recently. With the changing regulations, cannabis is rapidly becoming a resource that is now readily available to grow, research, process, and extract elements for widespread applications. This is the catalyst for countless businesses starting up and operating across the entire international supply chain, and in turn impacting and forming industries in their own right.

This transition toward widespread legal access to cannabis is fueling commerce in all facets of industry, much of which is being defined in real time as it happens. If we start from the ground up, quite literally, the cannabis plant is a natural resource in its primary form. The iterations and use cases of this resource will impact countless industries in their own right. From agriculture and farming of this resource and introducing it into the global economy, cannabis will have a permanent and profound impact from education and research to retail and consumer products to nonprofits and government agencies (just to point out a few industries).

A good analogy for what is happening with the growing access to cannabis is to look historically at other resources that were otherwise inaccessible in marketplaces of their day. For example, with the discovery of oil, all facets of commerce were influenced by oil making its way from sourcing, production, transportation, and ultimately into the hands of the consumer. All the existing industries of the day needed to adapt to and accommodate this new resource and the industries it was impacting and influencing from logistics and transportation, innovation and technology, finance and regulations. Today, would you consider the automotive industry part of the oil and gas industry? No, you wouldn't. Automotive is its own industry, but it is a part of the energy economy that was created through global access to oil. Today, cannabis is reaching all facets of modern industry in a similar way. In short, it is an economy.

DEFINING THE CANNABIS ECONOMY

According to Investopedia, an *economy* can be defined as "a system of inter-related production and consumption activities converting resources into wealth through systems of trade." Economies are then segmented into sectors and industries within those sectors. We can then adopt this definition and identify the Cannabis Economy as: "A global system for exchange of goods and services facilitating cannabis-enabled commerce, education, and policy."

As such, the global introduction of this new resource is so widely applicable that it is impossible to narrow down cannabis to one industry. When viewed as an economy, the benefit to entrepreneurs is the clarity this provides in defining their ventures not in terms of being a business in the cannabis *industry*, but rather in the context of being in an industry that is part of (or will be part of) the global cannabis *economy*. The concept of the cannabis economy forms the basis for entrepreneurs and investors to communicate through mutually defined and agreed-upon perspectives. Through the cannabis economy lens, discussions between investors and entrepreneurs can shift away from defining the "cannabis industry" to thinking about "industry of cannabis." This clears a path to discussing a business opportunity within the framework of the industry it operates within as opposed to being so unique or different that best practices don't apply.

CANNABIS INDUSTRIES DEFINED

An *industry* is typically defined by identifying a group of companies that conduct their primary activities within the same primary business activity. These companies are typically classified by their main source of revenue. The system used in North America to classify businesses is called the North American Industry Classification System (NAICS), which uses a code system to identify sectors and industries within the overall economy.

If you take the airline industry as an example, the companies that operate commercial airlines are classified within the primary "Transportation and Warehousing" sector. Within that sector, categories are defined further that include "Scheduled Passenger Air Transportation" (NAICS Code 48111), which includes the companies such as American Airlines Group Inc. whose primary business function is to provide air transportation for passengers or freight.

If you look more closely at American Airlines, they categorize their core sources of revenue as main and regional passenger ticket sales, cargo, and "other." This "other" category is where they capture revenue generated from their loyalty and frequent flyer programs, which can be as much as 12 percent of revenue. Selling programs, such as credit cards, is arguably one of the most profitable sources of revenue for the company. Would you consider American to be an airline or a credit card company? Who is their customer?

This is an interesting debate and no more relevant than in the cannabis economy today. If we take the time to identify sectors and industries in a similar way within the cannabis economy, the operating metrics for success become more explicit.

Figure 1.1 applies a traditional hierarchy for defining the sectors and industries within the global cannabis economy. Within each sector, we can group together the companies that will make up an explicit industry. These are the companies that have a common source of revenue and business activity.

Now that we have a series of identified industries, it becomes obvious that none of these industries are in fact new, but rather are just now being impacted and adapting to the introduction of access to cannabis. Where

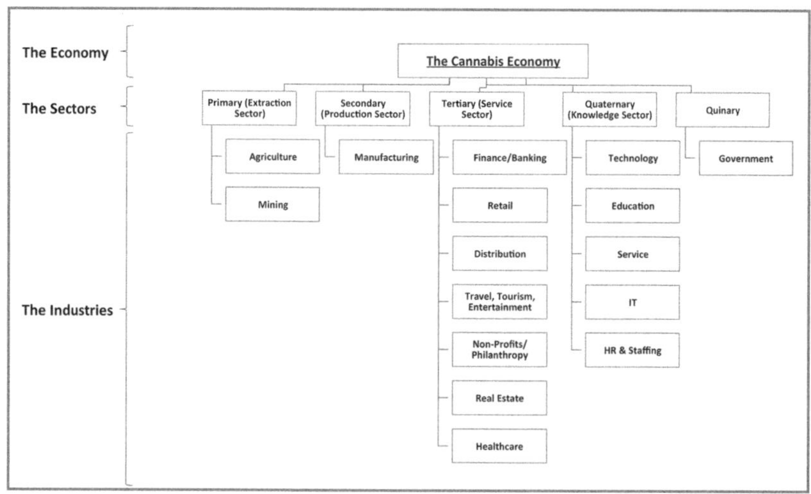

FIGURE 1.1—The Cannabis Economy Hierarchy

does your company operate? Is your core expertise in understanding cannabis either technically from a regulatory and compliance perspective, philosophically, or do you otherwise have expertise within that sector and industry independent of a working knowledge of cannabis?

A foundational approach to business is to not fall into the trap of throwing out best practices for the sake of rushing to defining cannabis as something separate from the industries it is impacting. You should avoid assuming that experience in other industries won't bring value to a cannabis company, as leveraging historical successes in non-cannabis industries will indicate a high probably of success in your venture. So don't be in a rush to throw out entrepreneurial disciplines and experiences under the assumption that cannabis businesses can't be defined in a traditional sense.

When participants in an emerging sector rush forward without taking the time to identify the foundational elements, markets become temporarily inflated. Irrational exuberance of public investors is a likely predictor that many companies will ultimately fail, and investors will lose their capital. This is true across all industries and we should not expect cannabis to be any different.

Every aspect of managing a business should be informed by a clear understanding of the industry a company operates within. This frames sales and marketing strategies, pricing and product development, supply chain and infrastructure, partners and competitors, and compliance with related rules and regulations. These are the drivers that form the basis of a well-thought-out business plan. Throughout this book, I'll repeat that it is your mission first to build a great business and then adapt that model to a core cannabis strategy.

THE CANNABIS ECONOMY AND YOUR VENTURE

The danger in defining cannabis as an industry is that it implies that there is some special skillset that requires a deep understanding of cannabis. This idea implies that if cannabis is an industry unto itself, only insider experts understand it. It is true that experience matters and industry knowledge is critical to success. It is common, however, that insiders and outsiders focus on and emphasize cannabis over business fundamentals. This skews the discussion and thinking away from a foundation in building businesses based on first principles of company management (which will be discussed in greater detail in Chapter 7). We can avoid that trap by thinking first about what a well-run company needs to be successful, then apply the nuances of cannabis.

It's time to move beyond the concept that only a chosen few understand cannabis. Yes, there is real merit and value in domain expertise, but this tends to be an excuse for entrepreneurs or operators to forego foundational business practices. This is where the communication between inventors and entrepreneurs begins to break down. If an entrepreneur dismisses feedback from investors as being uniformed as to the nuances of cannabis (which is a symptom of referring to it as an industry), then they likely won't be open to listening to the feedback and evaluating the business on the merits of how it is being run.

Of course, cannabis is unique in that new precedents are being set, new operating procedures are being designed, and new innovations are happening everywhere you look. If you step back and explore the history of each sector within the cannabis economy, this has happened throughout time with new innovations, technologies, and changes in regulations impacting the global economy. For example, in the U.S., travel and tourism went through a deregulation in 1978, and similarly in 1996 telecommunications was impacted. The industrial revolution started a global introduction of regulations and government oversight of emerging industries. In each of those situations, many businesses were adversely affected, but opportunity was created for new innovations in technology and systems.

Every industry has its own unique generational precedents of successes and failures that every business owner can learn from. By adopting the cannabis economy as the macro marketplace, you can break away from the confines of thinking that there is some secret knowledge that only a few can have. Yes, as with any venture, market knowledge is critically important. But the foundational business acumen and an understanding of how economies and the industries within them work is a skill and perspective at the core of great entrepreneurs and CEOs throughout history.

Operating a business requires an acknowledgement of the constraints that define the boundaries that a company operates within. Constraints are a positive thing when planning and building a business, in that it requires focus and discipline to build within set parameters. Only a clear view of those boundaries will allow you to strategically push those same boundaries and reframe them over time.

THE CANNABIS ECONOMY'S IMPACT ON RAISING CAPITAL

The complexities of the cannabis economy are important—as much so as the operational knowledge you need to succeed. So it's important to familiarize yourself with how the cannabis economy affects the investment process.

Communication starts with alignment, and taking the time to define the cannabis economy and the industry your business operates in will allow you to move beyond the disconnect quickly and get to a discussion of why your business will succeed. Remember that most companies fail, and investors are on the lookout for failure points (risk), so creating a common ground for communication is imperative to advancing the discussion with an investor.

Investors arrive at a point in their careers where they can invest capital in companies largely because they have been successful in building wealth through entrepreneurship in the past. Pitching to them can be akin to moving up to the major league from the minors. One of the foundational approaches to pitching well is to understand the investors' perspectives and be able to create common views. Being able to demonstrate a sophisticated understanding of operations and management is as important to investors as showing that you understand cannabis. With the investors' likely track record of success as entrepreneurs, they will look for indications of how you think about building your company and if those best practices and tactical approaches match their understating of how that maps to success.

The surging investments in cannabis reflect the growing recognition of the scale and opportunity that legal cannabis could represent. New Frontier Data estimates that cannabis consumers spent more than $340 billion globally in 2018 alone as shown in Figure 1.2 on page 10. With

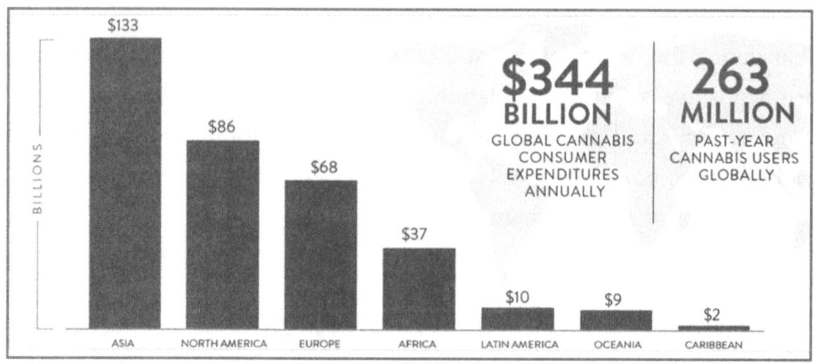

FIGURE 1.2—The Global Cannabis Economy

legal sales only accounting for less than $20 billion to date, the upside opportunity for legal market expansion is very significant.

North America has been the epicenter of that expansion, with Canada's legal market anchoring the global cannabis economy, and the U.S. patchwork of adult use and medical markets serving as hotbeds of cannabis innovation. But as the debate around U.S. federal legalization gains momentum, a growing number of investors and entrepreneurs are investing today with the expectation of catalytic growth following federal legalization.

According to Giadha Aguierre De Carcer, founder and CEO of New Frontier Data, "This type of growth (and opportunity), is reminiscent of the tech and internet boom, and has attracted an increasing number of entrepreneurs and investors. But growth has also created an expedited

GIADHA'S PERSPECTIVES ON INVESTMENT IN THE CANNABIS ECONOMY

If you think of how old the legal cannabis markets are, at least in terms of seeing material investment and new businesses coming into it, one could argue that it kicked off in a significant manner between 2013 and 2014. Whether via mergers and acquisitions (M&A) or going public, businesses are facing the need to expedite growth to remain competitive.

GIADHA'S PERSPECTIVES ON INVESTMENT, continued

This industry-wide synchronicity has translated into an entire market shift, so we are now looking at blanket consolidation across U.S. and Canada in massive numbers.

Speaking of massive numbers, this market shift is also having a material impact on entrepreneurs' and new business owners' ability to raise capital. Because of larger market entrants acquiring and investing in cannabis operations, as well as existing businesses merging with one another to withstand increasing external competitive pressures, the level of sophistication and complexity required to raise even seed capital has risen beyond some new entrepreneurs' skill sets.

This expedited market shift has also impacted the investment environment. Cannabis Investment 1.0, which occurred around 2015 and 2016, happened when a "good" idea and a 12-page deck could get you a $25,000 to $100,000 check from an angel investor. That quickly evolved to Cannabis Investment 2.0, between 2017 and 2018, whereby *family offices* (private wealth management advisory firms for very high-net-worth investors) and dedicated venture funds began to cut $250,00 to $1 million checks in return for proven revenues and 10 times the return on investment (ROI). Today, in Cannabis Investment 3.0, we are looking at billion-dollar funds, including publicly traded ones and multinational investment banks, and looking at refined fundamental business metrics. This new environment has begun to force existing management out of current positions and shrink the number of new entrepreneurs able to establish themselves. Along the same lines, investors are now pushing back on what many deem to have been highly inflated early valuations. Whether private or public, cannabis companies are now being put through much more rigorous valuation exercises, whereby revenue multiples, customer life value, and actual market penetration figures are expected.

market and business lifecycle one should be aware of before diving into what is today less of a green rush and more of a maturing global economy."

CANNABIS CAPITAL TAKEAWAYS AND ACTION ITEMS

Defining the cannabis economy (and knowing where you fit into it) allows you to seek out best practices and principles of operating that others within your particular industry have already figured out. It also allows you to refine the elements of your strategic plan and inform your market analysis, define competitors, and identify strategic partners and key collaborators. You can clearly apply discipline and focus in building your business within the sandbox that you have identified and shed light on the key regulatory and transactional trends. This in turn will highlight how to push those boundaries, adapt to change, and innovate.

But most importantly this allows you to set the conversation with investors through an economy, sector, and industry model that they can understand. This inoculates any debate about what cannabis is and any question that the opportunity is big enough or will produce long-term success. This allows for agreement with the capital providers and the entrepreneurs who are seeking capital quickly, which allows you to have the conversation you really want to have with investors early: That you know business, AND you know cannabis.

With this improved thinking, you can start to break down the opportunity in front of you. Cannabis is dynamic, large, and an expanding global opportunity. The introduction of the cannabis economy is sparking industries that will attract large investments and produce massive global economic impact with billions of dollars involved. Where do you plan to plant your flag?

Action Item: Research Your Industry

Take some time to think about your company as if it was not related to the cannabis economy. Are you a dispensary? Then you can use the retail industry as a benchmark. Are you a cultivator? Agricultural industries will present a reasonable analogy. Credit card processing? Think about financial services. Do you have a branded product? What similarities are there in the consumer products, or food and beverage industries? Are you developing compliant inventory-tracking software? If so, have you explored the existing software-as-a-service (SaaS) industry? See the pattern?

If you can identify a core incumbent industry that your business would operate in, then you can take some time to identify which investors are most active in that industry. Are there venture capital funds that invest exclusively in that sector (like you find in health-care technology, for example), and what companies have they invested in? Take some time to explore their portfolio of investments and see if there are elements of those companies that you could replicate. You can also ask yourself:

- $ How far along were they in their development when they raised capital?
- $ Did they have strong intellectual property or some other unique competitive advantage?
- $ Did the founders have prior successes before starting the company that secured the investment?

The profile of the companies that raise capital and go on to be successful can provide an initial template for the things you should aspire to build in your venture.

CANNABIS VENTURE CAPITAL

Through the cannabis economy lens, there is a specific industry that all entrepreneurs will endeavor to understand, and that is the emerging cannabis venture capital (CVC) industry. This chapter walks you through an explanation of how private companies get funded and how venture capital plays a key role. If you know how venture funds operate, what they look for, and how they generate investment returns, you will have a key insight into who is on the opposite side of a funding request.

Today there are more and more CVC funds launching to invest in cannabis businesses, yet it is still nascent compared to traditional VC. Many VC funds will continue to be restricted from investing in cannabis businesses (due to the federal illegality), so the committed CVC funds along with family offices/private investors will be the main sources of meaningful investment for the near and medium term. When traditional VC is able to invest in cannabis companies, investors will likely follow the industries they already invest in, resulting in a limited number of cannabis-economy-first funds. It is those funds that are investing in today's cohort of cannabis entrepreneurs.

To put it bluntly, cannabis financing is in a moment of post-prohibition purgatory. Regulations are being passed that are opening specific regions for medical and recreational use, so many companies are starting up to supply that regional demand. This increases the demand for funding, but traditional investors are either precluded from investing or remain so concerned with regulatory uncertainty that they cannot justify the risk-return profile of the companies they are evaluating. Similarly, it is difficult to navigate operating in different regions without the scale of functioning logistics and operators across the supply chain of the emerging industries in the cannabis economy. There is, however, significant investor demand as seen in the appetite of the public to invest in publicly traded cannabis companies. This creates an environment where it is even more difficult to bridge investors with companies in an inefficient private-capital market. This creates a perfect storm with an explosion of entrepreneurship, significant and growing investor demand, constraints of a fragmented regulatory oversight, and only a few explicit investors.

Professionally investing in cannabis companies is still emerging, and the challenge remains that there are more private companies raising capital than there are sources of capital. You can conclude that investment capital is still difficult to gain access to and will continue that way for some time. Why is this important? This confluence of market elements means that a cannabis entrepreneur like you, by necessity, needs to manage raising capital as a well-run and professional process. The company and management team both need to stand out from the surplus of investment opportunities that investors have in front of them. So how can you do that? You do it by knowing the investing landscape and adjusting your company's pitch to fit the needs of the market. Let's start by reviewing how private companies get funded, who the types of investors are that fund certain stages of companies, and how the emerging CVC industry is investing.

HOW PRIVATE COMPANIES ARE FINANCED

The one challenge facing every entrepreneur across all industries and all stages of growth is identifying the optimal plan to finance and properly resource their company. Access to these sources of capital and how they approach investing is critical to the success of privately held companies. *Private equity* (PE) has emerged as the category for investors who professionally invest in private (not publicly traded) companies. PE consists of funds, private investment offices, and individuals that have an investment strategy to own equity in private companies. These investors develop strategies and expertise that align with companies who are operating at certain stages in their lifestyle. At each stage, there are correlations between risk, valuation with the profitability, and options for financing and exit strategies.

Within that PE group, VC is made up of a specific group of firms managed by a general partner (the VC) that invest at an earlier stage of growth, can get comfortable with a greater degree of risk, and build investment portfolios to achieve target return expectations. VC has its roots in financing innovation and are the professional investors most associated with funding entrepreneurs and taking early-stage risk. In general, investing in PE over time will outperform all other investment strategies.

As companies mature, they have different financial profiles and associated risk and return profiles. What does "risk" mean in this case? You can think of risk as:

- $ Probability of failure
- $ Ability to return invested capital
- $ Potential for a liquidity event and magnitude of that exit event

As companies grow from the startup stage through expansion to a significant exit or an initial public offering (IPO), different types of investors focus on investing at those related stages. Figure 2.1 shows the stages of companies and how investors perceive risk at those stages.

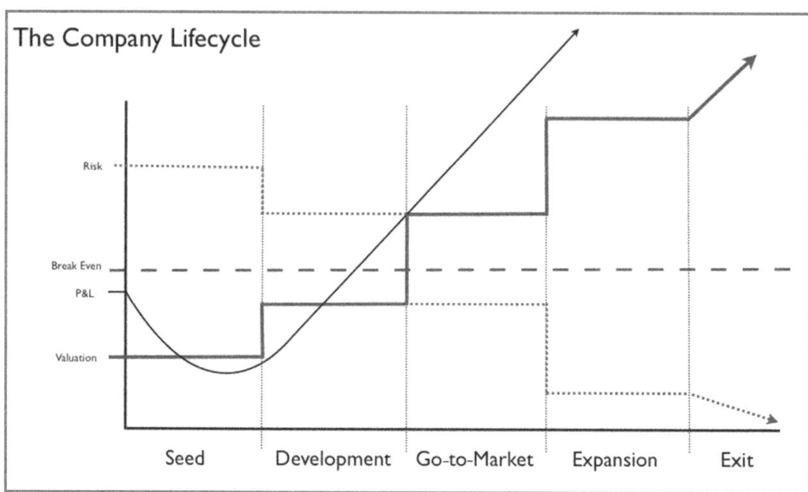

FIGURE 2.1—Company Lifecycle

This is important to understand because investors are looking for what is referred to as a "risk-adjusted rate of return," meaning that the greater the risk, the greater the return on the investment needs to be. The investor who accepts the least amount of risk are lenders. They provide loans with a guarantee of certainty of repayment, have a lot of security (protection) either through assets or personal guarantees, and almost all their downside is protected. They also receive an interest rate in return for taking credit risk, get paid monthly, and only lend to companies that have a very high certainty of being able to repay—or service—the debt. Only companies that have the ability to secure and repay debt will qualify for financing, which means that debt is not an option for early companies without proven cash flow. If you follow the profit and loss (P&L) line in Figure 2.1, the company won't have sufficient cash flow to support operating expenses and service debt until midway through the development phase when the P&L line moves above the break-even point, implying that there is sufficient cash to service debt.

At the complete other end of the spectrum are *angel investors* who make small investments in companies that may be nothing more than an idea. Companies at this stage are very risky investments as there are uncertainties about how the company will develop and what the outcomes will be, so the ability to generate a return on an angel investment is largely based on faith or a "gut" feeling of the angel. Investors at this stage require more than an interest rate to compensate them for the risk that their investment will be lost. The "Risk" line and the "Valuation" lines in Figure 2.1 show that when the company is at an earlier stage, the risk is extremely high, meaning that the company's valuation is significantly below that of a later-stage company with less associated risks.

Venture investors are seeking the ideal combination of risk and returns, which is typically achieved by investing in companies that are in the development and the go-to-market phase. They have to acquire meaningful equity in a company, so they capture as much value as possible to be monetized through a liquidity event, or exit. As the company successfully matures, the concept is that the probability of returning economic value to the investor through an exit event increases dramatically. And what a company is willing to pay for capital decreases in tandem. This means that an investor's return targets need to compensate for losses in the portfolio so that on aggregate, the returns of the winners wipe out the losses.

THE INVESTMENT LIFECYCLE OF A COMPANY

There are countless stories of entrepreneurship that can be traced back to a point in time when the founders wrote out their business plan on the back of a napkin. So much so, in fact, that it has become a common trope for describing the ideation and planning phase of a startup. It is a great example that often a business is little more than an idea; it's so small you can write it on a napkin. When you have the ability to take that initial napkin idea and develop it into an operating company, the business will grow and change. At each phase, there are specific dynamics that need to be managed and common strategic options and outcomes along with sources of financing that are specific to the needs of a company. It is helpful to understand how companies develop not only for the purposes of raising capital, but also for managing and building value over time, as outlined in Table 2.1.

Stage	Company Elements	Types of Financing
Seed	Founders are developing ideas about what the company will be. There are limited resources with no product or service ready and no revenues being generated. The company is run by the founders and is not capitalized to acquire staff or other resources and is without contracted suppliers, customers, or vendors.	Equity from founders' friends, family, and angels Debt from credit cards (founders' personal resources)
Development	The founders are refining the product or services to deliver along with the operating model. Any R&D and technology development is scoped out and underway. The operational plan is defined and resourcing requirements identified. Early adopter customers are identified and in discussions, but the company is still in a pre-revenue phase.	Equity from founders' friends, family, and angels Equity from high-risk venture capital

TABLE 2.1—Company Lifecycle Stages

Stage	Company Elements	Types of Financing
Go-to-Market	The company is generating revenue, but not yet profitable or just at break even.	Equity from founders' friends, family, and angels Debt from credit cards (founders' personal resources) Equity from high-risk venture capital Equity from private equity funds or family offices Bank debt
Expansion	The company achieves profitability and meaningful customer adoption.	Equity from high-risk venture capital Equity from private equity funds or family offices Bank debt Strategic financing from corporate partners
Exit	When a company has core value drivers such that a buyer will want to acquire it, exit opportunities are pursued, and early-stage risk is largely mitigated.	Equity from high-risk venture capital Equity from private equity funds or family offices Bank debt Strategic financing from corporate partners Access to the public markets

TABLE 2.1—Company Lifecycle Stages, continued

Two important terms that reflect where a company is in its lifecycle are "pre-revenue" and "post-revenue." These terms are widely used by investors to quickly identify a company's stage. When a company has demonstrated that it can produce revenue, it implies that there is a developed market-ready product or service and all the work has been done to get to a point where an external customer is willing to pay money for the product or service. If a company has not yet reached that point, it is considered a *pre-revenue company*. Many investors define their investment parameters by stating whether they will invest in pre-revenue companies, meaning they will take on earlier stage risk.

A *post-revenue company* will require investment for a completely different set of activities, so using revenue as a benchmark allows investors to quickly characterize what their investment will likely go to fund, what the next set of outcomes will likely be, and in what anticipated time frame they will occur. Companies with revenue are broadly managing how to scale while pre-revenue companies are managing developing products and an organization in anticipation of scaling.

THE INVESTOR LANDSCAPE

There are groups of explicit investors who allocate to companies at certain stages. You already read that VCs invest in innovation and growth-stage companies, but there are several groups of investors, some organized and some less so, who also finance private companies. The following is a list of investors who are unique from VC funds and may be a source of financing.

$ *Friends, Family, and Founders*. At the initial stages of a company, the first investor is the founder. As a founder, you have made the decision to invest your time, money, and resources into a business that you believe gives you the best return on those investments. As such, many companies are funded through the network of family and close friends who also believe in the founder. A company at this stage is mostly ideas and will have little more than some concepts and little to no infrastructure. As a result, the company would never fulfill the criteria of a VC fund and the investors are simply betting on the founder. These are typically small and mostly informal investment rounds.

- *Angel Investors.* When the company needs additional capital beyond what friends and family can provide, a group of investors defined as "angels" invest as individuals in these types of situations. Angels are most commonly retired executives or individuals with enough wealth to invest in a few private companies at a time. These investments are coming from their personal wealth. The investors make the investment decision themselves without much structure, although don't underestimate how important a spouse can be in the decision. Angels are difficult to find and get access to outside of some organized groups who accept applications. Angels may be involved in their investments at the board level and bring some relationships that may be helpful. It is also common that if a company starts to grow rapidly and attract more institutional investors, like funds that the angel investors, as well as the friends and family, will be diluted and may not have the available capital to participate in subsequent rounds to maintain their ownership. As a result, angel rounds will have similar terms, will usually have more structure, and will require negotiating key terms such as board participation and dilution provisions. But overall, the structure may be less detailed or onerous than the terms a VC would seek.
- *Family Offices.* There is a term that has become commonplace in finance and that is a group of investors that are defined as family offices. This structure has emerged beyond the Ultra-High Net Worth Individual (UHNWI) definition largely due to the significant individual wealth they are managing. In summary, when an individual is managing a significant amount of personal wealth, they start to establish some infrastructure to manage their assets, lifestyle, and business ventures. This can include everything from managing assets, such as homes and real estate, to wealth management to overseeing estates and property and developing tax-advantaged structures that facilitate wealth transferring from generation to generation. Many families group together in multifamily "offices" and leverage consolidated wealth management strategies and pool

resources. Family offices are very difficult to access as many want to remain obscured from public access. They are, however, a group of investors that are making significant investments into the cannabis sector.

The group with the highest level of scrutiny and investment rigor are VC funds, so in theory if you can meet the investment parameters for a VC, then you will meet the expectations of these other potential investors. For example, let's say a VC will need to see a projected financial model going out five years and an angel investor is fine with one that just covers the next 12 months. As a practical matter, planning for the five-year model and doing the work to build something that has a realistic potential will fulfill the needs of the angel investor while also standing up to VC-level scrutiny.

Raising capital is not about doing the minimum amount of work or having a "minimum viable product." Raising capital is a symptom of doing the hard work needed to build a great business and, with that, identifying the market of investors available to the stage and type of businesses you are combined with knowledge and research.

Depending on what stage of growth your company is in, there will be certain investors who are available to you as outlined in Table 2.2 below. If you correlate the stage of your business with the types of investors, you can focus on the groups that are suitable.

Investors	Stage
Friends and Family	Seed
Angel Investors	Seed and development
Venture Capital	Development, go-to-market, and expansion
Private Equity	Go-to-market, expansion, and exit
Lenders	Expansion and exit

TABLE 2.2—Investor and Company Stage Matrix

When Jon Trauben, founding partner of Altitude Investment Management, was asked at the Cannabis Dealmakers New York Summit 2019 about defining the types of investors, he explained how his fund thinks about the types of investors in private equity (PE):

> *Venture is investing in non-control positions and generally earlier stage; private equity is investing in controlling stakes and generally later stages. When I think of a hedge fund, I think liquidity. We're just fundamental investors in this industry. We spend the time, we look across the industry, and we're not pre-picking the verticals, strategies, companies, and geographies that are going to ultimately win. We're students of it, and we're following along.*

What Jon is describing is how his fund views the markets that they invest in and the clear lines of delineation between the stage and style of investing. He quickly aligns venture with non-control investing, which means that VCs are "minority" (less than 50 percent) shareholders in the companies they invest in. Although PE is the same strategy as venture (investing in private companies), he quickly points out that PE funds are different in that they take controlling interests (more than 50 percent) of an investment. For Jon's fund, this would indicate that they invest across stages because of how developing cannabis companies may or may not fit traditional definitions.

HOW VENTURE CAPITAL WORKS

In order to understand how a venture investor thinks, you need to look at how a venture capital firm operates and is structured—especially if you are raising capital from a VC. When an entrepreneur sits across the table from a VC investor, it's common to think about that individual as being the investor who will be writing the check. In reality, the VCs that you will be meeting with actually manage a fund of other people's money that they in turn use to finance the investment they structure with you.

VCs are categorized as institutional investors, meaning that they have formed a general partnership between investors, with themselves as the general partner. This partnership represents a pool of capital, or fund, that is formed to invest in specific types of companies. The general partner is the management team of the fund. It is their job to find investments that meet the criteria of the fund and go through a rigorous evaluation process to ultimately approve the funding of companies that meet that criterion. The key distinction between funds and family offices or angel investors is that the people managing and running the fund are using the capital they have secured from their partners as opposed to their own capital. So, their job is to allocate the capital they have arranged access to in a way that produces the largest possible returns back to the fund investors. The *general partner* is referred to as the GP, and the *limited partners* or investors are the LPs.

Over time, they will develop a portfolio that they expect to generate outsized (large) returns. To be successful in that pursuit, they create very sophisticated investment models and processes and have the highest level of scrutiny in their due diligence process (which you'll read more about in Chapter 10). The VC generates economics by charging a management fee and something called a carried interest. The *management fee* is a percentage of the funds that the LPs have committed to invest. *Carried interest* is where the VC makes the bulk of their economics as it is calculated as a percentage of the profits of the fund's investing activities. After the GP repays with a return on the capital the LPs have committed, the profits are split. VCs typically earn 20 percent of the profits of the investments. This is important because you should know how VCs are incentivized. The general rule is that the cost of identifying investments, performing due diligence on those investments, and having the team and infrastructure in place to do so is paid out of the management fees, but the real profits are generated through the performance of the fund. The theory is that incentives are aligned between the LPs and the GP so that the GP picks the best possible investments to produce the largest possible return for their investors. This also means that VCs have no incentive to deviate from their investment parameters or shortcut an investment process. Do not spend any time wondering if an investor will shift their goal posts just to invest in your business.

Where the messaging does become valuable when seeking VC investment is when you are aligned with an *exit strategy* for your business. An exit strategy is simply how you will produce a significant return for the fund and its investors by selling the company in the future. In other words, it's the end goal, the end game that will hopefully earn a solid return for both you and the investors. The hard truth is that, on average, 50 percent of a VC's investments will go out of business and produce a zero return. This means that the professional investors only get it right half the time. Angel investors have even higher failure rates. So why do LPs keep investing in VC funds?

What happens most often is that there is a massive exit event for one of the companies in the portfolio that not only recoups the losses of the failures but will also contribute to the bulk of the performance of the fund and produce the income they earn. When venture investments are successful, there are few other investments that can produce such significant returns. This is the risk-adjusted rate of return concept from earlier in the chapter. What does this mean for you?

- $ When you are raising capital from a fund, the people you are talking with are most likely not putting their own capital at risk; the
- $ GP of a fund is staking its business on the companies they invest in having a significant liquidity event; and
- $ VCs won't take unplanned or cavalier risks or deviate from their investment parameters, as there is too much riding on making only the best investments.

In the cycle of venture investing, each fund has a finite timeframe and set amount of capital it can deploy. The saying, "I'd rather invest in no deal than a bad deal" simply means that investors can wait to find the perfect deals to invest in. The long-term goal of VC is to raise additional funds, and their ability to do that successfully is predicated on the returns they generate in their current fund.

WHY TRADITIONAL VCS DON'T INVEST IN CANNABIS

Traditional VC funds are governed by the terms of their partnership agreements. These agreements between the GP and LP contain the terms under which the GP is allowed to invest the LP's capital. These terms include adherence to an established investment thesis, required reporting and compliance, and something called a *moral clause.* This is a clause that prohibits funds from investing in companies that are in the tobacco, firearms, or pornographic industries. And as long as cannabis is a federally illegal Schedule I narcotic, those clauses will continue to prohibit traditional VC investors from investing in cannabis businesses.

That said, there are some gray areas here, but investors don't like the gray areas and, for the time being, traditional VC funds will be steering clear of investing in cannabis with few exceptions. When this does change—and it will over time as many funds are already ramping up to start exploring cannabis investing—it is plausible that they will stay focused on the industries they have invested in historically. For example, a health-care fund will have the systems, relationships, and teams in place to invest in health-care companies. They will then continue to invest in health care but will at some point open up to cannabis health-care businesses.

The cannabis economy will impact the industries that venture investors have historically invested in, and once they are clear to invest in companies that are in those industries, they will look at companies that leverage cannabis in their business model. We can think about them as "industry first, cannabis second" investors.

THE CANNABIS VENTURE CAPITAL INDUSTRY

According to the National Venture Capital Association (NVCA) and research firm PitchBook, there are over 1,000 VC firms that invested north of $100 billion in 2018. There are currently approximately 125 explicit venture capital funds in the U.S. today investing exclusively in companies in the cannabis economy. Given the restrictions for traditional VC, the financing void is also being filled at a meaningful level by family offices and private investors that invest in deals directly. As the industry matures, a group of cannabis-committed funds are coming into the mainstream as well. Examples of some of the leading funds that are making significant investments are Gotham Green Partners, Altitude Investment Management, Tuatara Capital, Phyto Partners, Merida Capital Partners, Casa Verde Capital, Lerer Hippeau, Privateer Holdings, Poseidon Asset Management, Treehouse Global Ventures, T3 Ventures, and Hypur Ventures. Each has distinct investment strategies and invest across segments and companies at various stages of scale.

In addition, there are a number of firms that started as funds but migrated into holding companies and consolidated groups of operating businesses. This is how Canopy Growth Corporation, TILT Holdings, and Acreage Holdings started out. The investment industry for cannabis started emerging at the same time as Colorado and Washington legalized adult use, and according to MGO & ELLO PitchBook's 2019 "Cannabis Private Investment Review," there are approximately 125 cannabis VC investors (see Figure 2.2).

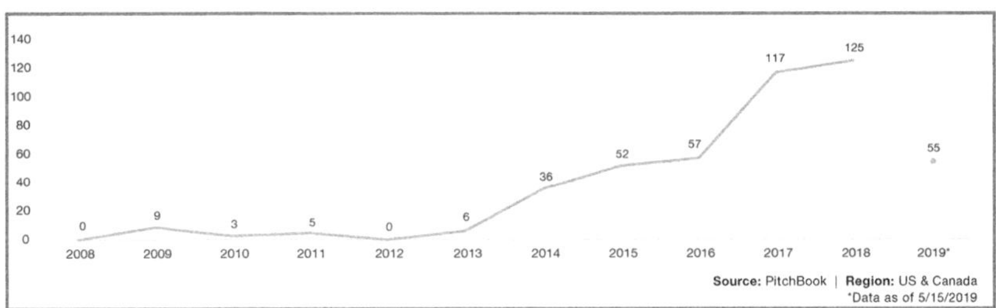

FIGURE 2.2—Active Unique VC Investors in Cannabis

As the number of investors dedicated to cannabis started emerging, there was also a concurrent explosion in entrepreneurship. Leading with the states that had made the most progress towards legalizing medical and recreational use, pockets of startups and investors began emerging. If you look at the data provided by PitchBook for CVC activity in Figure 2.3 on page 30, you can see that the number of transactions that secured investment has grown dramatically along with the amount of capital being deployed. It is, however, safe to assume that these were only a handful of the companies that were seeking capital at that time and many large transactions were materializing through other sources of private capital, such as family offices.

The year 2018 represents a banner time in financing with 149 deals collectively securing over $1 billion in CVC backing. Comparatively outside of cannabis, the PitchBook-NVCA Venture Monitor research tracked 8,948 VC deals closing in 2018 with total investments topping $100 billion in value for the first time since 2000. This would indicate that although CVC is expanding and many funds are raising their second-round funds already, there are still very few deals being funded in the cannabis

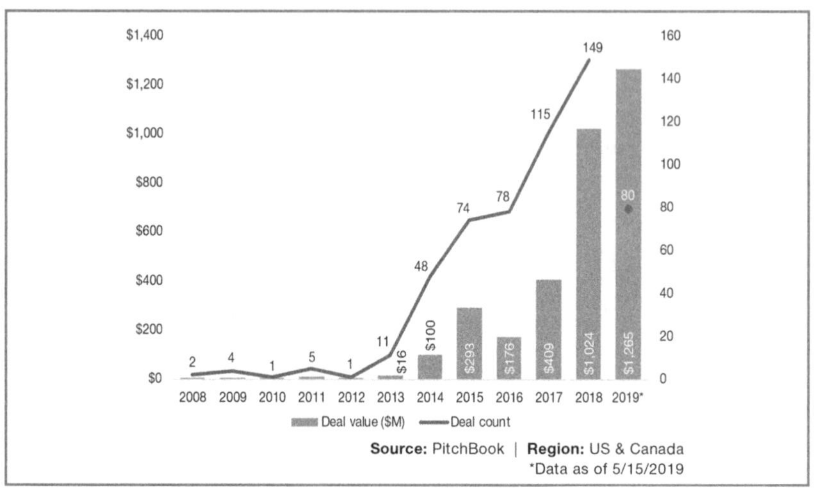

FIGURE 2.3—CVC Deal Activity

sector. This is despite the explosive growth and significant legalization momentum with medical use now legal in 23 states and recreational use permitted in 10 states.

The types of transactions that CVCs are consummating is also coming into view. As the sector matures, both early-stage investing and late-stage investing will increase as companies stay private and secure follow-on rounds of funding and investment funds secure more capital to deploy. Figure 2.4 on page 31 shows the momentum in first-round financing activity in cannabis.

As the markets continue to expand, there will also be more companies seeking CVC for both first financings and subsequent financings. Financings in private companies are described as "series," and the first institutional or VC round is commonly referred to as the "Series A" round. This round usually comes after you have requested funding from any friends and family or angels. Each subsequent round is given the next letter, so round two is a "Series B" round, and so on. Late-stage CVC are those companies that have closed multiple series and continue to open up new series of investments. For example, the company Pax Labs raised $420 million in a Series C in the first half of 2019. In looking at the total deal volume by stage in 2018, you will see that early- and late-stage funding are nearing similar high-water marks, and 2019 is projected to be the first year

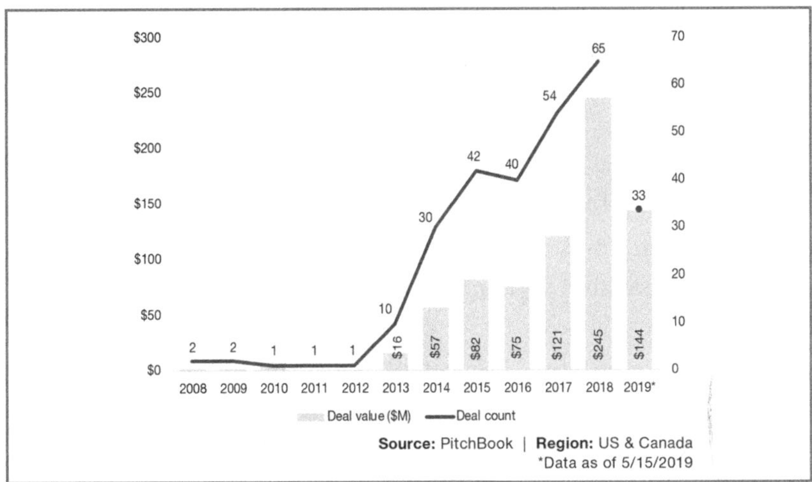

FIGURE 2.4—CVC First Financing Activity

that late-stage investment will exceed early-stage investing. As outlined in Figure 2.5, through mid-May 2019, there were $660 million investment in late-stage CVC rounds (including the PAX deal) across nine deals and over

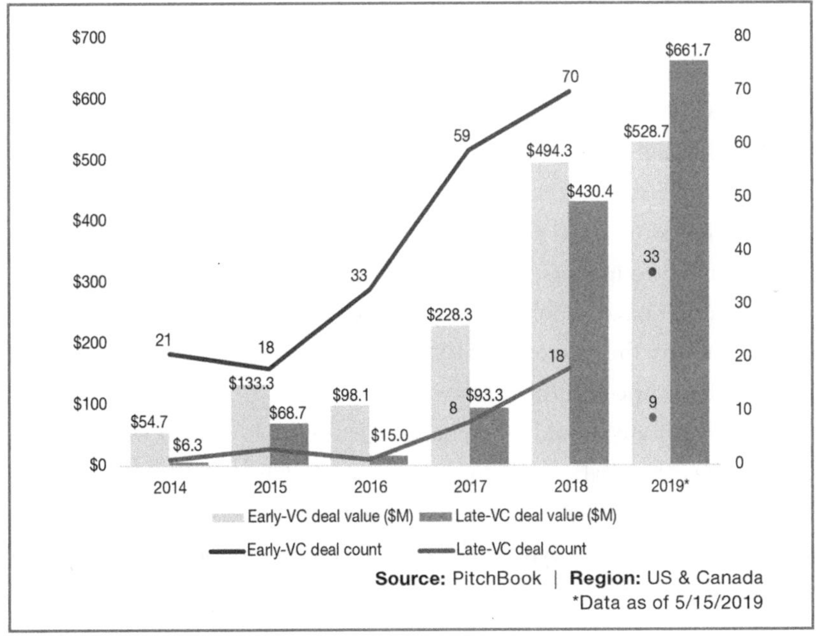

FIGURE 2.5—CVC Deal Activity by Stage

$530 million invested in early-stage rounds across 33 deals. This shows that the CVC world is growing at a steady rate as more companies receive funding at various stages.

SYNDICATIONS

When you hear investors talk about "syndicating" a deal or a "club deal," this means that a group of investors work together to invest in the transaction. Think of it the way TV shows are syndicated—many channels offer to air them. It's a similar case here. This is most common in investments that are under $20 million and almost always the case for seed rounds and Series A and B rounds. What this means is that one investor will typically take a "lead" on the transaction, set the terms, and quarterback managing the transaction on behalf of a group of investors who will invest less than the lead.

It is common practice to set up something called a *special purpose vehicle* (SPV), a legal entity set up for the sole purpose of collecting a group of investors to invest in the company. This means that one investor (the SPV) will own a portion of equity of the company and that SPV may have several investors in its own right. Having one entity investing in your company reduces the management of the investors significantly. Typically, the SPV will nominate one person to interact with the company on behalf of the syndicate.

As Troy Dayton, founder and CEO of Arcview puts it, "Managing a group of investors, such as angels or high-net-worth individuals, is a little like managing volunteers. They don't always know how they can best help, and they don't have to do anything at the end of the day if they don't want to." That's why the role of the SPV is vital—they have to understand and manage the nuances of those relationships.

The syndicate should be managed so you don't end up with a whole group of investors who want to be actively involved in your company. At times, it may make better sense to negotiate directly with the individual investors one-on-one. Syndicates are very common and a structure you should be familiar with.

UNDERSTANDING NORTH AMERICAN MACRO CANNABIS INVESTMENT TRENDS

by Scott Greiper, president of Viridian Capital Advisors, LLC

Through 2018, the transactional activity in Mergers and Acquisitions (M&A) by both buyers and sellers were Canadian-focused. What that means is that on both sides of the transactions were Canadian-domiciled private or Canadian-listed companies. For the first time in five years of tracking data, the most active region for buyers and sellers was the U.S. This change happened for the first time as shown in Table 2.3 based on proprietary transaction data from the Viridian Deal Tracker©.

	2018 Total	Q1 2019	Q2 2019
Lead Buyer Region (most active)	Canada	United States	Canada
Lead Target (seller) Region	Canada	United States	United States

Source: Viridian Capital Advisors Deal Tracker

TABLE 2.3: Viridian Deal Tracker M&A Buyer and Seller Regional Trends

What that means is that we are seeing a return to the U.S. cannabis marketplace by buyers, sellers, and investors, both public and private. There are four reasons for these trends:

1. The U.S. market is the largest in the world and continues to open up more and more states to cannabis.
2. Over the last three or four years, a flight of capital and companies to the Canadian marketplace was due to cannabis being federally legal in Canada. Investors did not have to price in the risk of being federally illegal like they do in the U.S. That uncertainty is waning.

CANNABIS INVESTMENT TRENDS, continued

3. At the time of this writing, there is legislation moving through the U.S. Congress that is providing some clarity for the banking industry to finance legally licensed cannabis companies and recognize the rights of the states to protect the rights of the legal companies from federal influence. This is the first attempt at enacting legislation to protect the rights of legally licensed state business to operate freely without the threat of federal action.
4. The Canadian marketplace has become very crowded. Investor rationale is better in the U.S. today because it is a more fertile market with more acquisition targets. It is not yet quite as competitive as what is happening in Canada, so you can negotiate good terms if you are a U.S. company.

So, what does this mean for an entrepreneur as they think about their exit strategy (which you'll read more about in Chapter 8)? Here are a couple of considerations:

1. With the Canadian market correcting (valuations and market caps) and with a slowdown of the companies going public in Canada, it is not as alluring for U.S. companies to go public in Canada. Therefore, U.S. companies are staying private longer.
2. The more attractive exit strategy is now a sale of the company and finding a buyer through the traditional M&A process.

CANNABIS CAPITAL TAKEAWAYS AND ACTION ITEMS

Knowing your audience is the first rule in raising capital. There is a broad spectrum of investors that back early-stage companies, and each has their own specific investment criteria, motivations, and approaches. By starting with VC investors and analyzing their approach, vetting methodologies, and really understanding how they operate, you can begin to formulate a strategy for how and when to approach investors. Less than 1 in 300 deals will achieve funding, meaning that less than 1 percent of companies will meet the expectations of VCs and secure funding through them. The key conclusions for a cannabis entrepreneur to consider are:

- $ CVC is an emerging industry within the cannabis economy.
- $ Although the number of CVC funds is growing and the capital they have access to is increasing, those inventors won't access enough capital to invest in the exponentially expanding opportunity set of emerging cannabis companies.
- $ Know your audience. A VC is a specific type of investor and has specific parameters. It has no incentives to deviate from its investment thesis, so start with identifying the fit and focus on investors that match your business.
- $ Companies access different sources of financing as they mature, so knowing the stage of your company will help you identify the best fits today, and you should plan for future financings as you grow.
- $ Traditional VCs aren't actively investing in cannabis today, so the CVC market is the best choice for cannabis entrepreneurs. However, when VC firms do invest, they will likely be "industry first, cannabis second" investors, and the CVC funds that are just establishing themselves will emerge as "cannabis first, industry second investors."

Action Item: Create an Investor Profile and Suitability Template

It is never too early to start doing your research on investors. If you start now by creating a database and learning about who is investing and whether they might be a good fit for your company, you will have better information when you start to develop your offering and preparing your process to raise capital. You can start this process by creating an initial suitability template for your internal use and using it a screening tool for the investors you are currently researching, as seen in Figure 2.6 on page 36.

	Investor Criteria	**My Company Parameters**	**Suitability**		
Cannabis	Y / N		Poor	Average	Good
Sector Fit	Y / N		Poor	Average	Good
Investment Stage	☐ Seed Stage ☐ Venture Pre-Revenue ☐ Venture Post-Revenue ☐ Late Stage		Poor	Average	Good
Investment Size	☐ <$1 Million ☐ ≥$1m ≤$5m ☐ $5m - $10m ☐ $10m+		Poor	Average	Good
Historical Transactions in Sector?	Y / N		Poor	Average	Good
Competitors in Portfolio?	Y / N		Poor	Average	Good
Equity/Debt	Eq. / Dbt.		Poor	Average	Good
Investor Viability	**Bad Fit**	**Average Fit**	**Good Fit**		

FIGURE 2.6—Investor Suitability Template

REGULATION, POLICY, AND BANKING

by David T. Mangone, Esquire, Cannabis Lawyer and Lobbyist

Opportunities available in an expanding global cannabis industry are at the forefront of conversations in family offices as well as among private and institutional investors around the globe. As part of these conversations, it is critical to understand the dynamics of federal cannabis policy in the U.S.—and the political landscape for reform—as key factors to risk assessment for investors.

Cannabis policy and politics in Washington are evolving as quickly as the industry itself, and real-time events are defining the future trajectory of federal cannabis policy and law. Because cannabis policy is a starting point for agricultural, economic, and health policies for many federal lawmakers, the discussion about when federal law will change is frequently a subset of a broader political discussion. Despite uncertainties about the timing and trajectory of comprehensive cannabis reform, the success or failure of any one cannabis investment is unlikely to be negatively affected by this fluidity. The purpose of this chapter is to provide you with the necessary understanding of the cannabis landscape at the federal level in order to credibly convey to investors the potential evolution of the cannabis industry. Keep in mind that policy and reform issues change frequently, so it's always best to check with your local, state, and federal resources for the latest information.

Despite its status as a federally illegal substance in the U.S., 33 states have enacted comprehensive medical cannabis paradigms and 11 states have enacted comprehensive adult consumption and commercialization programs as of this writing (likely with more to follow). Forty-seven states have enacted laws that have legalized some form of cannabis, including permitting cannabidiol (CBD) as a treatment for specific medical conditions or decriminalization for certain amounts of cannabis possession or consumption. For an updated list of each state's laws addressing decriminalization, possession, medical and fully legalized jurisdictions, you can visit the National Conference of State Legislatures site at www.ncsl.org.

With this conflict between federal illegality and state law, how can cannabis business owners—and the investors on whom these entrepreneurs so heavily rely—evaluate the progress of change in federal law? When and how will the conflict between federal and state law be resolved? When and how will urgent problems caused by federal illegality—such as access to banking—be addressed?

POTENTIAL PROBLEMS FOR INVESTORS

As of July 2019, there are two provisions of the Controlled Substances Act (CSA) about which investors should be particularly mindful as they consider entering the cannabis space: section 846 and section 854. Section 846 deals with conspiracy to commit offenses under the Controlled Substances Act. Depending on the level of direct or indirect ownership, an investor in a cannabis business could be deemed to be conspiring to commit an offense resulting in potential incarceration or fines. However, as of this writing, there have been no notable federal prosecutorial actions taken against investors in companies operating in compliance with state law solely by virtue of their cannabis investment. Section 854 is reproduced in part below:

> *It shall be unlawful for any person who has received any income derived, directly or indirectly, from a violation of [the CSA] . . . punishable by imprisonment for more than one year in which such person has participated as a principal . . . to use or invest, directly or indirectly, any part of such income, or the proceeds of such income, in acquisition of any interest in, or the establishment or operation of, any enterprise which is engaged in, or the activities of which affect interstate or foreign commerce.*

While direct or indirect ownership in a cannabis business can trigger this provision, it appears that certain stock and securities arrangements do not immediately trigger this provision:

> *A purchase of securities on the open market for purposes of investment, and without the intention of controlling or participating in the control of the issuer, or of assisting another to do so, shall not be unlawful . . . if the securities of the issuer held by the purchaser, the members of his immediate family, and his or their accomplices in any violation of [the CSA] after such purchase do not amount in the aggregate to 1 per centum of the outstanding securities of any one class, and do not confer, either in law or in fact, the power to elect one or more directors of the issuer.*

Fortunately, since 2014, a Congressional Appropriations Rider has prevented individuals from being prosecuted under these provisions. However, the Securities and Exchange Commission (SEC) has taken enforcement actions against cannabis business for traditional infractions like fraud. Other federal legal considerations for private equity investors in the cannabis space include:

- $ Access to the business banking
- $ A cannabis business' access to capital outside of private investment
- $ Taxation (as there is no IRS exemption for illegal income, so investors who receive investment income from an illicit business under federal law must still pay taxes on appreciated investments such as capital gains and dividends)
- $ Registration of securities through the U.S. Securities and Exchange Commission (SEC) if applicable

CURRENT FEDERAL PROTECTIONS

Despite the concerns highlighted above, certain aspects of the U.S. cannabis industry have limited protections from federal interference through annual congressional spending bills. Since the restriction of district-specific earmarks in 2015, lawmakers have used annual appropriations bills (also known as federal spending bills) to extend their policy priorities (or policy prohibitions) by inserting language that prohibits the expenditure of federal funds towards a specific program or activity.

Since 2015, Congress has consistently enacted law that limits the ability of the Department of Justice (DOJ) from interfering with states that have adopted medical cannabis laws by placing legal restrictions on their spending of federal dollars. Spending bills protecting the medical cannabis industry have to be renewed every year or must be carried forward in the event federal spending bills are not successfully enacted. Despite this onerous process, this legal baseline has established a consistent policy of respecting states' rights to set and implement their respective medical cannabis laws by preventing federal agencies, including Department of Justice (DOJ) and the Drug Enforcement Agency (DEA), from prosecuting medical cannabis stakeholders operating in compliance with state law. However, this appropriations language does not prevent other federal agencies like the IRS, the

Federal Deposit Insurance Corporation (FDIC), or the SEC from taking enforcement actions.

The impact of this restriction on spending statutorily strips the DOJ from prosecuting medical cannabis stakeholders and patients in states that have enacted medical cannabis laws. This restriction has also been upheld in the courts. In *U.S. v. McIntosh, 833 F3d 1163, 1178* (9th Cir 2016), the 9th Circuit Court of Appeals held that all stakeholders of state medical marijuana programs, including states, patients, operators, and investors, that comply with the rules and regulations of a particular state medical cannabis program enjoy a protection from federal prosecutorial interference.

While there has been progress to expand spending prohibitions to apply to the entire cannabis industry (and not just medical cannabis industry stakeholders), no efforts have yet been successfully signed into law, though the House of Representatives approved this provision in 2019 in a 267-165 vote, including efforts to prevent the DOJ from interfering in any state legal cannabis business, not just those that are medical in nature.

Former Attorney General Jeff Sessions rescinded a key DOJ policy (commonly referred to as the "Cole Memo") in 2017, which set forth the DOJ's enforcement priorities with respect to medical and adult-use cannabis stakeholders, focusing on issues like access by minors. However, since the rescission of this key policy document, the majority of U.S. attorneys in relevant jurisdictions have clarified that they will continue to exercise prosecutorial discretion in a manner consistent with the Cole Memo.

When the Cole Memo was first introduced in 2014, the Department of the Treasury Financial Crimes Enforcement Network (FinCEN) implemented guidelines predicated on the Cole Memo to address the bankability of proceeds from state-compliant cannabis activities, referred to as "FinCEN guidance." The FinCEN guidance sets forth specific standards for banks working with state-compliant cannabis companies to mitigate the risk that these financial institutions would be prosecuted for money-laundering violations. Though the Cole Memo was rescinded, the FinCEN guidance remained in place, which is important for investors.

CHANGING FEDERAL LAW AND POLITICS AROUND LEGALIZATION

For more than a decade, dozens of bills have been introduced in Congress to address federal cannabis reform. Consider these bills in two categories. In the first category are bills with the objective of legalizing cannabis at the federal level, either by descheduling cannabis as a Schedule I substance or rescheduling it to a less-restrictive category within the Controlled Substances Act. The second category of bills aims to address all the ancillary issues that have been created by the conflict between federal and state law. These include, but are not limited to, access to banking, cash treatment, federal benefits, immigration, veterans, and so on. With this active and evolving legislative environment, the question on everyone's mind is: When will cannabis be legalized at the federal level and by what legislative mechanism?

While entrepreneurs and investors look at the trajectory of legalization through the eyes of business opportunity, millions of Americans, advocates, and activists are looking to legalization because of the disproportionate impact that longstanding drug policies have had on minority and impoverished communities. Because of a commitment to correcting the disproportionate impacts of the War on Drugs, a constituency within the cannabis community is prioritizing legislative solutions that include social equity and reparative justice components above other reform considerations.

For example, the ability of the cannabis industry to expand and continue to flourish is largely due to state-level work of the drug advocacy community starting in California in the mid-1990s. Before there was an industry to be had—and before there were commercial interests to protect and promote—cannabis advocacy was advanced by individuals who were concerned about disparities in the application of laws. As business owners and investors, social equity remains a key concern of many industry advocates.

While the importance of sweeping criminal justice and drug policy reform cannot be understated, industry advocates also look at another layer of reform, which is ensuring that existing and future cannabis businesses are treated like other existing businesses without unnecessary discrimination, including access to traditional banking. As cannabis businesses receive more protections from the federal government, they can feel comfortable reinvesting in their communities through inclusive hiring practices and capital infusions. For cannabis entrepreneurs, creating business models that incorporate criminal and social justice pillars within their organizations will benefit from this important element of comprehensive reform at the federal level.

Nevertheless, it is understandable that for business industry stakeholders and their advocates, the most politically pragmatic opportunity to advance reform is legislation to address access to banking. Under current law, cannabis businesses are often forced to operate in cash. However, there is a favorable climate to advance legislation that would improve banking access for cannabis businesses.

The most meaningful legislative measure advanced to date is the Secure and Fair Enforcement (SAFE) Banking Act of 2019 (H.R. 1595 | S. 1200). The SAFE Banking Act would create protections for depository institutions that provide financial services to state-compliant cannabis-related businesses and service providers. The SAFE Banking Act would not only codify protections for banks and financial institutions to service the cannabis industry, but it would ensure that licensed and legally operating cannabis businesses in the U.S. have access to traditional financial services. Because the bill allows cannabis businesses to access financial institutions while rectifying the public safety concern posed by cash businesses, SAFE enjoys strong bipartisan support and looks as though it will receive significant attention in both legislative chambers.

Beyond the federal appropriations bills and the banking bill discussed above, cannabis industry advocates are working to advance a bill that reflects the nuances in differing state markets and localities entitled the Strengthening the Tenth Amendment Through Entrusting States (the [STATES] Act (H.R. 2093 | S. 1028). In its current form, the STATES Act would codify the federal government's respect of each state's right to define what constitutes lawful business activity in its jurisdiction related to marijuana businesses and would carve out those acting in compliance with their respective state laws from the Controlled Substances Act (CSA). The

STATES Act has garnered a broad base of political support as it allows cannabis businesses to thrive in states where voters and lawmakers have created legal programs.

Ultimately, the trajectory of federal cannabis reform and the timing of this progress will come down to the complex equation of politics, policy, and personality. From a politics perspective, lawmakers in both chambers—and on both sides of the aisle—are reminded of the growing popularity for federal cannabis reform and the undeniable support of Americans for prohibiting the federal government from interfering with state programs.

Irrespective of the uncertainties in Washington, DC, cannabis entrepreneurs and investors are uniquely positioned to take advantage of early market opportunities, with a low probability of interference from the federal government. As the federal policy landscape moves closer and closer to deciding a post-prohibition regulatory framework, businesses with the right composition of managerial and strategic leadership, as well as sufficient capital, will only continue to improve their valuations and long-term outlook.

BANKING AND PAYMENTS IN CANNABIS: A VIEW FROM THE FRONT LINES

by Tyler Beuerlein, executive vice president of business development, Hypur

The topic of banking and payments in the state legal cannabis industry may be one of the most misrepresented and misinformed topics in any industry today. Some reasons for that include a lack of accurate information, financial institutions unwilling to talk, and special interests with an agenda feeding inaccurate or speculative information. It has widely been represented that there are over 500 banks and credit unions openly financing this industry throughout the country. That comes from FinCEN reporting related to SAR (Suspicious Activity Report) filings tied to cannabis operators. That is not an accurate representation of those truly funding this space.

BANKING AND PAYMENTS, continued

There are less than 40 financial institutions in the U.S. today openly banking the state legal cannabis industry. These are institutions with more than 10 "Tier 1," plant-touching accounts and full board approval to provide banking services to dedicated marijuana-related business programs. The majority of those are banks, although credit unions typically have some of the highest account concentrations in their respective markets. Every state with a legal cannabis program is vastly different from a licensing, regulatory, and banking perspective. In some states, there are as many as seven financial institutions openly serving the industry while others may only have one that banks every licensee in the state. In every state in the U.S. with a program, there is at least one option for the industry. The number of institutions is increasing at a steady pace due to two factors: new markets being introduced and institutions becoming more educated regarding the fact that this industry can and is being banked.

State Legal Cannabis Banking

As it stands today, the vast majority of cannabis licensees in the U.S. have a transparent banking relationship. Yes, this industry is already "banked." That is a fact that is being missed as this conversation progresses.

The SAFE Act (which you read about earlier in this chapter) has recently brought attention to this issue at the federal level but may have little effect on banking. The use of the word "solely" throughout the document gives it little effect on whether or not a bank or credit union will make the determination to bank the industry. If a regulator is examining a financial institution that is banking the cannabis industry and they are doing something wrong, it would be very easy for that examiner to cite any number of Bank Secrecy Act (BSA) or Anti-Money Laundering (AML) violations to couple with the fact that they were

BANKING AND PAYMENTS, continued

banking the industry. This is as much of a "highly regulated industry" problem as it is a "cannabis" problem. What I mean by that is there are massive industries that are perfectly legal that have essentially been shut out of the banking system due to the fact that they pose a significant regulatory compliance burden to financial institutions. These industries include but are not limited to check cashing, cross border remittance, the gun and ammunition industries, payday lending, etc. There are a very limited number of institutions serving those markets for the same reasons. Cannabis is and will continue to be a highly regulated industry for years to come.

The institutions that have made the determination to enter the cannabis banking arena have done so for myriad reasons. Those include a need for new revenue streams, personal experience with the product, the ability to access cheap deposits to offset large loan portfolios, and perhaps, most importantly to do what is right for the community.

Banking Regulations

From a regulatory perspective, we have seen a significant shift over the last five-and-a-half years as well. Many fail to realize that the only guidance for a bank or credit union looking to serve this industry is the 2014 FinCEN guidance that accompanied the now-rescinded Cole Memo. Bank and credit union regulators have been forced to learn along with the institutions banking the industry due to the fact there's no Federal Financial Insitutions Examination Council (FFIEC) handbook for examining an institution banking cannabis. Regulators have been forced into developing their own expectations and standards over the years when examining these institutions. At the onset, this created a tense and opaque process depending on the regulatory body and region in which the institution operated. There were many instances where the same regulatory body viewed the industry and expectations

BANKING AND PAYMENTS, continued

differently in each region. Since 2018, there has been a significant shift in regulatory stance and sentiment. I firmly believe regulators want what is best for the industry and these communities, regardless of personal stance on the product. That being said, can a regulator tell a bank or credit union it's OK to bank the cannabis industry? No. What they may be able to say, however, is something like "If you decide to bank this industry, we will examine you as if you were banking any other highly regulated industry."

CANNABIS CAPITAL TAKEAWAYS AND ACTION ITEMS

Law, policy, and banking regulation can be complicated topics for a new cannabis entrepreneur—especially because they change frequently as new laws are passed seemingly every day. As someone seeking funding, keep in mind that regulation, policy, and banking are all dependent on each other to some degree and may affect:

- $ Access to the business banking
- $ Access to capital outside of private investment
- $ Taxation
- $ Registration of securities through the U.S. SEC if applicable

Action Item: Research Your State's Laws

While federal protections may be few and far between, many states have taken up the mantle of legalization. Do some research on the intricacies of your state's cannabis outlook so you can better address the scope of any potential investment plans. You can start by checking out the following sites for more information:

- $ National Cannabis Industry Association's State-by-State Regulations Directory (https://thecannabisindustry.org/ncia-news-resources/state-by-state-policies/)

- $ National Conference of State Legislatures State Medical Marijuana Laws (www.ncsl.org/research/health/state-medical-marijuana-laws.aspx)
- $ NORML State Laws Interactive Map (https://norml.org/laws)

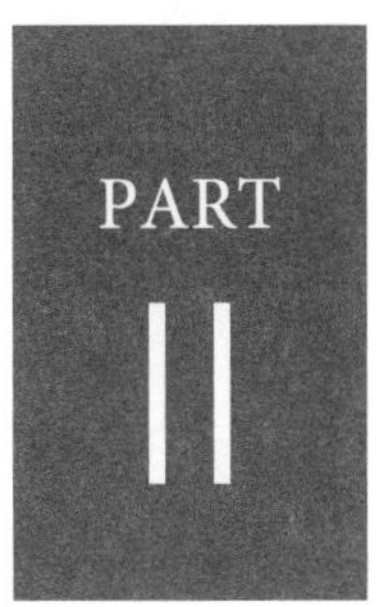

ENTREPRENEURSHIP AND PLANNING

CHAPTER 4

CANNABIS ENTREPRENEURSHIP

What does it mean to be the founder of a company? What is it like to be one of those people who describe themselves, and are described by others, as an entrepreneur? Over time, the concept of entrepreneurship has evolved through several market cycles from a relatively esoteric concept to being one the most aspirational career paths for a variety of generations. Those market cycles have gone through periods of massive growth and wealth creation and the turmoil of market crashes. Through all the volatility, great fortunes were made and lost, and we can expect that these market swings will happen again in the future.

During this time, *entrepreneurship* and *venture capital* emerged as terms associated with high-tech innovation. Silicon Valley has become the epicenter of venture investing that today glamorizes blockbuster deals with investors funding college dropouts who have gone on to build iconic businesses. These now-household-name billionaire founders have become benchmarks for the culture of defining entrepreneurship. This definition, though, is flawed. It is only a small expression of the universe of successful businessowners who represent the majority of entrepreneurs today. Most founders are not these outlier inventor-entrepreneurs who start a company based on a high-tech innovation, but instead are those who aspire to run profitable businesses iterating on experience and opportunity.

When you explore the research surrounding entrepreneurship, the data speaks to a group of business owners who are not young technology geniuses (or mostly male). According to the Kauffman Foundation, only 5 to 7 percent of successful startups make up those highly publicized tech-founder, venture-backed companies. Of these venture-backed businesses, statistically approximately 80 percent will fail within ten years. This would mean that approximately 95 percent of founders are running businesses that don't fit the public perception of entrepreneurship.

Most founders don't focus on large-scale innovations or disruptions but instead are *replicative*, a description that Economist and Professor William Baumol is credited with using to summarize the activity of taking existing ideas and copying them as a basis for building a successful (profitable) enterprise. These successful replicative entrepreneurs are different from the aforementioned stereotypes. They are older and more diverse, have spent more time working in other companies, and are more successful over the long term. As Carl J. Schramm, the former president of the Ewing Marion Kauffman Foundation, said in his excellent book *Burn the Business Plan* (Simon & Schuster, 2018), a large number of entrepreneurs did not attend college and waited until they were midcareer (and well over 35) before starting a business. He also goes on to highlight the probability that success increases with the age of the entrepreneurs. What is becoming evident is that the archetype of the entrepreneur is less about the flashy, headline-grabbing venture-backed stories and, particularly in cannabis, more about starting and operating a great business that has longevity, which is already incredibly hard to do regardless of the market you operate in.

This is good news for cannabis entrepreneurs. The cannabis markets are still new and looking for foundational business models where none had existed before. Simply opening a retail location for a dispensary is an innovation unto itself. The initial formation of the economy has been focused on building the infrastructure that cannabis industries will use to operate. This is the perfect opportunity for entrepreneurship outside the of the inventor-founder definition and inclusive of a more diverse group of business owners. CVC will need to adapt and iterate traditional VC strategies in order to finance the growth it seeks. In this chapter, we'll walk through some of the unique features of what it means to be a cannabis entrepreneur.

DEFINING CANNABIS ENTREPRENEURSHIP

An entrepreneur plays a critical role in their organization—to be responsible for the idea that the company was founded on commercializing it. The core competency is not to emphasize ideation, but rather being the leader who is responsible for bringing together resources and developing value for customers, employees, partners, their community, and ultimately investors. The type of person who can identify and access resources, such as capital and people, and then manage the deployment of those resources for profit is the model of a successful business owner and operator.

It is your job as a founder to identify the behaviors and charac-teristics of successful business strategies and experiences from other industries and adapt these best practices to your journey in cannabis entrepreneurship. Don't fall into the trap of believing that because your company is a cannabis business that the people with whom you do business from other backgrounds "don't know cannabis." This fatal flaw assumes that just because someone isn't as versed in the minutiae of a cannabis company they don't have the ability to understand the business of cannabis. There are simply a new set of problems to solve and a new set of evolving business conditions to operate within. Those are common challenges for entrepreneurs in any industry.

Emily Paxhia from Poseidon Asset Management describes the dynamic between cannabis and non-cannabis operators as the number-one issue facing operators and investors in cannabis today:

> *The number-one issue in cannabis is hubris. And that cuts both ways. People coming from other industries tend to assume that they can show—and I hate to use this word—the "potheads" how to run a better business. This marginalizes the experience that legacy industry practitioners bring to the table and almost always they are overwhelmed with how hard and complicated it is to run a cannabis company.*
>
> *From the legacy cannabis company operators' perspectives, people who have been in the industry tend to dismiss outsiders, stating that this is just how things are done. This creates a lack of ability to adapt to the transparency and communication that is needed to operate larger companies with more competition.*

Thus, it's important to remember that openly welcoming new ideas and outside perspectives while honoring the longstanding best practices of the industry are equally important.

One group straddling the line between history and innovation are advocates. The cannabis startup explosion is also being fueled by a migration of founders who were historically cannabis advocates focused on social and regulatory progress, transitioning into the role of cannabis entrepreneur. Were it not for the advocates who did the hard work to start the momentum towards legalization, showed up in their local elections, and voted in favor of legalization, the cannabis economy would be at best theoretical. Instead, it is a driving force for expanding global markets.

In addition, we are now seeing top talent transitioning from other markets and industries to start and run great companies in cannabis, enticed by the market possibilities and financial potential as much, or even more so, by any affinity for cannabis. One of the management teams that Mitch Baruchowitz of Merida Capital Partners, the "CEO Whisperer," described to me was made up of an experienced team that had people with operational cannabis expertise, financial management backgrounds in other sectors, and a lot of proactive interaction with regulators—a strategy that came from experience in other sectors as well. In other words, they had an affinity for strong execution.

EXECUTION: THE KEY TO SUCCESS

Constructing and running a great early-stage company with significant growth potential is all about who you hire and how you execute. Brett Finkelstein of Phyto Partners, founder of one of the first early-stage cannabis investment funds, says in describing one of the best presentations he saw for a company he invested in, "Their presentation was all about how they were going to execute, and only on the last page did they mention, 'By the way, we are focusing on the cannabis marketplace.'"

In short, execution is key, and you can learn a lot about how to do that successfully by paying attention to all the ways in which other business owners fail and succeed. The trick is to not make the same mistakes as those who came before you, but make new mistakes by pioneering new frontiers through the actions of entrepreneurial first principles. These start with some mixture of the three business manager characteristics shown in Figure 4.1.

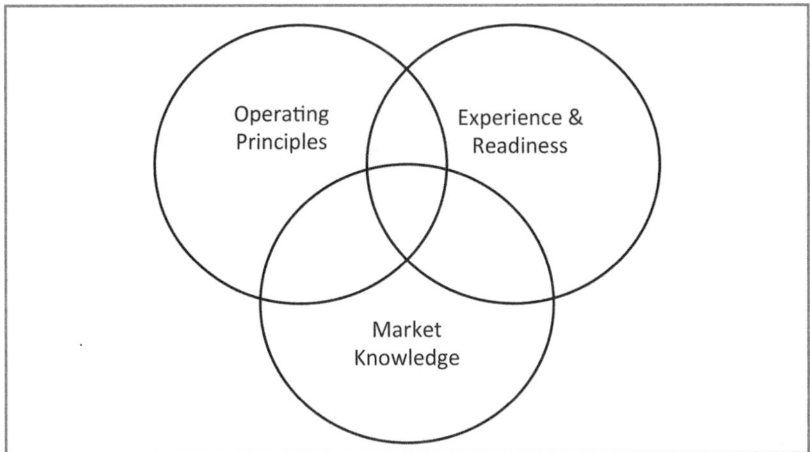

FIGURE 4.1—Business Manager Characteristics

If your company has the mix shown in Figure 4.1, you can showcase how that filters through your corporate philosophy (and how you, as the public face, live out your mission) when you are in the room with potential investors. You would be hard-pressed to find an investor who doesn't agree that success in venture investing really comes down to the people. So, what makes a great entrepreneur someone who investors want to back? More specifically, what qualities are signals for being a successful cannabis entrepreneur? There is no one answer to this, and when it comes to qualitative evaluations, many investors differ in their opinions. One constant remains, though, and that is that execution is the key to success as an entrepreneur, and the measure of success should start within the people and not become a goal simply to satisfy investors. Great companies and great entrepreneurs receive funding as a symptom of executing at the highest levels.

The unique capacity that successful entrepreneurs possess is the innate ability to scout opportunity. It's easy to define an entrepreneur through their capacity for risk or for being investors or innovators, but success in owning and operating a business is a symptom of seeing where there are needs not being met and pulling together resources to fill that need. In no sector is this core replicative entrepreneurship skillset more relevant than in cannabis.

The cannabis entrepreneur can be somewhat disadvantaged when approaching investors, as the majority of investors have decades of experience investing venture capital in other sectors. This is one aspect to the lack of fidelity in these discussions between investor and entrepreneur I stated in the introduction. It is imperative to first set guidelines and the operational principles that the cannabis entrepreneur can execute that would indicate future success in order to attract capital today.

MANAGING THE BUSINESS

Every investor will ultimately boil down their investment decision to people. Investing in a company all comes down to who is running it. Investors will be involved at the board level and can provide tremendous help and insights, but they are not running the company day to day. The success of the investment will only be realized after several years of being in business together, during which time the management team will be responsible for producing results. Starting and running a company is hard. If it was easy, everyone would do it and every investment would be successful. Standing apart in your ability to run your company successfully will be the difference between raising capital and going home empty-handed. When you are talking with investors, demonstrating that you have a grasp on how to produce results operationally increases the probability that your business will be successful for the long term and deliver value to you and your shareholders. This is a demonstration of operational acumen. As Mitch Baruchowitz of Merida Capital Partners says, "We want entrepreneurs to realize their dreams, and things go wrong in businesses all the time. So we look for how our CEOs handle friction and thoughtfully manage through it, which means we need to be clinical about our process and expect the operators we back to be clinical about theirs."

Management decisions come down then to a combination of people and processes, instinct and experience, chasing growth and managing risk. There are really only four reasons to act when managing a company:

1. To increase revenue
2. To reduce expenses (increase profits)
3. To fix something that is broken and not working
4. The government made me do it

Every organization needs guidance to help inform action, and it is the owner's job to set that guidance so that employees, customers, partners, and all the stakeholders are aligned in their understanding of your business. What you do, why you do it, how you do it, and for what desired outcome are the tenants of your corporate purpose. This starts by setting the vision for the business and a mission statement to inform decisions made within the organization. This, in turn, sets the culture of your business and is one of the most important ownership responsibilities that can only be led by owners.

Visionary Management

You will often hear about entrepreneurs being "visionary." What exactly does that mean? It takes a certain capacity to visualize a business where one does not exist yet. Metaphorically, an entrepreneur can look at an empty field and imagine a house there one day—one that is three stories high, with cedar frames, a four-car garage, the whole works. The level of detail they can visualize is extraordinary. But the idea of a house is only part of the story. If we can recognize that the ideation-entrepreneur, or inventor, is only a small fraction of the universe of entrepreneurship, the vision skillset for running a successful company lies in the ability to take the concept of the house and articulate it as a home. A home is not just a physical structure. It has purpose for providing shelter, for serving as place to convene family, a place to rest, a place to entertain, and the center of a person's world. A house is the "what," a home is the "why." Similarly, the entrepreneur has a unique capacity and vantage point to translate the why into a vison statement for their business.

You as a founder will define a vision statement for the company. This is the first piece to defining the company's mission and culture and can only be set by the owner. Your vision statement should capture the essence of why the business exists. What purpose is driving the organization, whom do you hope to impact, and what outcomes and place in the world does the business aspire to own?

Derived from the vision statement is the mission statement. The mission statement is defined and carried out by the organization. The "how" to the business should be articulated succinctly through this mission statement. Figure 4.2 on page 59 shows the transition from vision to mission. The mission statement is to be extrapolated by all the people involved in and impacted by the organization, ultimately leading to the operating principles that guide the day-to-day business and culture to deliver the objectives, goals, and tasks needed for your company to succeed.

The creation of the vision and mission is archived by setting up the organizational principles of the company. Driving these activities, understanding the interplay between them, and holding the organization accountable to deliver on the vision as a long-term strategic goal is vital to positioning your cannabis business for a successful pitch to investors.

Action is needed every day in your company, and the mission of the company should inform the actions of the stakeholders, both internally and externally. The mission statement can be set by you and your team and

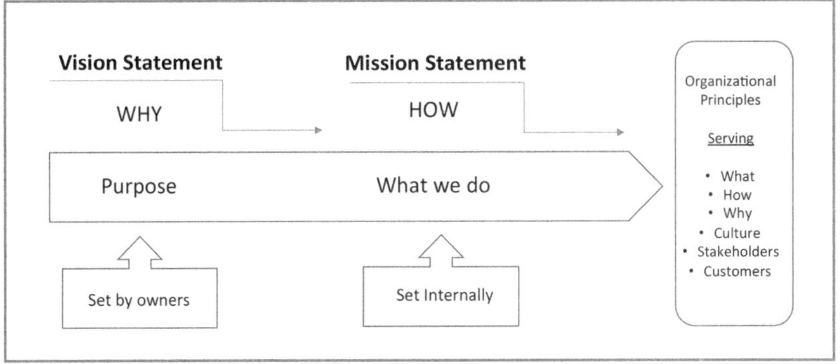

FIGURE 4.2—Vision and Mission Statement

should have input from employees at all levels of your organization. At the outset of a company when you don't have department heads, that's you—you're the single layer of input. Down the road, the team (and you will grow to have a team if you don't already) will look for guidance through the mission statement every day when they need to make decisions in the best interest of the organization. With that responsibility and ownership of the company's mission, you will also find that feedback from the team will lead to improvements and innovation.

Resource Management

There are only three resources in any business: time, people, and money. The dance of the business owner is to find the resources and then manage them. Because these are finite resources, the dynamic of running a private company will require you to make decisions with imperfect information and without the fullness of the resources you need. Reid Hoffman, the founder of LinkedIn, partner at Greylock Partners, a venture capital firm, and sage of all things entrepreneurial, describes entrepreneurial management as making decisions without the luxury of perfect information, without the resources to properly execute, and without adequate time to do it.

Figure 4.3 on page 60 serves as a graphic representation of the tension between these three resources that you need to manage. Figure 4.4 then adds the all-important element of the marketplace, showing the interaction between these resources and management of the organization.

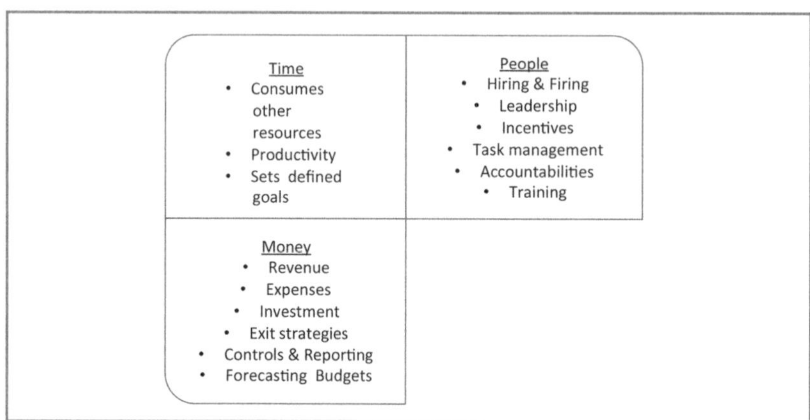

FIGURE 4.3—The Three Resources

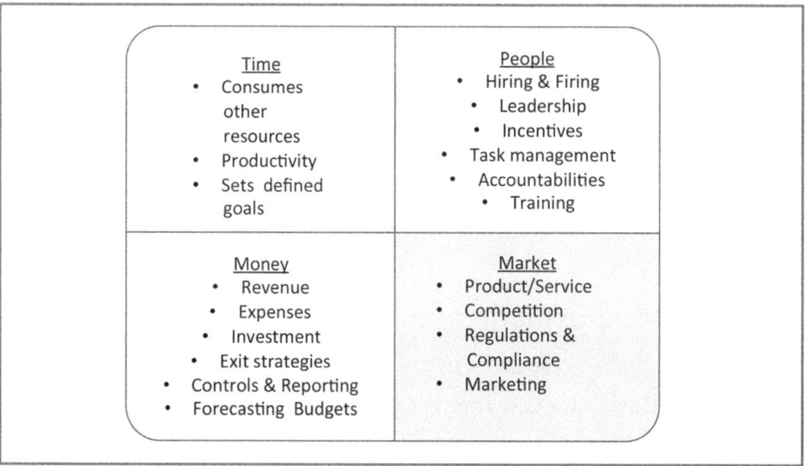

FIGURE 4.4—The Three Resources and Market Engagement

How you manage the market is predicated on the systems and operational controls you are able to drive internally. For cannabis entrepreneurs, this is essential to success.

The four reasons to do something and three resources you manage can all be mapped within the "Ten Operating Principles" seen in Table 4.1 on page 61. Keeping things simple cuts through the noise of operating a company. Many entrepreneurs run from one thing to the next without processing how to act or why they are acting. "Managing by the last phone call" describes how many business owners can fall victim to reacting to what just happened as opposed to being intentional in their actions. Running from one thing to the next because the phone rang is a recipe for disaster. Most successful investors come from an entrepreneurial

	What You Manage	How You Manage It
1	Revenue	• Budgeting and forecasting • Product or service
2	Profitability	• Gross margin • Expense management
3	Customers	• Customer satisfaction • Data and surveys
4	People (HR)	• Hiring and firing • Policies
5	Marketing	• Media and PR partners • Custodian of pricing
6	Sales	• Own the customer relationship • Executes the sales and marketing plan
7	Culture	• Training and personal development • Education
8	Systems and Processes	• IT • Reporting
9	Infrastructure	• Physical real estate • Equipment and fixtures
10	Policy and Risk Management	• Government relations • Insurance and contingencies

TABLE 4.1—Ten Operating Principles

background and have likely learned the hard way that this can be a death knell for a small company. The language of how you run—and plan to run—your company can be articulated through these guiding principles.

Goal Management

Entrepreneurs and investors ultimately share the same desired outcome. They both seek to build value for stakeholders and then extract that value. The mechanism to accomplishing this goal is the company. The results are measured by showing an increase in value of the shares and other economic outputs of the company. Delivering on this mandate is the mission of the entrepreneur who needs to direct the activities of the company towards an agreed destination. The starting point off the "what" and "why" will color what the future destination of the company looks like.

You'll notice that I am using the term "stakeholder" and not "shareholder" for a reason. This is intentional, as a company has both shareholders and stakeholders. Shareholders are exactly that: individuals or separate entities that own shares in the company. Stakeholders include the shareholders but are more broadly the groups and individuals who will benefit from the success of the company such as employees, vendors, customers, and community members. As attorney and license owner Sara Presler said at the 2019 Cannabis Dealmakers Summit in San Diego, "There isn't just the opportunity to build something great, but to do something great in cannabis. When we think about building value for ALL stakeholders, your entrepreneurial mission should be easy to identify and inform how you will execute."

Keeping that in mind, your vision and mission statement should inform your business planning and influence how you manage resources and adapt the Ten Operating Principles to your venture. How you think about managing the company and delivering value to your stakeholders will define the constraints through which you will operate. In this context, a constraint is a good thing, as it will provide you with direction on what to do but also force you away from what not to do so you can stay focused on your core vision.

When talking with investors, you can collaborate to define the start and the finish together. Do you want to build a company that supports a community of cannabis evangelists and one day pass it along to your kids or family? Or do you want to build a company that goes public in the next year and hire a public markets CEO to run it? What does your investor audience want to see happen and how does this align with creating value and extracting value? In reality, the finish line isn't actually an end point, but rather an agreed-upon next destination. How you align goals and then manage the race makes the difference between getting to the finish line first, second, last, or not at all.

Talent Management

Managing any startup or early-stage business is complicated at best. With growth comes a larger organization to manage, and soon you will find yourself transitioning from doing the bulk of the work to hiring people, and delegating and managing teams. This is not an easy transition for every business owner. The element of this equation that comes with the highest risk is the people you hire.

Recruiting great people is essential, and your success in doing so will be directly impacted by a variety of factors. How you incentivize people, the culture of your company, the benefits you provide, and the training you offer all come into play. It is in your best interest to have an active and ongoing recruitment process to have multiple candidates even when you may not be actively hiring. When you need people quickly, you will be grateful that you aren't starting the process too late as there will be a desire to move quickly, which comes with risks. As the old adage goes, "Hire slow, fire fast." That rings true for the cannabis entrepreneur as well.

Speaking from excruciatingly painful experience, there is no greater threat to your business than having the wrong partners or wrong employees. It took some hard lessons to learn that mistake. Although I was motivated by the upside and unlimited earning potential that entrepreneurship can provide, some people just want a job and are more interested in the security of a paycheck so expectations and incentives were misaligned. In the past, I was in a rush to bring people on and gave too many people way too much credit for what they said they could do. When they failed, which they invariably did, I was left with the responsibly of managing a business that was damaged by their actions or lack of execution.

The lesson was that doing background checks on people, listening to references, and creating success-based compensation was a difficult task. But had I paid more attention to it, I would have avoided some very expensive lessons and litigations. If I had taken the time to work with our attorneys upfront, we might have had the protections in place to protect our company from unethical employee behaviors. We could have better addressed instances when employees looked for easy ways to avoid the hard work by ignoring agreements rather than acknowledge they were beyond their capabilities.

Working in an entrepreneurial environment can be very difficult and not for everyone. Keep the following tips in mind:

- $ Don't be in a rush to hire.
- $ Take your time to develop performance-based incentive plans.
- $ Don't be in a hurry to give out equity to employees.
- $ Have very clear non-compete, confidentiality, and non-solicitation language in your agreements.
- $ Be concerned by people who create chaos and drama instead of delivering results.

THE CANNABIS CONUNDRUM—DON'T BELIEVE THE HYPE

In addition to nuts-and-bolts issues (like creating mission and vision statements, hiring smart, and focusing on smart management practices), you need to stay focused on what makes a cannabis business viable—not what it has been hyped to be. The cannabis economy has reached a tipping point and is here to stay. Prohibition is sunsetting and evolving regulations and polices are being enacted globally and regionally to open up markets and industries to cannabis. As with all new markets, there has been a significant amount of enthusiasm and an influx of new companies, and with that, retail investors in the public markets are driving up valuations based on an irrational exuberance for the sector as opposed to relying on fundamental analysis.

CANNABIS CONUNDRUM, continued

Much of the "Green Rush" is based on hype with investors flooding into the public markets at stratospheric valuations. When investors value the sizzle more than the steak, it's time to get back to basics and focus on the fundamental value drivers in successful private businesses. There are precedents that we can look to justify building and investing in a great business because it's a great business. It just also happens to be in cannabis. Both investors and operators win when they move beyond the hype and instead focus on the merits of an opportunity.

The term "Green Rush" is analogous to every other gold rush in history that attracted countless speculators seeking to find their fortunes. In reality, it was very rare that miners or speculators made any money at all—most were ruined financially, and only a handful of industry participants accumulated the majority of the economic upside of people's enthusiasm. This all but implies that speculators and hype are driving cannabis entrepreneurship. And like any other historical rush, there will be countless tales of greed, financial ruin, and the establishment of a few industry leaders who will largely control their sectors.

Luckily, we are much smarter in the modern economy now that we have seen countless cycles and ideally learned from the mistakes of the past. During the California Gold Rush, the term "entrepreneur" didn't even exist in the lexicon of the day. Today, not only do we understand that the diggers and miners of that time would have been considered entrepreneurs, we now have learnings and perspectives that would have helped define approaches to success when most failed. We also now know that, historically, the winners in any rush were the transportation, infrastructure, merchants, and suppliers who made the vast fortunes.

Using the word "rush" also implies speed and can trigger impulses to skip steps and miss adequate preparation, which can be a virtual

CANNABIS CONUNDRUM, continued

death blow to an entrepreneurial venture. Given the dynamic of cannabis entrepreneurship (lack of time, lack of resources, lack of data), we need to apply modern thinking about running a private company successfully as a primary function of building a great business first. These are the building blocks of the foundation from which to raise capital, and it will take time. The replicative entrepreneur strives to create a business, not just an application or single product. Put one way by Joe Mimran, a leading investor in the cannabis sector, founder of the clothing company Club Monaco, and a judge on the TV show *Dragon's Den,*

> *Beware of the Klondike mentality. When a sector is hot there is a tendency to rush in without properly assessing the business so as not to miss the opportunity. This is an age old problem in the early 1900s there were as many as 450 American car companies. By 1936 there only three that mattered. The day of reckoning will come and when the public market analysts start digging into the cannabis companies fundamentals there will be definite winners and losers. It's a competitive world . . . in the beverage market. There are some 400 new beverage launches every year; only 40 will make it through the first year or two and only four will be successful.*

Change Management

The one certainty in doing business in the cannabis company today is that things will change. They will change quickly and in ways that will be unpredictable. You should be able to align foundational components for building a successful business and attracting investment by demonstrating skillful change management tactics. As much as you prepare, you cannot predict the future and will end up reacting to things that are unpredictable and unplanned. Cannabis entrepreneurs will need to develop a keen sense of how to manage change, adapt, and thrive. You will need to develop a winning business plan that contemplates that the markets and regulatory overhang in cannabis will change on you rapidly (we'll talk about doing this in Chapter 5). The companies that are able to build operationally sound business fundamentals that can manage changes and unforeseen challenges will have the highest potential for success.

Many cannabis entrepreneurs have built businesses that are temporary fixes to temporary problems. CVC investors are seeking sustainable enterprises that are built for the long term. Cannabis entrepreneurs need to understand better than entrepreneurs in other markets how to manage for change and to survive the unknown. For example, we know that state and federal regulations will change; we just don't know when and in what manner. The companies that have the foresight to plan for those impending but unknown changes will be the companies that survive and ultimately produce a financial return for the entrepreneurs and their investors.

Change management intersects with risk management. You are your first investor, and as such will act just like any other investor in wanting to de-risk your investment and insure against known and unknown threats. My personal investment approach is to avoid investing in companies that are temporary fixes, or "Band-Aid" solutions. I am happy to invest in a novel solution to a problem in the marketplace; however, if that solution is temporary and otherwise unable to adapt to changes, that kind of company is not representative of a durable entity that can sustain changes and continue to create value over long periods of time.

CANNABIS CAPITAL TAKEAWAYS AND ACTION ITEMS

As you have read, being a cannabis entrepreneur has its own unique fingerprint in the business world. Yes, you share several similarities with other types of entrepreneurs, and you should certainly run your business using best practices that come from various industries and sectors. But you also have to keep in mind the unique challenges and opportunities that are part of the cannabis entrepreneur's journey.

Action Item: Entrepreneurship Readiness Test

Take a moment to imagine yourself as a successful cannabis entrepreneur. Visualize yourself in ten years and what your company and your lifestyle look like. Now imagine what it took to get you there. Did you have to make extraordinary sacrifices?

There are many resources you can use to evaluate your aptitude for entrepreneurship. There is much published about the innate characteristics of entrepreneurs, addressing such qualities as appetite for risk, ability to create ideas, leadership, humility, etc. The readiness test in Table 4.2 on page 69 is a simple checklist to ensure you have thought through what it will take to get to the starting line and what you will need to bring to the race. Take the time to rate each element from 1 to 5. A 1 means this is something that is not fully developed nor an asset that you can rely on when you take this journey. A 5 means this is something you have developed and can implement immediately. This is, however, a quick questionnaire that you can revisit and help you move quickly to the starting line if that is your next goal.

How did you score? If you ended up scoring higher than 40, you are well on your way. There is still a lot of work ahead, but you can focus on moving forward and filling the remaining gaps you need to address (the areas where you scored the lowest). If you are in the 30 to 40 range, you should focus on the foundation you need to move forward. Any score under 30 is high risk and you may want to go back to the drawing board or focus on building more of your own entrepreneurial skill sets before jumping in headfirst.

Action Item: Vision and Mission Statements

Set your vision and mission for the company. If you have already done this, revisit what you have and make any updates that are needed. Once you have defined the vision for yourself as an owner, share it with the rest of your team and solicit feedback. Also share it with your advisory board, other investors, attorneys, accountants, and customers. When everyone has provided input to your mission statement, publish the vision and mission statement publicly and hold yourself and your team accountable for producing results in alignment with your operating ethos.

	Question	Ranking
1	How many years can you go without earning an income?	1 2 3 4 5
2	How many years of experience do you have working for other companies?	1 2 3 4 5
3	How developed is your product or service; 1 (is an idea); 5 (is already generating revenue)?	1 2 3 4 5
4	Have you talked to at least five customers who have indicated they will do business with you?	1 2 3 4 5
5	Do you have at least five months cash on hand to operate the company at your current burn rate?	1 2 3 4 5
6	How many employees do you have?	1 2 3 4 5
7	How many companies have you started before starting your current business?	1 2 3 4 5
8	How many advisory board members do you have?	1 2 3 4 5
9	How much money have you raised (in millions or hundred thousands)?	1 2 3 4 5
10	How many years do you think it will take to reach your exit strategy?	1 2 3 4 5
	Total	_____/50

TABLE 4.2—Entrepreneurship Readiness Test

Action Item: Critique Yourself

It takes perseverance and discipline to succeed as an entrepreneur. One of the characteristics of the most successful entrepreneurs is that they demonstrate an unusual combination of stubbornness with the ability to be sanguine about the problems in their company and with their own capabilities. However, the number-one business killer is an unrealistic belief that an unsustainable business will somehow become a success. When an investor views a business that is DOA (dead on arrival), the founders can be accused of trying to "give CPR to a corpse."

The best critiquing can come from within yourself and your organization. Take the time to step away from yourself and your company and view what is happening from an independent third-party perspective. A way to approach this task is to utilize a concept called the "black hat." This is when you put together two teams: the red hat team and the black hat team. The red hat team will focus on all the positive elements of the business and advocate for the company's success, and the black hat team will identify all the challenges and risks and advocate for why the business will fail. Both teams will debate their findings and illuminate the strengths of the company and bring to light all the risks and deficiencies. In a capital-raising process, you are leveraging your assets and what the company is good at as a reason to justify that you can manage capital. It is the weaknesses and deficiencies, however, that you highlight as uses of the investment to improve, fix, or mitigate. The more you can go through its evaluation internally, the more prepared you will be for working with investors. It is their job to be the black hat and to identify all the reasons to not make an investment. Only when they can't find any more reasons to say "no" to the investment will they move forward.

BUSINESS PLANNING

There is some debate on the merits of writing a business plan in a company's very early stage. The primary concerns are that it can be very lengthy and intensive, and at an early stage there are so many unknowns it can be an exercise that quickly deviates from reality. Personally, I find that many entrepreneurs spend too much time making the case for the "opportunity" when writing their plan. Many business plans become little more than a detailed market analysis and theory as to why there is little doubt that demand for the company's product or service will produce a massive financial windfall. The "why" is important, but far more important for the purposes of business planning is taking the time to define in detail "how" the business will be managed and operated. If we expand upon the calculation presented in the introduction, we can add additional weighting to the business success algorithm like this:

Version 1.0: Success = (Execution x 9) + 1 Idea

Version 2.0: Success = (Execution x 6) + (How x 3) + 1 Idea

When it comes to business plans, how entrepreneurs plan to run their business and what investors want to see end up being best aligned when you focus on "how." And taking the time up front to prepare this before working with investors is a critical planning activity that serves both your long-term business goals and your capital goals. So, what should you focus on when writing your business plan?

If you think about the business plan not as a homework assignment but rather as a playbook for the business, it becomes a document that serves as an actionable tool and resource as opposed to an exercise in writing for the sake of writing. Don't get caught up the term "business plan" in the traditional sense and instead view this as a management resource that will guide your core activities and inform the plays you will call to advance your business. This "playbook" is your business plan and investors will want you to share it with them as part of your investment proposal.

Now, let's clarify who the audience is for reading a business plan. Some might believe that business plans don't serve a purpose because, many times, management teams spend a lot of time working on them only to file them away, never to be opened again. Yes, that is certainly an exercise in futility, but if you think about all the stakeholders who can benefit from interacting with your business plan, the effort becomes clearly valuable. And by interacting, I mean that a business plan is not simply a static document that is read front to back like a novel, but rather a dynamic and evolving tool that is continually being revised and adapted to actual outcomes and not just projections. So, the audience interacts with a business plan because it should not just be read but questioned, modified, iterated, and challenged. This is, of course, what investors do when they evaluate a plan.

But investors are only one audience. And clearly, they are being shown a business plan to help them identify the merits and risks in making an investment in the company. That is a clear and valuable use, but business plans are also great tools to share internally with employees. There may be some sections that are redacted pertaining to compensation or other sensitive information, but generally the operating team should be in complete alignment with the business plan. What you are doing, how you plan to do it, and the expected outcomes should all be factors in your company's narrative. Well-crafted business plans tell a story with purpose and should include the mission statement of the company and, directly or indirectly, capture the culture of the company so all stakeholders are familiar with your goals. For example, your attorneys should be clearly versed in the business plan so they can advise you on how to manage the legal requirements and prepare for the regulatory impact of how (and where) the business will operate. In addition, knowing your plan and mission allows them to prepare the documentation to appropriately structure and close an investment transaction. That's just one practical application of the business plan. I have also seen business plans used as great recruitment tools for hiring talent or board members, for example.

No two businesses are alike, so it is difficult to standardize business plans or use pre-designed templates. Great entrepreneurs identify the audience, purpose, and need for a business plan and then capture the elements that serve the specific needs of their company. There are, however, some core business plan elements that every entrepreneur should address that are also essential for investors to understand as well. Following in Table 5.1 on page 74 is an example of a framework that could be used to start building from for a cannabis business.

WHAT INVESTORS LOOK FOR IN THE BUSINESS PLAN

The matrix in Figure 5.1 on page 83 demonstrates a good way to articulate how your company compares to an identified competitive group of companies. This is not the only a way to simply and effectively

Section	Overview
Executive Summary	I recommend writing this section last as it is a summary of all the sections and work that follows. It's best to write a four- or five-page executive summary that can also be shared by itself. The content of the executive summary should be clear and make sense to someone who would read it independently of any context of the deeper plan or accompanying presentations. The executive summary is meant to summarize the entire scope of the business plan and company overview. It should be high-level but fact-based and highlight the key tenets of the business that are necessary for anyone to properly understand what the business does, why, who is involved, and how it will build from where it is currently. I also like to include the company's mission statement in the executive summary up front. The final section can include, for the purposes of raising capital, a summary of the transaction that is being pursued (amount of capital and what is being used for) and where the company is projected to be as a result of that investment. It's also helpful to conclude the executive summary narrative with a statement about the goals of the business with regard to an exit strategy.
Management Team	It is critically important for anyone reading a business plan to know the key people who are involved. This is more than just bios and backgrounds—it should include a description of the organizational chart outlining the reporting structure and a description of the key roles and responsibilities. Don't forget to include the advisory board or other key external members of the team like bankers and attorneys.

TABLE 5.1—Cannabis Business Plan Framework

Section	Overview
Product/ Service or Technology	Every company has a value proposition that most commonly is rooted in the identification of an unmet need in the marketplace or a novel solution to a significant problem. Investors need to clearly understand what your value proposition is and what you sell. This could be a whole roster of products and/or services or a single scientific development or proprietary technology. Clearly knowing what you have to sell will define how you build the business in the near term and long term.
Business Model	"Please now tell us how you will make money!" You would be surprised by how many business plans don't clearly articulate how the company plans to make money. For example, if you are a direct-to-consumer CBD brand, the profitability and long-term value you are creating will be predicated on your ability to do several things really well: 1) source the best quality CBD at the best prices; 2) create a recognizable brand; and 3) sell better than any of your competitors. This means that your business model will focus not on the production of CBD but rather buying it at one price and marking it up to resell to your customer. Within that margin, you will need to be able to deliver the best direct-to-consumer experience and technology to build sales and a brand that will stand out from the crowd.

TABLE 5.1—Cannabis Business Plan Framework, continued

Section	Overview
Opportunity/ Addressable Market	The opportunity section should start at a macro level and describe the sector and industry the business operates in. This should be brief as most readers will already know that your industry, as a sector of the cannabis economy, is rapidly growing. Don't spend much time reaffirming what is likely already known. Be sure to include statistics and research, and be sure to cite the source anytime you present data. Validating that you are in a large and rapidly expanding market is the objective for this section. Once you do that, move quickly into the "addressable market." This was discussed in Chapter 2 in more detail, but an addressable market is the market you can directly sell to or otherwise monetize. "All cannabis users globally" is not an addressable market because no company can sell to all people everywhere. With an understanding of the market, this section should also point out what needs your company is specifically solving, sometimes referred to as a "pain point." Many companies think they are solving a problem only to find out that the problem is not really causing enough pain for their customers to pay for the solution, no matter the price. When you know what your value proposition is, you can define an addressable market—the direct group of customers you can reach and convert to buyers. If your addressable market is valued at $100 million and you aim for sales of $200 million in year 5, that math does not work and your assumptions are way out of line with the real revenue potential of your business.

TABLE 5.1—Cannabis Business Plan Framework, continued

Section	Overview
Sales and Marketing	You have already identified the need or addressable market for your product or service, so going back to that rationale is redundant. What investors need to see and what the business needs, is a strategy for how to market and sell the product or service. Marketing is all the promotional efforts you undertake in order to create a potential client. Selling is then the conversion of getting your message in front of your customer and converting their interest into sales. At the end of the day, sales are the lifeblood of every company, and every company must sell. The founder who can convert limited resources and limited access into paying customers will win. Investors then want to see the playbook for how you will generate sales. This is much more than just identifying who your clients are; this section of a business plan should take into consideration how to scale and identify the key hires and how they will be managed. How do you pay commissions? How will you find the talent you need? Have you considered payroll taxes and benefits in your projections? How will your customers pay you? These are the thoughtful inputs that are required in the planning phase in order to create the basis of your financial projections. The more you add details about "how" your business will deliver on sales, the more believable your projections will be to the investor.

TABLE 5.1—Cannabis Business Plan Framework, continued

Section	Overview
Operating Plan	This is the all-encompassing "how." Once the plan answers the what and why, the how is the only thing that matters. How you will build the infrastructure for your business will impact the financial projections, the cost basis at which you will operate, and the ability to deliver profits in the near and medium term. This section should include all the organizational charts that need to be made clear, both functional (the roles and responsibilities) as well as reporting structure. Also describe the third-party companies and resources you will require such as accounting firms, law firms, and partners within the supply chain. Do you need to source products from a distributor? If so, who is that distributor and what terms have you negotiated? Do you need to leverage industry-specific software or regulatory compliance services such as testing or reporting? What are the costs and contract terms? Who will manage these key relationships?

TABLE 5.1—Cannabis Business Plan Framework, continued

Section	Overview
Competition	When you describe accurately where your company's place is within your industry, direct and indirect competition becomes clear. A word of caution is that EVERY business has competition, and to say that you "have no competition" is not only inaccurate in every situation but also shows a lack of maturity and understanding to investors. A good way to define your competition is to analyze your industry and highlight others who are trying to face the problems or have a similar value proposition. You can then select the industry-specific elements of the business that all the companies can be compared against. Figure 5.1 shows a competitive matrix, which is a good way to articulate your competitive set. It's also good to identify direct and indirect competitors including non-cannabis businesses. For example, if your company has a novel solution to processing credit cards, American Express, Visa, and Mastercard will be your competition at some point. You can categorize your competitors as direct and indirect competition. Direct competitors are companies that operate with a similar business model in your industry. Indirect ones are other businesses that would have an interest in participating in your industry if they are not already there.

TABLE 5.1—Cannabis Business Plan Framework, continued

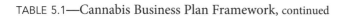

Section	Overview
Financials	The section dedicated to the financials of the company should include a profit & loss statement (P&L), cash flow statement, and balance sheet. For companies that have been operating for a year or more, this should include all the historical statements as well as projections. It's also good to include relevant financial information for a transaction here that should include a detailed use of proceeds (as discussed in Chapter 9) and a capitalization table (the current ownership of the company). Your objective here is to show that there is some real financial planning in place and that you are setting targets that can be used to measure success. Investors will always scrutinize the financials heavily, so it's wise to provide as much detail as possible and encourage a detailed evaluation.
Regulatory Considerations	Most businesses in any sector should be addressing regulatory risks or requirements, but this is especially relevant for cannabis businesses. The changing regulatory environment is extremely difficult to manage and the number-one concern from investors and operators alike in cannabis is regulatory risk (more on this in Chapter 3). Every cannabis entrepreneur should have their finger on the pulse of the regulations that impact them most directly and have thoughtful contingency plans and risk mitigation strategies that can be clearly articulated to anyone reading the business plan. The regulatory playing field needs to be defined in order to build the playbook for the company that can adapt.

TABLE 5.1—Cannabis Business Plan Framework, continued

Section	Overview
Exit Strategy	It is important for the investors and the company to be aligned on how the value will be created in a company and then extracted through some liquidity or exit event (see Chapter 8 for more on this). The exit strategy is important to include in the business plan because the desired outcome will inform how the company will be developed. For example, if a management team is really focused on going public, the company will build out resources and spend differently than a business that will remain private. This is a critical data point for the business modeling and financial modeling contained in the business plan and a section that investors will want to spend time reviewing to ensure that there is a reasonable expectation that they can receive a return on their investment.
Future Opportunities	One area that becomes a hang-up for entrepreneurs and investors is spending time on the future opportunities that the company believes they can capture. For example, if a company sells in certain states today but thinks they can sell internationally, it is common to try and convince the investor that this is a highly valuable business because of that "opportunity." I cannot stress enough that investors can get excited about some future upside, but they invest in what the business can do to achieve success right now and in the near future. The business that is considering selling in a new or foreign market must prove they can sell in the market they can most readily sell to today. That near-term success will allow them to pursue future opportunities, so it is good to show that there has been some thought about how the company might grow in the future.

TABLE 5.1—Cannabis Business Plan Framework, continued

Section	Overview
Appendices	A useful tool in a business is making use of the appendix to catalog or include information that would be distracting or not relevant to the core content but is informative and tangentially useful for the reader. Great examples of this kind of content are sales collateral, related media, and articles. No company is built specifically to make headlines, and everyone who is selling needs to have good sales collateral. Many times, entrepreneurs think that highlighting these items is important to an investor getting excited about their company. This is a prime example of "sizzle" vs. "steak," so instead of bogging down other sections of the business plan, those items can be added here and be inventoried and accessible to the reader. This is a great way to provide the sizzle where it can easily be found without distracting from the core merits of the business plan (the steak). There are no rules about what you want to provide or not provide here and, in some situations, contracts or customer letters or testimonials might even be appropriate to include.

TABLE 5.1—Cannabis Business Plan Framework, continued

communicate, but it's a great example of why this is important for investors to see.

When an investor views your company-specific competitive matrix, they will be looking for advantages, and comparisons, and that you have adequately done your homework in identifying the companies you present. It is highly questionable for an investor to do their own independent research and identify a group of competitive companies that you did not already identify. This indicates that you either aren't aware of the full competitive market pressures you are operating within or are disregarding other companies in your management of the business. Both are dangerous,

	Your Company	Competitor 1	Competitor 2	Competitor 3	Competitor 4	Competitor 5
Metric 1	✓	✗	✓	✗	✗	✓
Metric 2	✓	✓	✗	✗	✓	✗
Metric 3	✓	✓	✓	✓	✓	✗
Metric 4	✓	✗	✓	✗	✗	✓
Metric 5	✓	✓	✗	✓	✗	✗
Metric 6	✓	✓	✓	✗	✓	✗
Metric 7	✓	✓	✗	✗	✗	✗

FIGURE 5.1—Competitive Matrix Example

and an investor would perceive a lot of risk in a company that could otherwise be blindsided if they aren't preparing to create barriers to defend and protect their addressable market position.

In every section of a business plan, investors are really looking for a depth of knowledge about your industry and your business and the ways in which you are preparing to manage with all the considerations identified. When I evaluate a company, I am not always looking for "right" or "wrong" answers, but I'm looking to get a sense of:

- The management team's business acumen.
- How they plan to deploy resources and for what benefit.
- How they will manage in a fast-paced environment in which companies need to be agile and accept imperfect information. For example, investors will be looking at the risks associated with unanticipated regulatory changes and how you might respond.

These are all indicators of future success.

At the end of the day, investors want to see a well-thought-out and researched business plan. They are looking for what you are doing and why, who is involved, and how you will be able to execute. More businesses fail than succeed, and this is true because of execution risk. No business plan is perfect, and none will predict results in the future with perfect accuracy, but the business plan represents the most detailed understanding of the assumptions that went into the planning. How the team will otherwise execute against the plan is what investors need to get comfortable with. High-performance teams that are successful in entrepreneurship will develop a plan that outlines the playbook they will follow and then execute it. Investors are looking for a solid playbook that will serve as a set of operating principles to get them through unforeseen challenges when things don't go as planned.

HOW IT ALL SYNCS UP

Once you have a framework of a business plan developed, you will have the key data points to start developing a financial model that includes topics like product and pricing, cost of production and operating expenses, headcount salaries and benefits, the marketing budget, and projected revenue volume. Each element of the planning of your business goes into the planning of the offering you are taking to investors. It is not advisable to take one item at a time and try to push forward in your investor outreach without the full set of investor materials prepared. This is outlined as the "investment package," which you'll read more about in Chapter 9. When investors do the deep dive into analyzing you and your business, the quickest way to secure a rejection is to appear unprepared or be tripped up not being able to adequately answer questions. And answering questions does not necessarily mean being "right;" it means that you have done the hard work of thinking about how to successfully manage your business from the point in time you are currently at to the next inflection point of success and beyond.

Each element of the investment package serves two purposes. One, it is the base planning tool that any business needs to manage through to be successful irrespective of financing or the need to raise capital. And two, the elements of each document will influence each other. For example, you won't be able to put together a detailed or sufficient use of proceeds unless you have a detailed financial plan that clearly defines what resources are required and what the costs are. You won't be able to identify the resources you need if you don't have a clear operational plan that will have, as one aspect, a hiring plan. You will need to know who you are hiring, why, and what they will cost, along with the outcomes or impact on the P&L. For example, if you are hiring six salespeople, what do their base salaries and benefits cost? What will you pay for commissions? What are their sales goals over what period of time? Those core elements will highlight the capital needs and timing of those needs to deliver on the business plan. In addition, defining the sales resources you need is a function of understanding your addressable market and identifying your target customer, pricing strategy, and marketing budgets. As you can see, this becomes a detailed and deep analysis that is dependent on all elements of the business plan.

The way to think about the investment package that you prepare for investors is that each component has a specific lens into the aspects of your business. Through each perspective (finance, execute summary, structure and terms), you create another entrance point to drive deeper into the business in a way that leads back to the foundation of the operations. It is difficult to take someone through a clear story without incrementally developing the basis for how you are thinking about, and executing against, the core business you are building.

CANNABIS CAPITAL TAKEAWAYS AND ACTION ITEMS

The business plan is the master tool that any entrepreneur can use to do the appropriate planning, identify operationally how they plan to execute, and memorialize future predictions that can be measured against and used to create accountabilities. It is always interesting to go back and revisit prior versions of business plans. One thing that is absolutely certain is that what is projected a year or two prior to happening will always be different from what actually happens. So, for the purposes of planning, accurately predicting the future is important in the context of how far off the actual results were. For example, if you are reviewing a revenue projection, ask:

- $ Did you meet or exceed it within a 10 percent margin of error? That is certainly different than being 20 percent off from the projection because the larger the margin of error becomes, the more fundamental problems there are with the underlying assumptions you made.

- $ Did the plan project that a certain piece of legislation would be passed within a certain time frame?
- $ How does that compare with the actual legislation and timing?

These are just a few sample scenarios you might experience when considering projections. What investors are looking for is how a management team plans, executes, and then reacts when the results are different from what was planned.

Action Item: Build Your Competitive Matrix

Think about all the direct and indirect competition your business has. Which companies do you consistently see at the conferences and events you attend? Are they selling to your customers? Who do your customers buy from instead of you? Which metrics or qualities of your business differentiate you from the competition?

Be mindful of indirect competition. I hear companies all the time say things like, "We are going to be the Mastercard of cannabis." That's not accurate because Mastercard will be the Mastercard of cannabis, which would make them a competitor. Although Mastercard cannot do business in the cannabis industry yet, you can bet they are looking at ways to in the future. This means that you have an advantage if you can operate in the market before they can, but they are still competition and will make for a formidable adversary when they do start to compete with you.

Finally, you can think about how investors will view your competitive set. What will differentiate you should not only be elements of your business in the matrix, but also the foundation for much of your business planning. How will you create competitive advantages? How will you lead or follow in certain markets? How will you otherwise show knowledge of the landscape that dictates your business playbook? Take some time to think on these and write out your answers.

FINANCIAL PLANNING

The process of writing a business plan intersects heavily with creating a financial plan. To sufficiently model the prospects of the company, your management team will start planning the financial elements of the business. Separate from the business plan, which summarizes the financials at one point in time, a well-run company will need to develop a set of evolving financial models and statements in real time. The business plan is a snapshot, but the business changes each day. Financials are best viewed as "historical" and "projected." Historical financials are just that—the summary of the actual activities of the business: where the money came in and where it went. The function of your financial planning should be about building a forward-looking view into how the business is expected to perform over time.

Financial planning as a process identifies core assumptions and modeling the projected outcomes into the future. This is an intensive process that requires a working knowledge of finance, the ability to align the business plan and operations to financial outputs, and view the future through a sensitivity analysis that will guide the expectations for the actual results of the company. The organization needs to excel in financial planning in order to produce the optimal results. If you do not have formal financial training, it will be important to identify the right "numbers person" to lead this foundational area of the business. Financial planning is iterative and ongoing and should not be done solely for the purposes of raising capital, but serve to produce company-specific functional tools that every management team needs in order to effectively manage their enterprise.

As with all the elements of business planning, financial planning involves taking into consideration a variety of internal and external influences along with technical competencies to model the financial statements and develop a financial strategy for the business. Imagine walking into the boardroom of a multimillion-dollar international business as the CEO and presenting your financial plan for the company to the board of directors. What would you need to take into consideration to be confident that your decisions will produce the best financial results for your company and deliver value for the stakeholders? How would they hold you accountable for doing the right things to generate a return on their investment?

Financial planning is a specific activity within the broader financial management preview of any businesses. Going back to the entrepreneurial conundrum, founders and venture management teams need to be experts in all disciplines of business that larger organizations may have teams of people in place to handle. Some of the topics you need to master include forecasting and budgeting, expenses, capitalization, cash flow, and profit maximization. Great entrepreneurs always seem to be able to do more with less, so be prepared to get familiar with these topics.

When it comes to building your team, it is common that a financial expert, in particular when raising capital, is one of the first key hires of any growing business. In the absence, though, of a full-time CFO or CPA on the payroll, you can tackle the financial planning yourself by focusing on a few key statements and approaching the projected businesses performance that is required for raising capital. Figure 6.1 shows the inputs and outputs and relationship of the elements of financial planning.

Inputs	Operations	Outputs
• Cash on Hand • Investment • Historical Results • Sales Forecasts • Expense Projections • Debt • Needs Assessment • Cost of Capital	• Resource Allocation • Financial Management • Fact-Based Management • Cash Management • Policies	• Bank Balance • Accounts Payable • Accounts Receivable • KPIs and Reporting • Use of Proceeds • Raising Capital

FIGURE 6.1—Financial Planning Basics

In this chapter, I will walk you through the concepts, steps, and tasks required to undertake the financial planning process for your business. You will be able to confidently approach investors with your financial models developed and the intersection of finance and operations made clear. The first thing you need to understand is how to craft and interpret financial statements.

INTRODUCTION TO FINANCIAL STATEMENTS

There are three central financial statements you will need to become familiar with: the income statement, cash flow statement, and balance sheet. These statements interact with each other and together show the profitability of the company, cash needs and uses, assets and liabilities, and owners' equity for a period of time (usually monthly and annually). Companies manage their financial position by reviewing historical performance, comparing it to budgets and forecasted projections, and then make decisions about changes and modifications to how the company operates to optimize performance going forward.

Financial statements present a story of a business showing past, present, and future outlooks. To tell that story, founders should be familiar with the language of financial statements even if they are not preparing the reports themselves. I highly recommend finding resources to learn how to develop the reports yourself when you start your business. There are countless websites with advice and numerous organizations from the Kauffman Foundation (www.kaufmann.org) to the Small Business Administration (www.sba.gov) to business accelerators. You can also pick up *Start Your Own Business, Finance Your Business*, and *Write Your Business Plan* from Entrepreneur Press. The hands-on perspectives gained from doing the work yourself at first will help you develop an in-depth understanding of how your businesses finances function. The importance of having accurate historical figures gives the company creditability internally and with outside investors. The correct presentation of what money came in and how it was spent is the core of the accounting function. There are two main accepted ways accounting results are presented: on a *cash basis*, where revenue and expenses are noted when money changes hands (most common for early-stage enterprises), and the *accrual method*, where revenues and expenses are recorded when incurred, not when money is exchanged.

The financial statements are in some respect the most important section of the business plan. Many investors (including me) will skip right to the numbers when first reviewing a proposed investment. The story they tell is multidimensional in that it speaks to the decision making and assumptions that reflect how the management team believes the company will perform and how it should be run.

Let's walk through each of these statements. For the purposes of illustration, let's use a fictional company that is just launching called the Happy CBD Company, LLC (HCC). HCC sells CBD products direct to consumers and through dispensaries. In order to start the company, Betsy McKenna and her sister each put in $500,000 cash for a total investment of $1 million to set up the operations, buy inventory, and start selling their products. To their delight, the business grows quite rapidly from the first few months. They can tell from the amount of work and products being sold that they are on a growth trajectory, but they don't know how fast or with what momentum. They start to prepare the financial statements so they can have more insight into the business and suspect that they will need to raise capital at some stage. They meet with their accountant and start reviewing their balance sheet, cash flow, and P&L statements.

The Balance Sheet

The balance sheet summarizes the assets of the business and how they were acquired. The balance sheet must always "balance" in that assets will always equal liabilities and owner's equity. Let's say that on day one, Betsy and her sister make their investment of a total of $1 million resulting in the company having an asset (cash) of $1 million. Let's assume that Betsy's sister made her capital contribution as a loan, and since a loan is due to be paid back, there is now a liability of $500,000 on the balance sheet along with Betsy's owners' equity of $500,000. Then the company uses the cash to buy $250,000 of inventory to be sold, as seen in Figure 6.2.

Over the course of the next month, HCC has the following transactions:

- $ Rented office space for $10,000/month (reduces cash by one month).
- $ Spent $100,000 on marketing.

Assets			Liabilities		
Cash	$	750,000	Note Payable to Sister	$	500,000
Inventory	$	250,000			
			Owner's Equity		
			Betsy's Original Investment	$	500,000
Total Assets	**$**	**1,000,000**	**Liabilities & Owners Equity**	**$**	**1,000,000**

FIGURE 6.2—Opening Balance Sheet of Happy CBD Company, LLC

- $ Sold 6,000 products at $95 each.
  - Each unit cost is $10.
  - Cost of Goods Sold (COGS) is number of units sold (6,000) multiped by the unit cost = $60,000
  - Therefore, gross profit is equal to total sales (6,000 x 95) of $570,000 minus COGS of $60,000 which equals $510,000

Now we can enter the following transactions and produce an end-of-period balance sheet, as seen in Figure 6.3:

- $ Inventory is reduced by $60,000 for a new total of $190,000.
- $ Cash is increased by sales of $570,000 and then reduced by the added expenses of rent and marketing ($10,000 + $100,000 = $110,000) = $460,000.
- $ The company can calculate earnings for the period by deducting expenses ($110,000) and COGS ($60,000) from sales ($570,000) = $400,000.

Assets		**Liabilities**	
Cash	$ 1,210,000	Note Payable to Sister	$ 500,000
Inventory	$ 190,000		
		Owner's Equity	
		Betsy's Original Investment	$ 500,000
		Retained Earnings	$ 400,000
Total Assets	**$ 1,400,000**	**Liabilities & Owners Equity**	**$ 1,400,000**

FIGURE 6.3—Closing Balance Sheet of Happy CBD Company, LLC

What this would tell an investor about HCC is that the company is getting paid on time and generating a lot of cash from converting inventory into sales. The ability to generate cash means that the company should have the ability to pay its current liabilities (Betsy's sister's note). Retained earnings represent the cash on hand that could be distributed as profits to investors. It is common that early-stage companies use retained earnings to reinvest in the business, but in this hypothetical situation, the company could distribute profits to the investors if the business continues to convert inventory into cash, leveraging the minimal cost of goods and continuing to be paid on time.

The Cash Flow Statement

The second financial statement is the cash flow statement, which sources information from both the balance sheet and income statement. The purpose of the cash flow statement is to track the changes in the cash flow of the business resulting from operations and financing activities. The basic cash flow calculation is:

Cash at beginning of period + Cash received from sales =
Total cash – Cash disbursements =
Cash available at the end of the period

As you can see in Figure 6.4, the sample cash flow statement takes into consideration "investing" activities. For the purposes of this example, this is the equipment and other investments that Betsy has made in the first year. She also paid back a portion of her sister's note.

Cash Flows From Operating Activities	
Cash Received from Sales	$ 570,000
Cash Paid For	
Inventory Purchases	$ 250,000
Operating Expenses	$ 670,000
Interest	$ 40,000
Net Working Capital	**$ (390,000)**
Cash Flows From Investing Activities	
Equipment Purchases	$ 150,000
Net Cash Used in Investing Activities	**$ (150,000)**
Cash Flows From Financing Activities	
Proceeds from Issuing Shares (investment)	$ 500,000
Proceeds From Loan	$ 500,000
Payments on Long Term Debt	$ (100,000)
New Cash Flow From Financing Activities	**$ 900,000**
Beginning Cash Balance	$ 750,000
Ending Cash Balance	**$ 1,110,000**

FIGURE 6.4—Cash Flow Statement for Happy CBD Company, LLC

The Income Statement, Also Known as Profit & Loss Statement (P&L)

The income, or profit and loss (P&L), statement is the financial statement that is most scrutinized by investors when evaluating an entrepreneur and their company. It reflects the performance of a company by showing the flow of resources associated with generating revenues, the difference between the two producing either a profit or a loss. For illustrative purposes, the balance sheet examples on pages 91 and 92 for HCC do not contemplate the full spectrum of expenses that a business needs to manage such as payroll, technology/IT, equipment and computers, travel and entertainment, and third-party service providers like attorneys and accountants. The profit of a business can be articulated as *net income*, which is the difference between the company's total revenue and total expenses. The most commonly used calculation that represents the profitability of a business is EBITDA, or Earnings (net income), Before Interest (cost of debt), Taxes (payments on profits), Depreciation (non-cash accounting for the declining value of tangible assets), and Amortization (noncash accounting for intangible assets such as patents). *EBITDA* is a metric that is used by investors and business managers to evaluate the business' ability to generate cash. By removing how the company finances its operations with debt or equity from the balance sheet and eliminating non-cash expenses, EBITDA is the standard formula that represents the company's ability to pay cash for the owners. EBITDA is also the number that companies focus on for transactional purposes. For example, in M&A transactions when a company is paying a multiple of EBTIDA for a business, they are valuing the company on this ability to generate cash. In theory, as the new owner, they can make different decisions or may have a different cost of capital to finance the operations. So the new buyer is looking at the value of the company through the lens of its ability to manage expenses and convert sales into cash.

Things have been going well for Betsy and HCC, so she produces a P&L statement for the last four years. She wants to start looking at trends and think about forecasting the business going forward. She also includes some operating metrics in the P&L reports such as gross margin ratios (GM%) and year over year (YoY) growth rates (see Figure 6.5 on page 95). She is already thinking about raising capital and was told, correctly, that investors will

	Year 1	Year 2	Year 3
Revenues			
Product A	$ 570,000	$ 650,000	$ 700,000
Product B	$ -	$ 250,000	$ 500,000
Product C	$ -	$ -	$ 750,000
Total Revenues	**$ 570,000**	**$ 900,000**	**$ 1,950,000**
YoY %	*0%*	*58%*	*117%*
Cost of Sales	$ 60,000	$ 250,000	$ 750,000
Gross Margin	$ 510,000	$ 650,000	$ 1,200,000
GM%	*89%*	*72%*	*62%*
Operating Expenses			
Salaries	$ 180,000	$ 400,000	$ 600,000
Rent	$ 120,000	$ 125,000	$ 130,000
Marketing	$ 100,000	$ 200,000	$ 300,000
Legal Fees	$ 90,000	$ 50,000	$ 75,000
Accounting Fees	$ 45,000	$ 50,000	$ 55,000
Travel & Entertainment	$ 60,000	$ 120,000	$ 90,000
Facilities	$ 30,000	$ 15,000	$ 15,000
IT	$ 20,000	$ 25,000	$ 30,000
Miscellaneous	$ 25,000	$ 25,000	$ 25,000
Total Operating Expenses	**$ 670,000**	**$ 1,010,000**	**$ 1,320,000**
EBITDA	$ (160,000)	$ (360,000)	$ (120,000)

FIGURE 6.5—Historical P&L Statement for Happy CBD Company, LLC

want to evaluate the business starting with reviewing a consolidated recap of the P&L performance and trends since she started the business.

THE 280E TAX CODE

In planning your financial statements, you might want to keep in mind tax implications. I recommend that you always check with your CPA or tax accountant when making tax-related decisions, especially when it comes to your business. Most standard tax topics will apply to you, just as they would to any other business owner. There is one major tax consideration for cannabis businesses you should know about, and this is the Internal Revenue Service Code Section 280E. The code states that:

THE 280E TAX CODE, continued

> *No deduction or credit shall be allowed for any amount paid or incurred during the taxable year in carrying on any trade or business if such trade or business (or the activities which comprise such trade or business) consists of trafficking in controlled substances (within the meaning of schedule I and II of the Controlled Substances Act) which is prohibited by Federal law or the law of any State in which such trade or business is conducted.*

This means that any business that is operating legally within a state that allows the sale of marijuana and marijuana-derived products (cannabis and THC), although legal in that state, are not able to deduct normal operating expenses to calculate what they owe in taxes. For a non-marijuana business (such as a hemp company, which is now covered under protection of the Farm Bill), taxes are calculated on taxable income, which can simply be stated as:

Taxable income = Gross income – Businesses expenses

This applies to any business that derives their revenues from the sale of a Schedule I substance and are taxed on gross income. This means the IRS calculates the taxable income on gross income, which is gross revenue minus only the cost of goods sold, without applying any additional deductions of business expenses. Figure 6.6 on page 97 compares the implications of 280E to a business selling marijuana and one that does not. The only deductions that a marijuana business can deduct are cost of goods sold, which is inventory cost, cost to ship, and the cost of the product.

The critical takeaway is that you must understand your tax liabilities and consult with your CPA and accountants. The IRS is strictly enforcing this and is something all cannabis entrepreneurs should be aware of.

THE 280E TAX CODE, continued

	Marijuana Business		Non-Marijuana Business	
Gross Revenue	$	5,000,000	$	5,000,000
Cost of Goods Sold	$	2,500,000	$	2,500,000
Gross Income	$	2,500,000	$	2,500,000
Deductible Business Expenses	$	-	$	1,000,000
Taxable Income	$	2,500,000	$	1,500,000
30% Tax	$	750,000	$	450,000
Effective Tax Rate		50%		30%

FIGURE 6.6: Taxable Income 280E Comparison

For more information on tax planning and accounting, check out Mark Kohler's book *The Tax and Legal Playbook* (Entrepreneur Press, 2019).

INVESTOR EVALUATIONS OF THE P&L

Let's revisit the Happy CBD Company now that we have a set of financial statements that can be reviewed internally and externally. So how do investors read these reports? Betsy decides that due to her expanding revenues and having finally turned a profit in the previous year, she should give this financial statement to a friend of hers who is an analyst at a CVC fund to ask for advice. She sends her friend a copy of her P&L statement, and after reading it, he sends her the following summary of his initial observations:

> *Dear Betsy,*
>
> *I made a quick assessment of the report you provided to give you a sense of how our team would interpret the story as it appears. I hope this helps you think about the operational initiatives you would define as a part of the investment request:*
>
> $ *It appears that you had a good first year in terms of sales and that first product you sold clearly had a great margin. I can see why you continued with the business.*
>
> $ *I am guessing that in the second year you were seeing some attrition of sales from Product A and realized that diversifying your revenue by adding products was a good strategic move.*

- *It would appear that your second product did not come out of the gate with as much momentum as the first product. I saw that your gross margin has been decreasing each year, so we would want to learn more about each product's cost basis, sourcing, and how you are managing COGS.*

- *It looks like your third product was a major hit out of the gate so we would want to evaluate your sales trends for each product as you have flat year-over-year growth for Product A. Product B is growing consistently but appears to have brought down margin and profits, and if Product C will continue the rapid growth or flatten out like Product A did, you will run into problems. The last year's revenue growth rate is a concern.*

- *On the expense side, it appears that salaries are tracking with product and sales growth, but we will need to see a breakdown of head count and turnover.*

- *I assumed that marketing is essentially $100,000 per product per year, meaning that if the marketing spend is the same for each product, focusing on higher-priced products with more GM will positively increase your bottom line.*

- *It seems that legal fees were more in year one than in the rest of the years, which is understandable if you were tackling corporate formation and set up, establishing new contracts, and bringing on employees for the first time, which would have required an employee handbook, establishing policies and agreements. In addition, it is anticipated that there would be extra costs to set up third-party agreements with vendors for the first time, so it's also anticipated that legal fees would decline in year two while revenues increased. Did you have any lawsuits or legal matters that started in years three and four?*

- *It looks like you had to control your travel and entertainment expenses after spending twice as much in year two as you did in year one.*

- $ *The only consideration is your EBITDA. It looks like expenses increased more in year two and needed to be reined in with the addition of more people and more products to sell.*
- $ *The last two-year EBITDA trend is heading the right direction. Congratulations for turning a profit last year for the first time. By the way, are you subject to 280E tax treatment?*

Good luck,

Joe

Betsy was very appreciative of the feedback and discussed it directly with her friend. The CVC fund expressed interest in learning more about her company, so she started to think about how much money she should raise and what a new investment would allow her to accomplish.

PREPARING FINANCIAL PROJECTIONS

With a set of financial statements based on actual results, you can start to develop forward-looking projections. One area that investors most highly scrutinize are the financial models and projections you present. They are investing in you partly because of what you accomplished, and partly because of the potential for what your company could achieve with their funding. It's imperative that you have a clear budget and ways to track outcomes. The HCC example is a simple story to help add some context to the meaning of the financial statements. For me personally, finance only became real beyond the theory of accounting and business management when there was a reason or real-world story that impacted the math. Building a set of projected, or future-looking, financials is your opportunity to write your own story.

With proper planning and preparation, you and your team can make decisions about how to manage your business in the future to deliver stakeholder value. Those decisions will produce a set of assumptions, or inputs, into the projections and will ultimately represent the benchmarks you and your investors will hold the organization accountable to.

To accurately predict future performance, you must be able to predict the future with certainty. There is one *small* issue with this: No one can accurately predict the future. The one thing we all must accept is that no set of projections will ever turn out exactly as projected. The task then is to identify all the moving parts, dependencies, and assumptions such that your forecast for the future is within an acceptable margin of error. The financials you present will be the scorecard that will demonstrate how close you actually came to achieving your forecast. The amount by which you missed your projections (up or down) will be the real qualifier for investors.

One way to think about this is if you were a basketball team, and you projected that you would win the game, score exactly 78 points, and beat your opening by no less than 12 points. The probability of this happening exactly as you described is almost zero, but you would be able to point to a scoreboard at the end of the game and compare actual results to what you predicted. If you end up winning the game but only score 65 points and only win by three points, would this be considered a success? You can bet that the team's owners, coaches, and players would invest in going forward to play the next game and expect to win again. Your certainty of the outcome is predicated on the plays that you know you have drawn up, the team you have to execute the plays, and your understanding of the opposing team.

There are great resources that can teach you how to build financial models, and you can find further resources at www.cannabiscapitalbook.com. What is important at this stage is to understand the concepts behind modeling your financial projections and how to go about the process.

The intersection of financial planning and entrepreneurship is best highlighted though a concept I call P&L Impact. Every business decision can be processed by thinking about the impact it will have on the P&L statement. At the beginning of any day, week, month, or year, you will be making decisions about how to allocate resources and direct the activities of the organization. At that moment in time, if you produced a P&L statement, you would see the outcomes from the activities you've completed (or not) and can compare to the same prior period. Therefore, the decisions you make will each have an impact on the P&L. For example, if you decide to hire a new sales rep, adding them to the payroll will increase your salary expenses, payroll taxes, and benefits expenses, and increase variable expenses like cell phone reimbursement and travel and entertainment and commissions. These added expenses will decrease your profitability when put into the P&L statement. Your decision to add a sales representative was probably based on the need or ability to increase sales. Therefore, the P&L impact is fully evaluated when the projected revenues are added along with the projected expenses. Now you can compare your P&L to before and after the added expenses and anticipated revenues. Is the business more profitable? What happens if the sales are only 50 percent of what you projected? If you ask yourself the question, "What is the P&L impact of this decision?" you will be able to use your financial statements and projections as a mechanism to make and evaluate decisions.

Assumptions/Inputs and Techniques

The quality of your projections will be rooted in your understanding of how your company is working, should be working, and how your business will interface with your market. The best approach to preparing the projections is to model the inputs that will drive the outcomes and use those inputs as levers in the model that can be changed or adjusted to test how they impact outcomes. This requires that the model be dynamic and is capable of running formulas that automatically update with changes to the assumptions.

If you approach your financial analysis from the ground up, meaning that you start within your business and not from the external market perspective, this will force you to focus on the aspects of your company that you can control: the number of people you hire, the price you will charge for your product or service, the locations you will operate in, if you will lease equipment vs. buy equipment, and how much you will spend on essential businesses activities. This approach to building the expense base of the company will illuminate key decisions that are required to support the revenues, and ultimately profitability, of your venture.

When thinking about revenues, the most common mistake entrepreneurs make is to be overly optimistic about sales. Revenues in your forecast are not simply what you THINK customers will buy, but representative of your ability at predicting customer behavior. This is even more complicated and uncertain in a market that will have competition and considerable factors outside of your control like changes in regulations and tax policy (which you read about in Chapter 3). The question then is how can your business influence customer behavior (marketing, for example) such that predicted behaviors can become reliable assumptions? Naturally historical data becomes a key input in planning for sales outcomes.

In general, your assumptions reflect your judgment and should represent a balanced, realistic view that can be used to extrapolate outcomes. Investors look for projections that are tangible and concrete and not centered around emotion, enthusiasm, hope, or aspirations.

One strategy for presenting projections to investors in this format is to provide a spectrum of results. When testing your assumptions, certain inputs will be impactful in the outcomes and can be presented in a base case, worst case, and stretch case format:

1. *Base Case.* The set of financials you are managing against that is not too optimistic and not too pessimistic, but rather the middle ground with most things going the way you predict. Also contemplates unanticipated bumps along the way.
2. *Worst Case.* If you dial back all your assumptions, you can present a version of the forecast that essentially represents that the plan does not produce what you expected. Customers don't buy, competition cuts prices and undercuts you, regulations change, or a variety of headwinds materialize. It is a common practice for investors to simply cut a forecast in half to start their analysis of what might actually happen. In general, as time goes on, things take longer, cost more, and produce less than what the plan predicts, so this scenario can provide insight into what the business might look like in a decline and, ultimately, if it can survive.
3. *Stretch Case.* To provide a counterbalance to the worst case, if your company takes off, and expands more rapidly and outperforms projected revenues, what does that do to the underlying operations and what strategic options might materialize sooner than planned? For example, will you be fielding acquisition offers sooner than anticipated? If so, will this accelerate the potential investor returns, or will you be a buyer instead of a seller?

Investors will use the projections and financial statements you provide to cast their own version of how they think your business will perform. By providing a range of potential outcomes with the base case, worst case, and stretch case scenarios, you are doing some of this work yourself before approaching investors and will have already thought through how you would manage the business as you see the actual performance tracking and trending towards any one of those scenarios. This also creates visibility into how your business is performing so you can make adjustments and be proactive.

DETERMINING YOUR FINANCIAL NEEDS

Every company reaches a point where the activities required and resources required to continue building the business outstrip the cash the company currently has access to. This is the point at which most entrepreneurs rush out to find investment capital, often thinking "If we only had a million dollars in the bank, nothing could stop us!" The financially competent manager will stop right there and look at the overall financial plan for the company to decide if raising capital is the right next step. Can you otherwise self-finance the business through cash flow and reach another milestone that will positively impact the valuation and terms to raise money later? Are you reaching a point where you have no cash in the bank and can't make payroll without securing some financing in a matter of weeks?

A common theme throughout this book is being able to identify the foundational planning tools and tactics that you can develop to create systems and processes that produce the outcomes you desire. It's important that you continually identify what the company needs to execute on the business plan. There are a variety of ways to articulate these needs, so what follows will take you through some approaches and pitfalls in the planning phase so that you can communicate to investors a specific set of activities, the capital needs to support them, and the expected outcomes.

Two key questions will come up in managing your business:

1. Should I raise money?
2. How much should I raise?

If you start by answering the second question first, you will be able to define exactly how much money you need, which will impact the suitability of raising capital today and from whom to raise it.

The "Use of Proceeds" Report

A *Use of Proceeds* is a summary report that clearly states what the cash shortfalls are in a business needed to execute on the plan. A way to think about this is that the use of proceeds is the output of a modeling and budgeting process that produced the inputs needed to produce the summary. Those inputs are a function of a detailed analysis that the management team should be conducting on a regular basis that includes analysis of historical spending and revenues (or lack thereof).

Many entrepreneurs are unsuccessful in raising capital because they don't have a detailed request for investors to evaluate. Developing this specific "ask" for funding and the terms under which the funding will be structured relies on a detailed understanding of how much financing the company actually needs. Starting with a needs-based analysis of your business can help you avoid many of the pitfalls entrepreneurs make when presenting a use of proceeds to an investor. Many projections show a cash requirement that is different from what the company will actually need to sustain a growing company if the use of proceeds is only for added expenses and does not take into consideration working capital requirements, which are also a use of cash.

Your plan for raising capital needs to include a detailed understanding of how you plan to effectively deploy the capital to produce the highest benefit for the business and build shareholder value in the process. It all comes together in the "Use of Proceeds Report," like the example in Figure 6.7 on page 105.

This style of report shows the total cash required, how it will be deployed in various categories, and what percentage each category represents in terms of the overall funding request. It is common to round up each line item to capture unplanned costs or expenses, but the starting point will be derived from your base case forecast scenario. Be prepared for investors to scrutinize this heavily when working through the investment structure and have thoughtful planning behind each number. You

Use of Proceeds Report		
	$	**% of Total**
Total Investment Sought	**$ 3,000,000**	
Planned Uses		
Capital Expenditures		
Equipment and Fixtures	$ 650,000	22%
Software & IT	$ 250,000	8%
Total Capital Expenditures	**$ 900,000**	**30%**
Working Capital		
Salaries & Wages	$ 900,000	30%
Professional Services	$ 125,000	4%
Product Development	$ 350,000	12%
Marketing	$ 275,000	9%
Certifications & Licenses	$ 190,000	6%
Business Development (incl. T&E)	$ 175,000	6%
Other	$ 85,000	3%
Total Working Capital	**$ 2,100,000**	**70%**
Total Uses	**$ 3,000,000**	**100%**

FIGURE 6.7—Use of Proceeds Report

should be ready to discuss at length with any interested investor why the investment will produce the results you are projecting and where you can sensibly delay or shave some costs.

In our fictional example, let's say Betsy from HCC starts thinking about what she could accomplish if she had more resources. The feedback from her contact at the investment fund was thoughtful, and she now has an interest in talking more with them. As a next step, she organizes a meeting with her financial and management team to talk about what they would need if they took in some investment capital. There are a lot of considerations that they discuss such as should they raise money, when should they raise, and how much and at what valuation.

SHOULD YOU RAISE MONEY?

This is the moment of truth. Are you raising money because you think it is just what you should be doing or because everyone else is doing it?

Are you raising money because you have tapped out your resources and can no longer operate the business without financial support? Or are you raising money because you missed your sales targets or have not developed a viable revenue stream? None of these are good reasons alone to raise capital. There is a perception that when you don't need money everyone will invest, but when you need it most investors will highlight all the reasons they can't or won't invest. Let's start with the clear situations that investors stay away from.

The scenario investors like the least is to provide financing for a company that misses its sales targets or is underperforming. The most expensive capital for a company is equity, and the most expensive time to raise this kind of capital is at an early stage. Therefore, raising money because sales aren't materializing comes with the possibility of hiding a flaw or deficiency in the business. Is the product working? Are the customers willing to pay?

In other words, are you raising capital for the right reasons? Your investors will want to know. For example, if your business was out of cash and you couldn't make payroll, that would not be an ideal investment scenario. Those kinds of situations are considered to be "distressed" and, unfortunately, venture capital is not in the business of funding distressed companies. This is the domain of turnaround experts who will come in and take over a company that can be rescued. This is why so many startups fail. The companies are at a point where they run out of financing, and there isn't a significant enough operating business to secure rescue capital. This is all the more reason to focus on planning and then actively managing the business finances. In addition, even if an investor would be interested, the structure of the transaction would likely not be palatable for the entrepreneur. So, always be asking: *Should we raise capital?*

When Investors Like to Invest and When They Don't

VCs, angel investors, and early-stage financiers are primarily interested in financing internal growth. *Internal growth* can be defined as the activities that internal resources can be allocated to in order to deliver expanded results and build value. When an investor funds a company, the cash can then be allocated to activities like product development or R&D, adding resources to expand sales, adding equipment or infrastructure to expand production, or securing licensing or approvals to start operating in a new region. As the company expands through this financing, the valuation increases along with the ability to identify an exit strategy.

Situations that don't fall into the category of internal growth are financings where the investment leaves the company but does not return value. For example, there are some transactions in which the founders take some money for themselves, or take some money "off the table." In early-stage companies, investors typically have no interest in derisking the venture for you outside of an external party validating the business through an acquisition or buyout. Investors want founders to align with the outcomes and have a vested interest in the success of the company.

Another example of a misalignment with VC and a potential business objective is to acquire another business. As discussed in more detail in Chapter 7, in the cannabis market there are a lot of transactions happening in all kinds of forms and they seem to be happening for companies much earlier in their lifecycle. It's not improbable that even at an early stage, acquisitions or mergers may be part of your strategic plan. VC in other mature markets is reluctant to finance a company so it can go and acquire another company for a number of reasons:

1. An early-stage company needs to focus on driving internal growth, and an acquisition can be distracting.
2. When buying another company, much of the purchase price will go to the founders and investors of the target company and not be allocated to internal growth.
3. Even in large companies, the majority of acquisitions end up failing because of complicated operational integrations.
4. As it is likely a smaller transaction, the investor might be better off investing in the target company than the buyer.

A small company taking on an acquisition is a major risk. Managing one business is hard enough but when you add in the layers of complexity to manage two organizations, what seems like a good idea can ultimately be the catalyst for both companies to fail.

EARLY INVESTING IN CANNABIS Q&A WITH LORI FERRARA, CO-FOUNDER OF TREEHOUSE GLOBAL VENTURES

Q: As one of the earliest investors in the cannabis sector, what was it like in the early days? What were some of the major hurdles that your investors struggled with, and how did you get through those issues?

A: As an angel investor in 2013, the earlier days of investing was, let's just say, early! It was exhilarating to meet other investors coming from different industries who believed as I did that cannabis would be the next great industry with the potential to help many people.

As in any startup industry, the frustrations of great ideas with average management were prevalent. The earliest days are both exciting and fun, but also the most dangerous. Unfortunately, some ultimately failed because either revenue was too slow to grow or CEOs were overwhelmed. Being one of the only women investing at this time was incredibly rewarding, yet filled with some difficult times. Getting through those days took lots of strategic planning, hard work, and sweat equity.

Q: Once you started making investments, what was it like working with entrepreneurs at an early stage of venture capital for cannabis? What unique elements of investing in cannabis did you identify early on, and what advice would you have for entrepreneurs who are raising capital from cannabis-dedicated investors?

A: Advising and mentoring early-stage companies became a full-time job, and this is how I learned many of the do's and don'ts of the industry. Entrepreneurs can be so passionate about their business but often have not figured out how to translate their passion into sales.

Also, if you have previous experience as an entrepreneur, be prepared to talk about and highlight your background. Cannabis entrepreneurs need to be great communicators. They need to be able to paint the

LORI FERRARA, continued

picture they see in their mind with words to convince investors that their plan is reasonable and has the potential to be the next great adventure. Also, they need to project confidence to be able attract and motivate employees. No one can do it alone. So, their ability to build a team is crucial.

Many investors believe in investing in people more than a product. No matter how great your product is, if an investor doesn't believe you are the right person to lead the company, they are not going to invest.

One bit of advice: Your projections need to be realistic and believable. Things inevitably go wrong. Things take longer and cost more than you think. You need to make sure you have enough money to execute your plan.

My last piece of advice for entrepreneurs is to get a board of strategic advisors and or strategic investors. It's expensive for this kind of advice when you are an early-stage company, so being surrounded by the right people can be of great value. Regular contact with your team will propel the company forward and give you a much greater chance to succeed!

Q: You have a focus on backing women entrepreneurs and have stated that diversity is important in investing in and operating cannabis ventures. What advice do you have for those entrepreneurs who may just be starting out or transitioning from other industries?

A: I believe that women are incredible motivators and collaborators. Identifying C-suite women to round out your team can prove invaluable! Women are proving their skill set for running companies and generally tend to have stronger business ethics. Finding capital for women and minority investors can be very challenging, and our goal is bringing awareness to this highly overlooked population. According to data from

LORI FERRARA, continued

the M&A, women and minorities receive less than 2.2 percent of capital, while all-male and mixed-gender teams receive about 86 percent.

Here are some actionable steps emerging women entrepreneurs can take to build their profile within the cannabis economy and get early-stage funding:

- $ Find a lead investor.
- $ Find women and minority networking events to attend.
- $ Seek out female and minority influencers in the industry.
- $ Be open to collaborations.
- $ Have a substantial marketing budget to build out the brand.
- $ Volunteer to speak on industry educational panels.
- $ Align yourself with a great cannabis attorney.
- $ Look into loan and grant opportunities for woman- and minority-owned businesses (both government and private).
- $ Seek out local angel funds with a women and minority focus.
- $ Build a team of good advisors and mentors.
- $ Meet as many people as possible.

HOW MUCH SHOULD I RAISE?

Many cannabis entrepreneurs fall into the trap of coming up with the amount of capital they are raising based on what they think investors have an appetite for, not what the business needs or why it needs it. In the current environment, it is common to think that a company should raise as much capital as possible. There are two schools of thought on this and it is a topic hotly debated in all industries. One camp believes that you should only raise as much capital as you need to reach the next milestone of growth. The other perspective is to raise as much money as possible when it is readily available.

This is not a challenge unique to cannabis operators. There are certain scenarios where investors will provide more capital than what the company is seeking for a variety of reasons. In addition, some companies will raise significantly more capital than they need if it is available to them.

It may seem intuitive to raise as much money as you possibly can, and there is definitely a strong argument to take in money when it is available as you may not have that luxury down the line. There are, however, a number of concerns and issues in raising more capital than you need, starting with valuation. When you raise more money, you will either need to sell more of the company or inflate the valuation. For example, if you are raising $1 million on a pre-money valuation of $2 million, the investor will acquire one-third of the company. If you raise twice the investment from them and accept $2 million, the post-money valuation will be $4 million (up from $3 million in the previous example) and the investor will acquire a full 50 percent ownership. The alternative is to increase the pre-money valuation to $3.75 million, which would give the investor 35-percent ownership which is closer to one-third of the initial structure. The problem is that if you artificially raise your current valuation by $1.75 million, or almost double the current value of the company, new investors would have no reason to accept the higher valuation should you raise an additional round of investment. This can create a situation of financing a "down round," meaning that you would take in additional capital later at a valuation lower than what you closed this current round at. There are both optical reasons to not let this happen, but also practical reasons in that the purpose of the business is to build value, not diminish value over time. Table 6.1 on page 112 shows the pros and cons of raising more or less capital that you can consider.

ADDITIONAL ROUNDS OF FINANCING

When you are looking towards the future needs of the business, it is most common that companies raise financing through several rounds

	Pros	Cons
Raise exactly what you have planned for	You have a budget and remain streamlined and focused on reaching the next milestone. Remain judicious with equity, and valuation will continue to increase with subsequent rounds. Raising capital is a huge milestone that you can complete.	You can run out of money if things don't go exactly as planned. Capital may not be available when you raise more later.
Raise more than planned	You shore up the balance sheet and not have to raise money again for a considerable amount of time. It shows investor confidence in the company.	Inflated valuation that may be problematic for future rounds Overspending Cash sits unused on the balance sheet Stifles creativity Access to cash may mask problems in the company

TABLE 6.1—Capital Raising Considerations

of investment and through multiple sources of capital. When you are planning your current round of financing, it is always worth considering if you will raise more capital in the future. The answer is most likely "yes," so you should think about how your current round will impact future rounds.

One significant issue is dilution. What you need to consider now in the financial planning phases is that if you have to raise capital at a lower valuation in the future, what impact that will have on your current investors? If an investor acquires 10 percent of your company today, they will want to ensure that if more capital comes in later they won't be diluted heavily down from that ownership. You will want to be judicious with how much capital you raise and at what terms so that your current investors will participate in future rounds and don't end up at odds with you or your other investors if their position is losing value not gaining value.

CANNABIS CAPITAL TAKEAWAYS AND ACTION ITEMS

Financial management is a career-long discipline, and as with all aspects of your business, as the entrepreneur/founder/manager, you need to execute at the highest level. Part of managing the financial aspects of your business is the process of raising capital, which requires the baseline financial reports and forecast to develop correctly. Should you raise money, from whom, when, and for how much are all questions that are answered through astute financial management and planning. Projections are always going to be fluid, but are still your scorecard for success. The trick is to have enough detail and understanding of your core assumptions such that the difference, plus or minus, to your projections and actuals is within a range that is tolerable for the business to succeed and for your investors (and you) to be happy with.

The key considerations for financial planning are:

- $ Learn how to read and prepare your financial statements.
- $ Financial statements tell a story and investors look for the story that shows how the company will convert assets to cash flow and produce liquidity for their investment.
- $ Assumptions need to be made to create the inputs for a dynamic and iterative projection.
- $ You can gauge the volatility in your results by stress testing your projections and presenting a base case, worst case, and stretch case sensitivity analysis.

- $ Know what you need, why, and how the investment will help you reach your next milestones.
- $ You are not ready to raise capital if you don't have your financial management systems and reports in place and certainly not before you know how much money you are requesting and why.

Action Item: Raising Capital Suitability

Not all companies are a good fit for raising capital, and most companies that are raising capital are not suitable for venture capital. Table 6.2 on page 115 is a quick questionnaire that in no more than a minute can give you a litmus test for your suitability for going after CVC investment.

If you were unable to answer "yes" to eight or more of the questions, I would recommend looking at alternatives to CVC. This does not mean your business won't have a shot at raising capital one day, but it just may not be today. As an entrepreneur you don't want to spend your most valuable resource—time—on any activities that don't have a high possibility of succeeding.

Suitability Questions	Yes	No
Can you self-finance growth initiatives from current working capital?		
Are you willing to sell a reasonable amount of equity and accept financing terms to secure capital?		
Are you prepared to have another person or group of people be involved in decision making?		
Do you want to create a return for yourself by growing quickly and selling the company?		
Will the investment be used to finance internal growth initiatives?		
Are you generating revenues?		
Do you have at least 12 months of working capital on hand?		
Have you made a significant investment in your business already?		
Are you planning on selling equity yourself or directly from the company?		
Is your team experienced and ready for investor road shows?		
Has your company shown significant growth and can deliver even greater growth by using the funding to scale?		

TABLE 6.2—Raising Capital Suitability Assessment

CHAPTER

7

VALUATION AND ARTICULATING RISK

What is your business worth? What level of risk is involved to make it a success? These are questions you will have to answer before you get in the room with potential investors.

Valuation is largely negotiated between the parties in a transaction and considered both an art and a science. Ultimately, an investor will take into consideration all the tangible and intangible value drivers and risk factors of a privately held company when they make an investment decision. Through the transaction, the investor and current owners will agree to a valuation that accurately reflects their shared perspectives on what they feel the inherent risk is in the business, each taking into consideration the existing and future value of the opportunity. It is important that you as an entrepreneur have a sophisticated approach to understanding the value of your company and are able to communicate this information to investors through the language of valuation methodologies. This is one of the most contentious aspects of negotiating a transaction, and only when both parties are armed with the same set of information can they come to an agreement and consummate an investment. This chapter explores the important concept of risk in private companies, how investors perceive risk, and how they assign a valuation to a company for the purposes of making an investment. In this chapter, you'll read about several valuation methodologies and useful frameworks that can help you to articulate risk and value both quantitively and qualitatively.

WHAT IS RISK?

Risk is inherent in all aspects of every business. It is an expression of the uncertainty of future outcomes. It is this exposure to known and unknown threats that investors evaluate when defining the risk specific to each individual investment. The cannabis investing market and private company markets in particular are populated by entrepreneurs and investors who have a very high tolerance for risk. That's good news for you as a cannabis entrepreneur.

When thinking about risk in the context of cannabis investing, *risk* can be defined as the tolerance an investor has for taking on the financial and operational burden of owning equity in a privately held company. Private companies have an extremely high failure rate, and many that don't fail still don't achieve their full potential. Due to the correlation to operations and the success of the investment, private company investments are not viewed as passive investments, as the operational success and management team are intrinsic to building and extracting value for equity owners.

Cannabis investors view the profile of their investments in the context of putting their capital at risk at the outset of an investment, compared to the potential to create a return in the future. The desire of the cannabis investor is to take as little risk as possible in an investment for the greatest return. This is the risk-adjusted rate of return that is acceptable considering that the investment is *illiquid,* meaning that there is no readily available marketplace to sell the shares and liquidate your investment like you can with a publicly traded stock. The result is that there is little to no ability to be redeemed and convert the investment to cash until an exit event at some future point in time.

One unique aspect of cannabis businesses of note is that despite being very early stage, many companies achieve positive cash flow quickly, which is unusual in other investment markets. This can be a beneficial situation for investor and entrepreneur alike; however, it can also be a threat to the business as revenues and profitability can hide operational deficiencies and regulatory risks. When things are going well, stress testing the business for unforeseen risks is not always a priority. When predictable cash flow is available for dividends or other investor redemptions, this should be taken into consideration when performing a valuation assessment, but this is why cash flow in cannabis is not the only metric that is applicable.

Risk is a complex issue, and investors will continually strive to identify risk in all aspects of any investment opportunity. They will continually ask probing questions such as:

- Does the company have outstanding lawsuits?
- Do they get sued a lot?
- Does the company need any regulatory approvals that they don't have?
- What is the probability they don't receive those approvals and what is the contingency plan?
- Do the founders work well together?
- Has the company taken on too much debt and struggling to service that debt?
- Does the company have a concentration of sales with one customer?
- What happens if that customer goes out of business?

As you can see, opening up any discussion around risk can take the investor down a seemingly endless path of exploration and identification of market and company specific risk. Cannabis investors will continually evaluate risk before, during, and after any transaction, as they should. After all, this is the job of any investor. How an investor views the perceived risk of a proposed investment will inform their negotiations and create a structure for moving forward in the process. It is the job of the entrepreneur to help the investors fully understand the risks of the investment, but also to put those opinions in context and explain the mitigation strategies and planning for any unforeseen eventualities that are contingent to the company's business plan. Many complex issues arise post-funding in the event that a major unforeseen risk materializes, which in the emerging cannabis industry will be a likely certainty.

PRIVATE COMPANY RISK

There is some level of risk to investing in any company, public or private. Macroeconomic trends can impact the largest, most stable businesses, and unforeseen natural disasters can happen. When they do, there is little a management team can do other than react and have contingency plans in place. When investors evaluate the risk of a private company specifically, there are several categories of risk that investors will focus on:

1. Management team risk
2. Market risk
3. Regulatory risk
4. Product or service risk
5. Operational/strategic execution risk
6. Financial risk

Your cannabis business is mostly likely a private, not public, venture. As such, it's important that you understand these various risk categories. Let's walk through them.

Management Team Risk

When evaluating a management team, investors look for people who clearly work well together, have some track record of success, and ideally have a history of producing financial returns for investors in the past. An example of this is that many early-stage venture capital investors will prioritize an investment with a team of individuals who have successfully built and exited a company in the past over an investment in a first-time entrepreneur.

Market Risk

As investors define the addressable market and industry of the specific company under review, they will also be evaluating the overall market, sector, and global cannabis economy risk. This includes consolidation trends, competition, international market trends, customer buying trends, and sector maturity. For example, in a mature market with larger, more established competitive businesses, is there room for innovation or new developments? Will that innovation be a threat to the business or create an opportunity?

Regulatory Risk

This is the area investors are most likely to focus on when considering a cannabis investment. The regulatory issues are broad, complex, and changing rapidly as outlined in further in Chapter 3. Fifty percent of investors surveyed over a two-year period for this book identified regulatory issues as the number-one consideration when investing in a cannabis company as seen in Figure 7.1 on page 122.

Product or Service Risk

Does the company have a product or service that is unique and addresses a major point of pain for its customers? Is the company's solution difficult to replicate or compete against? Is the product in a decline due to new offerings, which requires the company to invest heavily in research and development? Will heavy spending also be required to bring new products to market, not all of which will succeed? You will need to ask yourself if you have evaluated your direct and indirect competition, unique selling proposition, and costs in line with a competitive product.

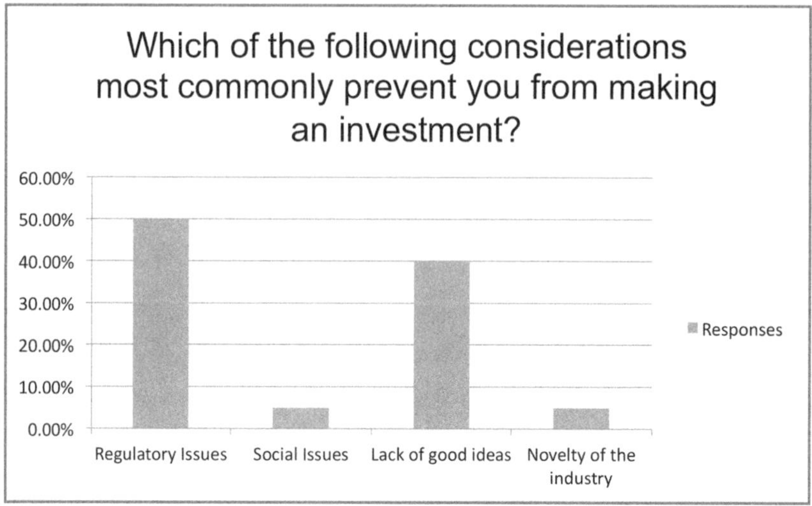

FIGURE 7.1—Investor Survey Results: Perceived Hurdles
Source: Bonaventure Equity, LLC, Investor Surveys

Operational/Strategic Execution Risk

Execution risk is a common theme across the cannabis investing spectrum and in venture capital. The key concept is that all companies have operational risk with varying degrees. Cannabis investors will need to spend a lot of time understanding this risk and determining if the management team can identify and execute against a defined strategic plan to reach the milestones and goals for the business.

Financial Risk

When determining the financial risk of a cannabis investment, investors will take a 360-degree approach to the financial structure of the company. This full scope view will take into account everything about the business that flows though, or is managed by, the finance department. Does the company have the appropriate alignment of financial resources, structure, and operational controls? This is increasingly complicated in cannabis venture investing in that many companies may not be able to have traditional bank accounts or have to comply with 280E federal tax requirements.

ASK THE IMPORTANT QUESTIONS ABOUT RISK

Financial risks are most heavily scrutinized by investors throughout the investment process as the numbers are the clearest articulation of any risk/return analysis. The initial place to start digging into a company's financial health is to look at the overall ability of the company to finance its operations. Investors will likely want to know:

- $ How is the company capitalized and what are the sources of the required financial resources? How much equity is on the balance sheet?
- $ Is the company financed only through equity or investor capital, or do they also have debt?
- $ Can the operations be supported through cash flow alone?

Asking the question, "Are there adequate resources to support the operating expenses of the business?" will reveal factual data about the relative health of the company. Entrepreneurs should be asking this question at every stage of growth. Looking at things like the company's outstanding payables and aging will indicate if they are paying their commitments on time or are floating operating expenses by extending the terms with their vendors. Conversely, looking into the company's receivables and aging will indicate how sound their clients are and if they pay on time. How a company manages its finance department is a good indication of how professional the operations are. Some other important questions to ask are:

- $ What reporting do they produce?
- $ Is it for management review or investor reporting?
- $ Do they have an outside accounting firm, and if so, what is the firm's reputation?
- $ Do they have an annual audit?
- $ What controls and polices do they have in place?

To expand upon the general areas of risk evaluation, many private companies can be assessed on a company-by-company basis with unique characteristics related to a variety of additional risk factors, a sample of which are outlined further in Table 7.1 on page 124.

Risk Factor	Private Company Characteristics
Stage of Maturity	Private businesses can be defined as any company that is not on the public exchanges. This broad definition includes everything from startup companies to very late-stage companies. The earlier the stage, the greater the risk profile and higher the failure rate of a private enterprise. Early-stage companies have less financing options and will typically pay more for debt if they can qualify.
Concentration of Shareholders	Private companies typically only have a few investors with a lot of access and ability to influence the management of the company.
Long-Term Investment Strategy	To realize a meaningful liquidity event, many companies require a multi-year period of growth and building value before realizing a liquidity event.
Owner Operated	Most private companies have management teams with significant ownership and control over the operations of the company. Shareholder disputes in smaller companies can be very distracting and erode value.
Quality of Information	Public companies are under strict timelines to disclose information to the market. Private companies do not have this same pressure and therefore investors will find a wide range in reporting capabilities, or gaps within private companies.
Market Liquidity	Private company liquidity is primarily generated through a strategic sale which takes many years to achieve, during which time the value of the company's equity is illiquid. In the public markets, investors can trade their shares in a company in real time.

TABLE 7.1—Examples of Private Company Risk Factors

THE INVESTOR'S RISK ASSESSMENT LENS

The greater the perceived risk of a business, the higher a "risk premium" the investor will apply to the investment. Compared to less risky investments that an investor can allocate capital to, the premium will be provided to the investors as acceptance of the perceived risk. Investors will price risk into a transaction taking into consideration that the risk is larger with a private company investment and they only have two ways to generate a return:

1. Equity through either dividend yield or the company's ability to distribute profits to shareholders
2. Capital gains or liquidity created through an exit or liquidity event

When investors evaluate and price the risk of owning equity in a private company, they will apply a variety of discounts to the value of the business to offset the risk. This is considered to be a "private company discount" meaning that because a public company has a liquid and efficient market for its shares, comparatively the private company would have be assessed a discount to its valuation to take into consideration that owning equity in a private company has more risk to the investor.

Cannabis investors will take into account many discounts and factors when articulating the risk of a business. Beyond company risk, venture investors will assess risk across a portfolio of investments and, in managing the risk of their investments, look to allocate capital across investments with different risk and return profiles as part of a broader portfolio strategy. Angels and high-net-worth investors may not have a portfolio to manage so the concentration of risk in one company becomes a major consideration when making an investment.

The articulation of this risk is embedded in the valuation assigned to the company for the purposes of executing a transaction. This is how risk translates to valuation through a transaction and is the source of much negotiation and dialogue between the investors and the management of the company.

There is risk in all business ventures and investments. With private companies in particular, the general risk profile and company-specific risk factors are assessed by investors through the investment process. With a developed view to the risk in their own business, you can inform how an investor will value an investment in your cannabis company. The risk the investor takes is then priced through an agreed valuation between the investor and current owners of the company. When you and the investor are aligned, you then need to figure out what the investor will pay for the equity. The work the investor does to come up with this analysis is based on a variety of valuation methods for private companies.

VALUATION

When a cannabis investor feels certain that they have a good understanding of an investment's risk profile, it gets priced by assigning a valuation to the investment. Valuing a private company and an illiquid asset with a limited market is extremely difficult and is the primary domain of the cannabis investor. With a perspective of the risk profile of the investment, the investor will embark on assigning a valuation for the equity of the company rooted in assigning a value to the overall enterprise. This valuation that the investor and current owners agree to will have long-term implications and will impact the type and magnitude of any return the investment will provide back to the shareholders.

The discussion will very quickly revolve around a pre-money, and post-money valuation. *Pre-money valuation* is the value of the company today, and a *post-money valuation* is the value including the investor's capital and their ratio of ownership post-closing. It is in your best interest to use every possible approach to convince the investor that the company has all the elements required to award the highest possible pre-money valuation. You have an incentive to retain as much equity as possible as there is a direct correlation of how you might monetize the intrinsic value of the business through your share in a liquidity event in the future.

The investor has the same desire, but is ultimately competing with the founders for equity in the post-money valuation. The more equity either party controls through the transaction, the greater the ability to generate a return on their efforts and resources. The reality is that investor capital is a scarce resource, and cannabis investors have a lot of leverage in the valuation negotiations simply by controlling the ability to write a check.

Looking into the future and anticipating what the investment might produce down the road is a worthwhile exercise when studying the possible return on investment. No one can accurately predict the future, and the reality is that more venture capital investments fail than succeed, which means that investors require a greater anticipated return for putting their capital at risk through an investment in a privately held company. The inverse of this equation is that when a private equity and venture capital investment does perform, the returns generated for the investor can outperform any other investment class. This is why valuation is so important—it maps directly to the risk-return profile for the investor and the long-term ability for the entrepreneur to create personal wealth.

In cannabis venture capital investing, transaction negotiations ultimately come down to what both parties can agree on, and no two investors will come out with the identical valuation of a target company. All investors are seeking a "risk-adjusted rate of return," which means that valuation is an articulation of perceived risk measured against the prospective returns that are adjusted to compensate the investor for the risk they are accepting when locking up their capital in the investment.

PRIVATE COMPANY VALUE DRIVERS

In the case of a publicly traded company, the value of what investors will pay to own shares in a company is decided through a transparent, efficient, and liquid market. Investors can buy and sell shares through the exchanges and decide what they will pay to buy and own equity in the company. In the public markets, this is the *market cap*, which is the value of the company on any given day of trading. When this happens on a large enough scale, a consensus is formed about the value of the company based on what investors will pay to own the shares. When making a decision on how to value the shares of a public company, investors take into consideration the return they will get based on readily available information through public filings and historical performance. Public companies report on a variety of operating metrics such as earnings per share, revenue, revenue growth, and book value of the assets among other reporting requirements. In the case of a private company, which may or may not have historical performance, how do investors form an opinion about the value of the company?

It starts with understanding what will drive the creation of value in any given investment. To achieve the strongest exit possible, the company will build upon as many of the value drivers as possible that will maximize the future value of the company. When a new investor becomes interested in owning the company, they will look at the various aspects of the business. It is in the company's interest to build in as many of the value-creation aspects of the business as possible. Doing so will create the highest value in the future based on what metrics a prospective buyer is willing to pay a premium for.

There are many quantitative and qualitative metrics that an investor will look for in a private company. The primary strategy for extracting the value of a private company is to sell to a strategic buyer (which you'll read more about in Chapter 8). To create liquidity for the equity an of a private cannabis business an investor owns, there needs to be a buyer. When a company is unable to buy or sell its shares on a public exchange, the only way for inventors can only sell their shares if they can find a private buyer who is willing to negotiate a transfer of ownership. These buyers and transactions are very difficult to effectuate on terms the parties will agree to. Or the company will ultimately access the public markets through an initial public offering (IPO). When considering the key drivers that a company can manage in order to build value, the shareholders and management team will plan to build value in the company that is aligned with the exit strategy they most desire. Some investors will seek a short-term gain and want to exit their entire position quickly through a sale or IPO. Other investors will be happy to stay involved with the company for ten or more years, collect dividends, and perhaps sell part of the business as it grows while staying involved for the long term. Table 7.2 on page 129 summarizes some examples of valuation drivers in private companies.

PRIVATE COMPANY VALUATION METHODS

Cannabis investors will employ a variety of valuation methodologies and tools at their disposal, which provide data points the investor will ultimately rely upon for their judgment. In the absence of an explicit market where

Value Drivers	Private Company Characteristics
Assets	Ownership of the business should be equivalent to the fair market value of the assets of the business if the company was to divest of those assets. Many private companies however are light on assets.
Intangible assets	Assets that do not have an explicit value such as patents, copyrights, and trade secrets and intellectual property. Private companies can build value and create a protection to their market position through intangible assets.
Historical and future cash flow	For private companies that have several years of operating history, investors can evaluate the consistency and levels of the cash flows generated by the company and estimate the probability of the company continuing to generate these cash flows in the future. For companies with significant year over year growth rates that have a high probability of continuing, investors will typically apply a premium to the present value of the business.
Management team	It is all about the people. CVC investors like to see a cohesive team of talented and complementary people who ideally have a track record of successfully running and growing companies of a similar size and structure. A history of providing returns for prior investors by the management team is a strong value driver for new investors who are evaluating the risk and return profile of the business.

TABLE 7.2—Private Company Value Drivers

investors buy and sell equity in companies with a stated valuation, the CVC investor will triangulate the value of the investment by using a combination of several methods for valuing a company. There are five main analytical approaches that are relevant for valuing a private company:

1. *Asset/Equity Valuation Methodology.* A review of the net asset or equity value of a business, otherwise known as "book value" or "liquidation value."
2. *Income Methodology.* A review of historical performance combined with the company's projections with a discount rate applied to future cash flow used to indicate a present value on an income basis.
3. *Market Comparable Analysis.* A review of external data sources to identify acquisitions in the market of similar companies indicating what metrics were used to value other similar companies, such as purchase price to revenue and EBITDA data.
4. *Sensitivity Analysis.* Using appropriate discount rates, conduct a review of what impact on valuation underachieving or overachieving revenue, EBITDA or transaction multiple projections.
5. *Replacement Value.* What would it cost to start from scratch and build the infrastructure you currently have?

Let's take a closer look at each of these.

Asset/Equity Valuation Methodology

This is a valuation approach that is most relevant for companies that own explicit assets that can be assigned a value. For example, a manufacturing or product-focused company may have a significant inventory on hand, which is an asset that appears on the balance sheet. That inventory will have a cost that the company has paid for the inventory and will therefore have some value if it was disposed of and can be converted into cash. The more unique the inventory, the less likely that it can be sold at or above the cost of the inventory; however, commodity products can be sold relatively quickly. There are other assets that can also be disposed of if the company was liquidated, such as equipment and furniture.

When taking the value of the tangible assets into consideration, the investor can calculate the book value of the company. Book value is a common calculation that is also known as net book value (NBV). *Book value* refers to what is carried on the balance sheet of the company stating the cost of the assets minus the accumulated depreciation, which is theoretically what the equity owners would receive if the company were liquidated. Net asset value is then the value of the total assets (not including intangible assets such as trade secrets, patents, or goodwill) minus liabilities. Here is what that formula looks like:

Net Asset Value =
Total Tangible Assets – (Intangible Assets + Liabilities)

With a stated net asset value, the CVC investor can perform a comparison to the company's valuation. Simply stated, if the value of the company is greater than the ability to dispose of the assets, the valuation would imply that there is greater value in the intangible assets of the company and would need to be justified through alternate valuation approaches.

Income Methodology

Using a company's income in order to value the business is most relevant when the business or asset has a steady history of revenues and earnings together with a level of certainty that the revenues will continue. The more certain the future revenues are, the more relevant an income analysis will be. One common analysis investors use is to articulate the present value of future cash flows in a *discounted cash flow (DCF) model.* The model assists with identifying the intrinsic value of a company by placing a value today on the future cash flows of the company. This takes into consideration the "time value of money" implying that the value of receiving a dollar today is greater than the value of a dollar paid in the future. Therefore, the future dollars generated will be discounted to a present value today.

Creating a DCF model can be a very complicated process that needs to consider interest rates, discount rates, a terminal value, growth rates, operating cash flows, capital expenditures, and the *weighted average cost of capital* (WACC), which is how much a company expects to pay to its security holders in order to finance its assets. What the DCF model aims to quantify for investors is the trade-off for what their investment could earn in an alternate investment vehicle vs. what the potential cash produced by the proposed investment would be discounted to a value today.

A DCF model is useful as a method to check the current value of a company today, but due to the volatility and uncertainty of future events, a DCF model is rarely the sole method for formulating a valuation for a private company in cannabis investing. This is in part due to the significant uncertainty in predicting the future cash flows and expenses of a private company. In addition, there are many assumptions that are needed to construct and analyze an income-based valuation methodology and, therefore, investors are encouraged to understand the various inputs and business metrics used in this evaluation. The higher the volatility in outcomes, the less reliable a DCF analysis is for use in early-stage private companies.

Market Comparable Analysis

The most common method to developing a valuation for a private company is to study the market of what other buyers or investors have paid for other private companies that are similar to the intended target. As with all the valuation analysis techniques, there are several issues to consider. The primary issue is that the type of information the investor is looking for is difficult to access. Unlike the public markets, there isn't one source of consolidated publicly available information.

Take, for example, a private investor who is looking at an early-stage CBD company with the following characteristics:

- It is a single-product company.
- The business generated $4 million in revenue over the last 12-month period, and is growing at 15 percent per year.
- It is privately held by the founders and management team.
- The company sells through two large distributors and has no single customer with more than 15 percent of total revenues.
- The company has a 25-percent EBITDA margin, or $1 million over the last 12 months.

- $ The company has $250,000 in outstanding bank debt and $500,000 in cash on the balance sheet.
- $ The product is protected by multiple recently awarded patents that the company owns outright.

To compare this company to other peers who also went through a transaction, the investor will prepare a list of precedent transactions to evaluate. The more data that is available, the deeper the analysis can be. Most investors will start with creating a list of suitable public companies to begin the comparative analysis process. The information that they will evaluate is a set of metrics that can translate to a private transaction. For example, they will look at *total enterprise value (TEV)*, which is the calculated value of the company on a debt-free basis, which in turn can be compared to other companies on a debt free basis. TEV is calculated as:

TEV = Market Capitalization + Debt – Cash

With a TEV, investors can then create a series of ratios (multiples) of the enterprise value compared with certain metrics such as a multiple of revenues over the last 12 months or multiple of EBITDA over the last 12 months. With these ratios calculated, the investor can compare the target company with other like businesses. When comparing public companies as a benchmark, it is appropriate to apply a discount to take into consideration that the target is a private company.

The single most common method for valuating a private company is to perform a similar exercise as above with a database of private company transactions, or comparable transactions. Investors discuss the market "comps" (comparable transaction analysis) of a private company as a gauge of what another buyer or investor would apply as a value to the target investment.

Figure 7.2 on page 134 is an analysis for the example CBD product company that outlines certain public companies, applies a private company discount, and compares a series of comparable transactions of other private companies. This sample analysis creates a sense of the market for similar companies recognizing that no two companies are exactly alike. With the analysis of the information in this evaluation, the investor can then apply it to the target company.

Company Name:

Cannabis Consumer Single Product Company Example

Comps
($ in millions, except per share data)

Company Name		TEV (Cap + Debt - Cash)	TEV/LTM Total Rev	TEV/LTM EBITDA	Number of Products	Description	Date
Acquirers and Micro Caps							
Representative Public Company A	84,529.0	$ 90,894.0	3.1x	11.9x	Multi	CBD	Feb-20
Representative Public Company B	25,486.0	$ 27,010.0	2.5x	10.2x	Multi	CBD & THC	Mar-20
Representative Public Company C	175,651.0	$ 174,604.0	2.8x	9.7x	Multi	CBD & THC & Retail	Apr-20
Representative Public Company D	48,604.0	$ 54,222.0	3.7x	10.6x	Multi	MSO	May-20
Representative Public Company E	12,855.0	$ 14,384.0	3.1x	10.8x	Multi	MSO	Jun-20
Representative Public Company F	206.0	$ 205.0	5.1x	0.0x	Multi	MSO	Nov-20
Liquidity (Private Company) Discount	50%						
High			2.6x	6.0x			
Low			1.3x	0.0x			
Mean			1.7x	4.4x			
Median			1.6x	5.2x			
Acquisition							
Representative Private Company A		$ 283	2.1x	3.6x	Multi	CBD & THC	Sep-20
Representative Private Company B		$ 225	4.2x	6.5x	Single	CBD & THC & Retail	Oct-20
Representative Private Company C		$ 2,744	2.4x	3.0x	Multi	MSO	Nov-20
Representative Private Company D		$ 300	4.0x	12.0x	Multi	MSO	Dec-20
Representative Private Company E		$ 194	1.9x	4.0x	Multi	CBD	Jan-21
Representative Private Company F		$ 150	1.0x	2.0x	Single	CBD & THC	Feb-21
Representative Private Company P		$ 425	4.3x	7.0x	Multi	MSO	Dec-21
Single Product Discount	20%						
% Single - Product	31%						
High			4.0x	11.3x			
Low			0.9x	1.9x			
Mean			2.7x	5.1x			
Median			2.3x	3.8x			

FIGURE 7.2—Precedent and Comparable Transaction Analysis
(Data in figure is fictional for illustrative purposes)

With the information from Figure 7.2, the investor can develop an implied valuation as follows in Figure 7.3 on page 135.

The data provided in the previous charts may be fictional, but the calculations are very similar to how an analysis like this might be

Implied Valuation		
	Company Estimates	
	LTM Total Rev.	LTM EBITDA
Operating Parameters	4,000,000	1,000,000
Valuation Multiples		
High	4.56x	15.16x
Low	0.61x	0.94x
Mean	2.38x	5.59x
Median	2.22x	4.90x
Implied Enterprise Value		
High	$ 18,225,000	$ 15,159,375
Low	$ 2,437,500	$ 937,500
Mean	$ 9,518,906	$ 5,586,758
Median	$ 8,875,000	$ 4,896,875
+Cash And Short Term Investments	$ 600,000	$ 600,000
-Total Debt	$ 250,000	$ 250,000
=Implied Equity Value		
High	$ 18,575,000	$ 15,509,375
Low	$ 2,787,500	$ 1,287,500
Mean	$ 9,868,906	$ 5,936,758
Median	$ 9,225,000	$ 5,246,875

FIGURE 7.3—Sample Comparable Analysis Implied Valuation Model

performed. In most cases, the investor will look to evaluate this business in terms of a multiple of EBITDA and use the market mean to start a sensitivity analysis of the company's value. In this case, the investor could very likely defend a view that the company is worth $5.6 million calculated as a 5.6x EBITDA (as an average multiple between the public and private comparable precedent transactions).

Sensitivity Analysis

It is with near certainty the CVC investor can expect that a company's projected revenues and EBITDA will not turn out to be exactly as expected. Therefore, many cannabis investors account for the volatility in outcomes by performing a sensitivity analysis of the future value

Company Name:

Revenue & EBITDA Mutliple Sensitivity Analysis

Multiple of Revenue Sensitivity

		Multiple of Revenue				
		1.5x	**2.0x**	2.4x	**3.0x**	**3.5x**
Revenue	**$ 2,000,000**	$ 3,000,000	$ 4,000,000	$ 4,759,453	$ 6,000,000	$ 7,000,000
	$ 3,000,000	$ 4,500,000	$ 6,000,000	$ 7,139,180	$ 9,000,000	$ 10,500,000
	$ 4,000,000	$ 6,000,000	$ 8,000,000	$ 9,518,906	$ 12,000,000	$ 14,000,000
	$ 5,000,000	$ 7,500,000	$ 10,000,000	$ 11,898,633	$ 15,000,000	$ 17,500,000
	$ 6,000,000	$ 9,000,000	$ 14,278,359	$ 14,278,359	$ 18,000,000	$ 21,000,000

Multiple of EBITDA Sensitivity

		Multiple of EBITDA				
		5.0x	**5.5x**	5.6x	**6.0x**	**6.5x**
EBITDA	**$ 500,000**	$ 2,500,000	$ 2,750,000	$ 2,793,379	$ 3,000,000	$ 3,250,000
	$ 750,000	$ 3,750,000	$ 4,125,000	$ 4,190,068	$ 4,500,000	$ 4,875,000
	$ 1,000,000	$ 5,000,000	$ 5,500,000	$ 5,586,758	$ 6,000,000	$ 6,500,000
	$ 1,250,000	$ 6,250,000	$ 6,875,000	$ 6,983,447	$ 7,500,000	$ 8,125,000
	$ 1,500,000	$ 7,500,000	$ 8,380,137	$ 8,380,137	$ 9,000,000	$ 9,750,000

FIGURE 7.4—Revenue and EBITDA Multiple Sensitivity Analysis

of the target company. In keeping with the fictional CBD company example, Figure 7.4 on page 136 shows what may be reasonable expectations for the future value of the company should one of two things happen:

1. The company misses their projected revenues or EBITDA or;
2. The multiples that a buyer is willing to pay either increases or decreases due to market changes or other events.

Companies that are valued on a multiple of revenue are typically valued as such because the buyer is most interested in the value of the top-line revenue profile of the company. Companies that are bought and sold on the basis of an EBITDA multiple are an expression of either the buyer or investor's desire to acquire an interest of the profitability of the business.

Replacement Value

Another way to come up with a perspective as to a company's value is to estimate what it would cost to build the business again from the ground up.

Investors will sometimes perform a build-vs.-buy analysis. This means that they will assess what it would cost to start at zero, hire the management team, and replicate the business. This is more difficult for a company that has significant intellectual property that may take years and millions of dollars to replicate. But in the case of a business that is operating a physical production facility that does not have anything proprietary to

WHAT THE INVESTORS SAY: ALTERNATIVE VALUATION METHODOLOGY AS A DECISIVE METRIC IN CANNABIS

by Ryan Ansin, co-founder of Revolutionary Farms

From my perspective, there is not an industry wherein the concept of "interest being cheap" rings truer than the cannabis industry. Most self-proclaimed "cannabis investors" have deployed de minimis levels of capital and many raise funds in lockstep with their deployment. If you break down this most prevalent strategy, it resembles a blended form of fund management and the assembly of single-purpose-vehicles (SPVs) to generate a track record of rising ships amidst a [hopefully] consistently in-filling tide. Large, professionally managed funds that do not transact in this way are very few in number, and should be held in high regard as they have accomplished something rare. But I'd like to focus now on the smaller investor, meaning sub-$5 million, to deploy directly into the industry.

Now, in Q3 of 2019, one could spend their entire year bouncing from one conference to another, gleaning free investment advice from early movers. That same person can very reasonably fill an entire agenda speaking with others, echoing sound bites from those on stage to an audience of $100,000 to $1 million check writers. In the age of AI, cryptocurrency, and cannabis, the one that has the most graspable business models and tangible assets seems to have prevailed in cocktail conversations in recent years: Cannabis has dominated the airwaves of hobby investors seeking their next tidal wave.

WHAT THE INVESTORS SAY, continued

Like so many overnight-upstart industries now and in the past, distinguishing the strong from the weak, the vapid from the capable, is very difficult. Even more perplexing is how to set an economic value on the opportunity in a vacuum, and with consideration of industry peers. The cannabis industry is particularly complex because each geography presents its own challenges, creating microcosms of opportunity. Where, as an example, the hope for artificial intelligence taking over a particular sector could be scaled across the world once proven successful, most operators in the cannabis industry cannot simply pour gas on the fire and replicate its exact model in an ever-expanding geography. This is true in vertical integrated cultivators, manufacturers, and distribution groups, but also reaches areas like ecommerce, "seed-to-sale" or point-of-sale systems, and well beyond. There certainly are a handful of expansive concepts that can cross geographies simply, but rarely is it so simple.

Meanwhile, to participate, you must generate a methodology of setting a relative value to the investments you are considering separate from a simple comparison-based consideration. There are no apples-to-apples comparisons and public market volatility is so great in the early days of the industry that your reasonable number today could be dwarfed or multiplied tomorrow—for better or worse hampering your ability as an investor to take decisive action with public-market comps.

speak of, tasks like real state, business licenses, hiring staff, and purchasing inventory can be done relatively quickly.

A good example of this is what happens in the franchise industry. It costs you less to buy a franchise than it would be to open your own independent business to compete with the existing multilocation franchises. This does not imply that the investor wants to compete with you, but rather that the replacement cost to replicate what you have is indicative of what the company may be worth today.

THE CVC METHOD

One final approach to valuation, specific to venture capital, is called the CVC Method. In this method, the CBD company in our earlier example is in discussions with a CVC investor to make an investment of $1 million to expand and grow the business. Is this a good investment for the investor?

With a look to the valuation of the company, the investor can now project what might happen in the future and how they can participate in a liquidity event. In Figure 7.5, we use the previous example where an investor makes the $1 million investment in the company and owns 15 percent on a post-money basis. If the company was to grow revenues to $8 million and generate $5.9 million in EBITDA, and the multiples in the market remain at the current levels, the investor can theoretically

Company Name:
Medical Device Example
Valuation Model

Precedent Transactions				
Current Company Value		Multiples	Implied EV	Weighting
LTM Revenue	$ 4,000,000	2.38x	$ 9,518,906	80%
LTM EBITDA	$ 1,000,000	5.59x	$ 5,586,758	20%
Blended Current EV			**$ 8,732,477**	

Exit Thesis		Multiples	Implied EV	Weighting
Revenues at Exit	$ 8,000,000	2.38x	$ 19,037,813	80%
EBITDA at Exit	$ 5,900,000	5.59x	$ 32,961,871	20%
Blended Exit EV			**$ 21,822,624**	

Liquidity Proceeds	
Proceeds Net of Debt*	$ 17,822,624
Equity Return	$ 2,705,827
Total Proceeds	**$ 2,705,827**

VC Method	
Amount of Investment	$ 1,000,000
Cost of Capital**	5%
Equity Ownership at Exit***	15%
Exit Proceeds	$ 2,705,827
Time (years)	5.0
Recommendation******	**YES**
IRR	22%
ROI	2.7x

Notes

*Assumes $4 million in debt at the time of sale that would be retired
**Assumes what expected returns would be if investing capital in other securities or asset classes
***Assumes no further dilution to the investor
****If required investment is less than expected return, then "YES"

FIGURE 7.5—Example CVC Method Calculations

participate in a sale of the business in year five. They would receive in return $2.7 million for the original $1 million investment. Therefore, since the potential return is greater than the capital to be deployed today, the CVC model would recommend moving forward with the investment.

The method described above is used across all sectors of VC investing. What makes this unique for the CVC is to overlay this yes/no company-specific investment thesis with a gauge for regulatory risk and then compare against multiple companies in the opportunity set that the CVC is evaluating. This allows for contemplating a preferred risk/return opportunity for each transaction but also takes into consideration constructing a portfolio. Figure 7.6 is a company-specific qualitative risk assessment tool. With this tied to each deal that the CVC is evaluating, the investor can then create a snapshot of the deals under evaluation as they progress through the process as outlined in Figure 7.7 on page 141.

CANNABIS CAPITAL TAKEAWAYS AND ACTION ITEMS

Each company is different so not all of these valuation methodologies will apply to every investment situation. Many early-stage companies

Company Name:
TBD, INC.
Valuation Factors

Qualitative	**Positive**	**Negative**	**Risk Assesment**	**Notes**
Management	25%	0%	Low	
Market	70%	0%	Medium	
Customers	60%	0%	High	
Product/Service	80%	0%		
Technology	75%	0%		
Competition	0%	25%		
Projections	0%	10%		
Channels	40%	0%		
Partners	0%	20%		
Cash Management	0%	30%		
Transaction Terms	0%	60%		
Risk Management	0%	60%		
Intellectual Property	50%	0%		
Company Unique Benefits	**Positive**	**Negative**		**Notes**
Marquee Customer	25%	0%		
Company Unique Discounts	**Positive**	**Negative**		**Notes**
Owner Dependent	25%	0%		
Total Qualitative Weighting	+	-		
	450%	205%		

FIGURE 7.6—Company-Specific Qualitative Risk Assessments

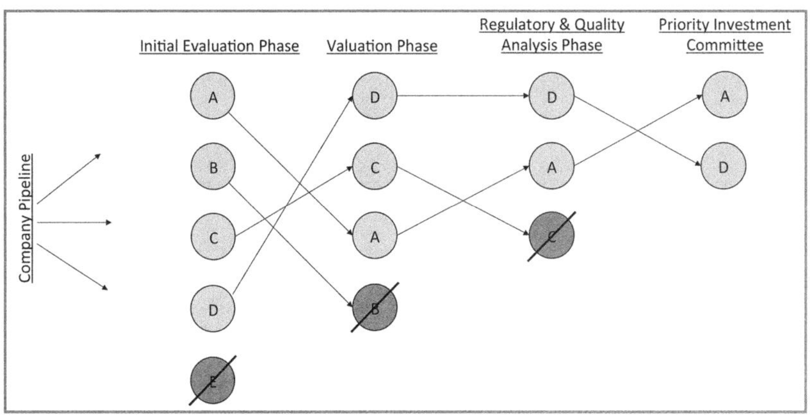

FIGURE 7.7—CVC Process Pipeline Management Tool

have few or no assets and will have a much higher volatility to future revenues and earnings, so the investor will rely heavily on their judgment in forming a valuation. In some situations, the investor will analyze the company using every form of valuation, and in some situations, they may use only one approach. To proceed with negotiating the valuation of your company with your prospective investor, you can now speak the language of valuation and speak to your case for your perspective on value with an understanding of how they will be assessing and pricing the risk in your business.

Action Item: Value Your Company Today

Take the some time to think about what your company is worth today. Try and be as dispassionate as possible in this evaluation and instead think about how your investors will perceive the value of the company. For now, you can focus on one or two methods as described above that best fit your situation. Figure 7.8 on page 142 will help you identify the most relevant methods to use.

If you're not sure where to start on this action item, let's use our fictional example to help illustrate one way to approach it. Betsy, the founder of the company HCC we discussed in Chapter 6, and her team decided that they want to move forward with raising capital to grow their business. They are now thinking about how to value their business

Valuation Methodologies		Assessment	Yes	No
1	Asset/Equity Value	Do you have significant tangible/intangible assets or have raised capital in the past at a set valuation?		
2	Income Methodology	Do you have historical revenues and profits?		
3	Market Comparable	Have there been a number of M&A transactions that you can benchmark against?		
4	Sensitivity Analyses	Do you have one or more methods/valuation metrics that you can apply?		
5	Replacement costs	Do you have infrastructure costs that someone else could replicate if they had enough resources (time & money)?		

FIGURE 7.8—Valuation Method Selection

and need to decide on an approach that will be similar to how investors will be assessing the HCC valuation. They are debating if there is enough historical income to use as a basis for the profitability of the company, but their financial team thinks it's too early to accurately value the cash flow of the company. The startup costs were not such that someone else with sufficient time and resources could replicate the infrastructure, so they are discounting any replacement cost methodology. There are some assets in inventory, but it turns over so quickly that numbers can shift dramatically from month to month. So, the team decided the best way to value HCC is to research some comparable transactions to see what buyers are paying for companies like HCC in an M&A transaction. If they were to sell the company in three or five years based on their financial projections, they can predict a range and estimate the future value of the business and what that would be worth to the founders and new investors based on their ownership percentages.

DEALMAKING AND EXIT STRATEGIES

The cannabis economy is moving rapidly with constant change and growth across all sectors and industries. This dynamic has led to deals being pursued at a record pace across a broad spectrum of transaction types. In addition to the myriad skill sets and focus areas, cannabis entrepreneurs must be proficient and excel at dealmaking. You will hear a lot about the importance of an "exit plan" or "exit strategy" for your business (which you first read about in Chapter 2). This is when you engineer a transaction that allows for some or all the investment to exit the company and convert the assets back to cash. The time to think about an exit plan is at the outset of the planning phase. With a clear understanding of how the company plans to achieve its targets, the management team can define a clear strategy.

One of the key themes around the development of an achievable exit plan for private companies is that there is a high correlation between how effectively the management team can operate the company and the ability to maximize value through an exit event. Given that there are multiple ways to grow a business to maximize the desired exit, a very important aspect of achieving the desired results is the alignment of the business plan (objectives) with the shareholders and the operating management team.

Preparing the exit plan can be tricky, though, due to a disconnect between what you might want and what the investor expects. If an investor seeks to deploy capital and exit the investment within five years, it is important to align the management team's objectives during that time frame. It is not uncommon for an existing owner or management team to want to stay involved in the company for the long term and for the balance of their career. This would imply that they may not want to sell within the five-year time horizon, as they will feel that there is more value to create over a longer period of time. It is not that this is a bad approach for a manager or founder, but it can create a disconnect with an investor who will be more attracted to selling as soon as possible. Many times, during an exit event, the management team may not remain involved for the long term and therefore will be disincentivized from selling even if the return for the investor is achievable.

In this chapter, you will learn about different growth strategies, how dealmaking is a skill set that you should develop and what deals or transactions can be part of your medium- to long-term planning. Ultimately you are looking to create value quickly in the short term, then extract that value for shareholders through an exit strategy or transaction in the long term. Dealmaking is an art and a science, and a leadership capability that, when executed currently, can exponentially accelerate the growth and value of your venture.

GROWTH STRATEGIES

All companies are looking for ways to continue to grow, iterate, reinvent themselves, or otherwise compete at a higher level over time. There is nothing static about business and this is especially true with cannabis businesses. When presented with opportunities or transactions that help you achieve your goals and mission, it's important to have developed a framework for growing the business so that these opportunities can be prioritized, pursued, or passed on.

There are several approaches to developing a growth strategy for your business. Many of these will typically occur at later stages in the company's lifecycle, although many cannabis businesses are pursing transactions much sooner than companies in their non-cannabis comparative industries. The basis for growing a company can be defined in two categories:

1. *Organic growth.* Growing the business with the internal resources.
2. *Inorganic growth.* Buying or partnering with another business.

There can be, and likely will be, intersections that apply to both categories in a specific transaction, but for the most part, any deals that you may consider can be defined as either organic or inorganic.

Organic Growth

Organic growth relates to anything that your company can pursue using its internal resources to drive growth in revenue and/or profitability. Staying with your core product or service can allow you to make additional investments in producing more revenue, reducing costs, or expanding customers. When a company can leverage the resources and current infrastructure to keep reaching new heights, the strategies deployed to achieve this are tied to internal or organic momentum. The decisions then fall to the management team, shareholders, and board members to decide on investing in those initiatives. When you can see that the company is trending positively, there will be an inflection point where you can reallocate resources that you already have, such as retained earnings, to finance those initiatives that will translate to more value. If we revisit the company lifecycle stages in Chapter 2, you will notice that there is a dip in the P&L line indicating that there is a period of continued losses that a company will finance in order to expand and grow sales and, in turn, mature as a business. It is at this time that most companies raise capital to finance the growth strategies that they are executing on. As the resources become more saleable, continuing in this vein will produce continued organic growth.

Inorganic Growth

An inorganic growth strategy will capture all the external initiatives that can produce scale, leverage, and value. This can take the form of acquiring another a company, forming a strategic alliance or joint venture, or divesting of a non-core business unit to free up resources to execute faster, better, or stronger. These transactions are typically the domain of investment banks who bring specific skills and relationships to help effectuate a deal. Today, a good entrepreneur should also have the vision and skills to not only identify these types of opportunities, but also be able to shepherd a deal through a process to get to a desired result.

Deals can be exciting, and entrepreneurs have no shortage of vision or enthusiasm for seeing big results in the future. Pursing transactions however can be extremely time consuming. If you are raising money, you should not try to pull off another deal at the same time. Taking your focus away from that critical process can be catastrophic. So, don't get distracted with something shiny and exciting that ultimately has a low probability of coming to fruition and can distract you from your core focus: running a successful business and raising capital for it.

Investors like to see that you put some thought into how the business will mature, so in some instances it may be enough to simply state that there are inorganic growth opportunities for the company in the future and what that may look like. This can be the "sizzle" of the story that you can include in your future opportunities section of the business plan and may be included in presenting to investors related to the exit strategy or plan to create liquidity. When a company is seeking venture capital, they are at a stage when the main focus is typically all on building and scaling organic growth. Investors at this stage do not like to allocate funds in a use of proceeds that will be used to buy another company. This can be a red flag that the company is failing at its core business and is trying to buy another company to fix a problem. When you get to a later stage in growth and your company is a suitable acquirer, that is typically when larger private equity funds will participate in order to fund an inorganic growth strategy. But again, this is long-term and almost always premature for a company seeking venture capital to contemplate other than suggesting that there is some point in the future when these types of transactions will be suitable for the business to actively pursue.

Aligning your strategic plan to your growth activities and then identifying and developing transactions to fit those objectives are all part of being a "dealmaker" CEO. Another common phrase is a "rainmaker," which refers to a leader who can engineer success through strategic transactions, or "doing deals."

DEALMAKING AS A DISCIPLINE

More deals don't make it to the finish line than do. Consummating a transaction takes a specific skill set most associated with investment banking. Identifying a suitable transaction is rooted in the companies' defined strategy. If there are two independent companies pursing a transaction together, then both businesses need to have an alignment of goals and objectives and both parties will need to see the benefits of pursuing a transaction. Deals are expensive in terms of both time and actual costs, such as legal or advisory fees, that many times are paid up front and are not contingent on a transaction closing. When a deal cannot be finalized, all parties walk away paying fees and adding expenses to be left with little to show for the effort.

As a cannabis entrepreneur and CEO, it is your job to ensure you don't get distracted prematurely and get "deal fever," as the rapid pace of transactions can be head spinning. So, the balancing act is to be prudent in what, if any, transaction focus you will have outside of raising capital. Be careful not to take your hand off the wheel of the core operating businesses and try to engineer something that has a low probability of happening.

As a cannabis entrepreneur, you have to develop some unique skill sets and core capabilities. Managing people, product development, selling, marketing, finance, regulatory compliance, and operations to name a few.

You can add dealmaking to that list. When you are actively raising capital, this is a process, in particular with earlier stage companies, that will be self-managed by the CEO (you!) and the management team. During this process of seeking capital from venture investors, the business needs to perform at its peak. There is nothing more damaging to the process of raising capital than to have to share that your company is underperforming. Every investor likes to see that sales are growing, expenses are staying in control, the markets are expanding, and that the company is not only hitting its targets but outperforming them. This is extremely difficult to accomplish with a small team when the founders and CEO are spending the majority of their time raising capital. If you then add another type of transaction to the mix, the company is at risk of trying to manage a toxic mix of activities that require complete focus and have extremely low probabilities of materializing.

The dealmaking discipline is a talent that certain CEOs have to be able to explore for inorganic growth initiatives, but be sure to quickly eliminate spending time on anything that isn't hyper focused on benefiting your organic growth initiatives. In that rare situation where something does come along that could transform the success of the business, the dealmaker CEO springs into action and manages a process. With the added dynamic of cannabis regulatory complexity and unknowns, the core discipline that the most talented dealmakers exhibit is finding solutions and tapping into their experience to find creative ways to ensure that they complete the deal and produce value for their stakeholders.

EXITING A BUSINESS

When you started your business, what was it that drove you to take on the significant personal financial risk to purse building your company? Was it because there was a major need that you identified in your sector and didn't see anyone else serving that demand? Did you always want to run a cannabis company and took the plunge as the regulations started to shift and allowed legal business operations? Most critically, did you start the company because you wanted to create a job for yourself or because at some stage in the future you anticipate creating great wealth for you and your family by selling the company? Investors will typically prioritize suitable exit strategies for a company in one of three main groups (which you'll read about later in this chapter):

1. Selling to a strategic buyer
2. Selling to a financial buyer
3. Going public (IPO)

There is no right or wrong answer, but you should be asking these questions of yourself so that you have a clear definition of the type of business you are building so investors will be interested. Many entrepreneurs lose sight of the fact that they are an investor in their businesses just like anyone they seek capital from would be. At some point in time, you made the decision to invest your time, experience, and likely your own capital to pursue building your company. Entrepreneurs typically think of investors as mythical people who, if they can just find them, would flock to investing in their company. So why did *you* invest in your business? And why would you be confident that the risks you took are going to pay off for you and all the investors over time?

This is where an exit strategy for the company influences an investment decision. Is there sufficient ownership for the capital that is at risk to produce an adequate return? How you perceive the business providing liquidity for investors (dividends, M&A exit, or IPO) will influence the value at which the investor is willing to invest. At the end of the day, investors have options on where to place their capital, and if they invest in your company, they will expect to see a return for their investment.

Why Plan Your Exit?

Having alignment with investors is a theme throughout this book and one that is imperative for informing how you will build the business together. When you set out to build your company, you had a desired outcome in mind and most likely that was to create wealth. Your investors will likewise be very explicit about a desire to create a return. Professional investors will articulate the future success of the business through a desired exit strategy. They ultimately want to translate the value created within the company at some point in the future and distribute that value back to the shareholders, thus creating liquidity for their investment. Private companies don't have liquidity for their shares like companies on a public exchange do, so the investor returns are calculated on how likely it is that the business will be sold or otherwise have excess cash that can be distributed back to the shareholders.

Why do investors focus on a liquidity event, and what does that mean to you and your founding shareholders? Investors will contemplate what the potential for a return on their investment is very early in the process and continue to evaluate this during the due diligence phase. These projections are exactly that—projections or forecasts. Similarly, many factors come into play such as economic conditions, market trends, regulatory changes, changes in the competitive environment, financial markets, etc. These factors may impact any given company positively or negatively. Therefore, forecasting investment returns is very difficult and full of uncertainty. Many investors do, however, set an expectation for what they want to achieve in terms of the return. For example, you may hear an investor state that they are looking for an 8x (times) a return on any specific investment. They are taking into consideration the high risk and lower success probabilities of investing in a private company and are stating that they expect 8x their original investment. The reason for making these types of risky investments is that there is a probability that the return generated will outperform other investments and produce an outsized return.

Returns for private company investments are traditionally viewed in terms of the total return compared to the initial outlay of capital. In addition, the return potential for any single investment can also produce a return that can cover other losses in a portfolio.

For example, an investor has two investments in a portfolio that each required $1 million investment. Company A goes out of business and produces a loss of $1 million. Company B goes on to be sold and produces a return of 4 times (or 4x) the investment and returns $4 million back to the investor. The combined basis for this portfolio is $2 million and the combined return is $4 million. The portfolio then returned 2x the investment including the total loss of Company A.

Figure 8.1 below shows a simple calculation for a single investment and how it performed over a five-year period. In this example, much like Company B above, the investor made an initial investment or $1 million and acquired 29.5 percent of the company. The business was sold after five years for $15 million, and the investor's stake in the business netted them just over $4 million, or 4.4x the initial investment. (This is a simple example that does not take into consideration many of the complex terms and structures that can be in place with these types of investments such as multiple classes of equity or employee option plans that will get exercised and dilute the shareholding of the company further.)

A word of caution for the entrepreneur: It is critical that you can speak the language of exits and return calculations, but your job is not to do the work of the investor and create calculated investment return expectations for them. In fact, it is not advisable to present to investors any expected outcomes on their investments. Many pitch decks will mistakenly show some calculation for how the investors will make money on their investment, and this is almost always a bad idea. It is guaranteed that things will not work out as everyone thinks it will from day one of the investment, and if you put in writing some target

Transaction Parameters	
Pre-Money Valuation	$ 3,000,000
Investment Amount	$ 2,000,000
Post Money Valuation	$ 5,000,000
Post Transaction Capitalization Table	
Founders (Pre-investment ownership)	60.0%
New Investors	40.0%
Liquidation Event	
Company Valuation at Exit	$ 20,000,000
Timeframe	5 yrs
Shareholder Proceeds	
Founders	$ 12,000,000
Investors	$ 8,000,000

Investment Return	Year 1	Year 2	Year 3	Year 4	Year 5
Investment	-$ 1,000,000	$ -	$ -	$ -	$ -
Liquidation Proceeds	$ -	$ -	$ -	$ -	$ 8,000,000
Total RV Proceeds	**-$ 1,000,000**	**$ -**	**$ -**	**$ -**	**$ 8,000,000**

IRR Calculation	68%
Investment Return Multiple	4.0x

Notes

FIGURE 8.1—Return Calculations

goal for a return on the investors capital, you run the risk of being held accountable for those projections in the future. You don't want to be in a situation where your shareholders are upset in the future because you didn't end up realizing the return you have promised if you set it up front. This is a complex and nuanced discussion because everyone wants to paint a positive picture for how the investors will benefit in the long term. In general, the way to address this is to share that the company will be looking at a specific exit strategy at some point in the future and that "management believes" there will be a suitable buyer or IPO within some range of times.

I will remind you again to acknowledge that you are your first investor and there is no right or wrong answer if you really believe you can achieve the stated results. Don't claim that the company will pursue an IPO if you have no interest in running a company. The worst thing that can happen is that you will state something for the purposes of appealing to an investor and you both go into the investment with misaligned expectations.

Let's assume now that you do want to sell your company at some point in time. Who then are the buyers and how can you plan around some potential exit strategies in the future?

TYPES OF BUYERS

Private companies at the expansion or exit stage of their lifecycle will most commonly pursue some form of a liquidity event, which will mostly likely take the form of selling majority ownership of their equity to a new entity. These buyers can be identified as strategic buyers and financial buyers. A *strategic buyer* is another business that is typically operating within the company's core or adjacent sectors. Most often this is a larger operating company that has its own inorganic growth strategy to acquire smaller businesses through M&A transactions. When a strategic buyer evaluates a company they have targeted for a merger or an acquisition, they will be looking for benefits that are of the highest value to them. As an operating business, the buyer will be looking to add revenue or top-line growth, acquire new customers, or expand their products or service offerings, and look to create synergies between the companies post-transaction. Synergies are a transaction benefit that are unique to strategic buyers in that they have an operating business. When the two companies are combined, there can be a reduction in redundant operations that can create greater profitability for both companies when combined. When two independent companies combine their operations, many expenses can be consolidated and even reduced. For example, each company would have been managing their own human resources and finance departments, and many times those departments can be consolidated and support the combined businesses going forward on a more cost-effective basis. The same can be achieved when marketing budgets are consolidated. These synergies can be very powerful and have significant benefit on the profitability of the combined entity.

The other type of buyer is a financial buyer. Financial buyers are groups like private equity funds who invest in expansion and exit-stage companies. Funds do not actually operate any businesses other than their investment fund, so they will not be able to see operational synergies unless they are the financial backer of a strategic buyer. When a financial buyer acquires a company, they look for purely financial metrics such as profitability or EBITDA.

The fundamental drivers for creating returns can be categorized as the value in the company. Value is subjective, so investors look at what value has been created in the given investment and what value can be extracted through a transaction. This is why the operational capabilities of a management team are so important to the investor and so much focus and time is spent evaluating management teams during the pre-investment vetting process. When we look at investments that have done extraordinarily well, the company usually had a matrix of underlying value drivers, such as the examples provided in Table 8.1 on page 154. During the time frame of the investment, the management team is continually building value so that when the company is in a position to engage in a transaction, it maximizes what a buyer will pay for and, in turn, provide the mechanism for the investors to extract the maximum value at that time.

Financial	
Revenue	Top-line revenues and scale are attractive to buyers who are rolling up industries or competitors.
EBITDA*	Bottom-line profitability is attractive for buyers who are expanding their profit profile.
Assets	Book value of assets equipment or hardware that has value to the buyer.
Management	Buyer looking to acquire talent and wants management to stay on post transaction.
Intellectual Property	Defensible science, technology, or patents that the buyer can get access to via a transaction.
Market Position	Competitors or market share consolidation through a transaction.
Tax Benefits	Carried over tax credits that an acquirer can benefit from.
Users or Customers	A buyer sees a cost effective way to acquire customers through an acquisition.
*Earnings before interest, taxes, depreciation and amortization	

TABLE 8.1—Sample Value Drivers

TYPES OF EXIT STRATEGIES

There are a number of other ways in which companies transact and create possibilities to extract value for shareholders. These include strategic alliances and joint ventures, divestitures, and today in cannabis you will hear many terms like "roll ups" and even crowdfunding. You already read a bit about mergers and acquisitions, but I'd like to dive a bit more deeply into that topic now, as well as talk about another common exit strategy, the initial public offering (IPO).

Mergers and Acquisitions

The most common types of transactions for private companies fall into the category of mergers and acquisitions (M&A). M&A can be considered the market in which private companies trade. Unlike in the public markets, these are negotiated transactions whereby the seller and buyer negotiate the value and terms of the transaction privately. There is, therefore, lack of publicly available information regarding valuations of private companies. So much negotiation around private M&A transactions involves quantitative aspects such as revenues and profitability, but also qualitative considerations that are difficult to put a defined value against. In the public markets, information is readily available about how investors value companies against the company's peers. When negotiating an M&A transaction, the buyer and seller spend a lot of time and effort coming to an agreement on what premium, or discount, should be applied based on the non-financial aspects of the company. This is, however, the most common and attractive exit strategy for private companies as the implied increase in the value of the equity of the business can be extracted by creating this kind of exit event.

M&A transactions can take many forms with the majority of deals being structured in one of several ways:

1. *Joint Ventures and Strategic Alliances.* Creating a partnership between two independent companies where each contributes assets or equity to establish a combined initiative. It may seem counter intuitive but JVs can be very powerful between two competitors within an industry.
2. *Mergers.* Two independent companies are put together where assets and equity are combined resulting in a combined operating business.
3. *Buy-Side or Sell-Side Acquisitions.* The outright purchase of an independent company by another company where the acquirer ends up owning all or a portion of the assets of the selling company. When a company goes on a buying spree, this is what's called a "roll up" when a larger entity rolls up a group of the industry.

Initial Public Offerings

IPOs for cannabis companies are happening more rapidly for earlier-stage companies compared to non-cannabis sectors. This is due in part to newly opened exchanges in other regions such as the Toronto Stock Exchange, where U.S. and international companies can go public. It seems as though there is a new IPO every day, but I would caution cannabis entrepreneurs to be very sanguine about looking at the current public markets and taking their company public. There is no question that public market investors have shown a major appetite for investing in cannabis companies. These investors are considered "retail investors," meaning that they are independent investors who are investing in public securities as part of their overall investment profile.

At the end of the day, every company at every stage of growth has stakeholders and accountabilities. It is advisable to consider the cost and resources required to manage a publicly traded company. There is a reason that in more mature sectors only a handful of the key companies within a given industry will end up going public. IPOs are expensive, require significant compliance and ongoing management, and the leadership team will spend a significant portion of their time managing the public markets and communicating with investors, many of whom can be very active and critical if they think the company can be better run or deliver better results.

The main concern that CVC investors are voicing today is the current enthusiasm for publicly traded cannabis stocks. With the demand of retail investors and many hedge funds combined with the relatively few companies to invest in, many companies are, as of this writing, investing in the story of the cannabis company rather than the fundamentals of the underlying business. It appears that we are in a capital market cycle where the exuberance for investing in cannabis companies is driving share prices into stratospheric levels of market cap multiples. Canadian company Tilray Inc. has a market cap of over $4 billion dollars. The company lost $67 million on $43 million in revenue in 2018 and has a negative earnings per share of –$1.05. This equates to a market capital of 93x multiple of revenues. Now, Tilray is one of the best performing cannabis stocks and many investors are betting on the future upside of the company and the health-care vertical focus that the business represents. Comparatively,

Pfizer has a market cap of $236 billion on $54 billion in revenue and $11 billion in earnings for 2018, or earnings per share of $1.96. This is a revenue multiple of 4.3x, which begs the question, should Tilray be valued by investors at 93x revenue when Pfizer is only worth 4.3x revenue?

There are many debates going on in the financial markets but what is most important to recognize is that a company like Pfizer is valued on its fundamentals as a business: great management, large growing

CROWDFUNDING

This is a topic that constantly comes up with entrepreneurs who are raising capital. There is plenty of research that you can do yourself to study the rules and regulations, but as a general rule, crowdfunding is not a suitable avenue to selling equity in your company. The successful crowdfunding platforms such as Indiegogo and Kickstarter are really online retailers who pre-sell a product before it is in final production. This is a fantastic avenue for consumer product companies that source working capital, but this is not a transaction where equity is being sold in the company. That function still needs to go through a broker-dealer if someone other than the company is sourcing investors.

You never "give away" equity—it is always sold and is a negotiated transaction for any security that has a high probably for outright failure and total loss of the investment capital. Everyone should go into a transaction with the perspective that despite best efforts the company may, in fact, fail. This type of investing is for a specific type of investor who knows the risks and has significant resources to construct a portfolio that takes this into consideration. Therefore, it is curious to me that the idea of taking small investments from the general public with little to no direct communication is a sensible strategy. The level of structure and negotiation does not lend to raising capital this way to the nuanced highly managed process that you will go through with sophisticated investors.

market opportunity, creation of products or services, intellectual property, revenue, profitability, and respective growth.

When public companies are valued on enthusiasm over fundamentals, this should ring alarm bells for investors and entrepreneurs alike. Investor demand and a public market that is not operating efficiently on the largest exchanges can spell trouble down the road if a company becomes publicly traded prematurely and does not have the operational foundation and financial wherewithal to sustain any major volatility.

For the purposes of raising CVC, it is fine to state that one of the options that you will evaluate in the future is the feasibility of going public. The CVC will prioritize a private M&A transaction. This is because there is a higher ability to influence this type of outcome, and historically strategic and financial buyers will pay more for a company in terms of assigning value compared to an efficient public market. One consideration for an IPO then is to understand the elements of the public capital markets.

CANNABIS CAPITAL TAKEAWAYS AND ACTION ITEMS

The cannabis markets are moving quickly, and there is a lot of investor enthusiasm in the public markets. An IPO is only one way to create some liquidity for the ownership of private company shares, and today cannabis entrepreneurs need to at a very early-stage start to consider and manage transactions not only to just raise capital but also to engineer inorganic growth and expansion. Raising capital is one of those types of transactions and how you structure raising investment capital will have implications for the options you will have in the future to create a return for you and your new investors.

Cannabis Capital Action Item: Design Your Exit Strategy

How do you anticipate providing liquidity to your investors (*Remember*: YOU are your first investor)? Are you building this company to create wealth for you and your family quickly? Are you trying to innovate and bring new benefits to your industry? Do you want to stay small and private, and collect dividends for your work year after year?

Take some time to investigate companies that have already accomplished what you intend to happen with your business:

- If it was that the company was sold to a strategic buyer, then who was that buyer and what did they pay for the business?
- If the company went public through an IPO, was it successful?
- Who were the investment banks that represented the company through the process?
- Did the stock perform well after it went public?
- What exchange is it traded on?

If you answer these questions and then apply the data points to your company, you will quickly highlight what is achievable, in what time frames, and what exit strategy or strategies will produce the outcomes that you (and your investors) are seeking. A good way to articulate your exit strategy to investors might look something like this:

> *Management believes that within three to five years a strategic buyer will value the company at a premium due to our strong revenue growth, industry leading management team, intellectual property, and profitability. At that time, we will evaluate selling some or all the business. Management also believes that the public markets may be a suitable option for the company once we archive certain revenue milestones and are already able to pay meaningful dividends to our existing investors.*

To give you an example of one way to tackle this action item, let's look again at our fictional example. Betsy from HCC and her team have been moving diligently through their internal planning in order to get ready to reach back out to her investor contact. They agreed that they would use a comparable analysis method and focus on selling to a strategic or financial buyer. They decided to create the following checklist in Table 8.2 on page 160 to see if the company represented the element that would attract a buyer in the future. They decided it would be a good idea to rank elements of the business in terms of "Low," "Medium," and "High" with respect to how they think a buyer would rank them today. The areas that they indicated with a "Low" ranking will become priorities to develop further in their business plan so they will be ranked higher when it comes time to explore an M&A transaction in the future.

Exit Checklist	Sell to Strategic Buyer	Sell to Financial Buyer	Initial Public Offering
Management Team (Experience and Track Record)	High	High	Low
Projected Revenues	High	Medium	Low
Projected EBITDA	Medium	Low	Low
Intellectual Property	Medium	Medium	Low
Brand Value	High	High	Medium
Buyer or Investor Demand	High	High	High
Freedom to Operate without Regulatory Hurdles	Medium	Medium	Medium
Strong Balance Sheet	High	Medium	Low
Other (TBD)			

TABLE 8.2—Happy CBD Company Exit Checklist

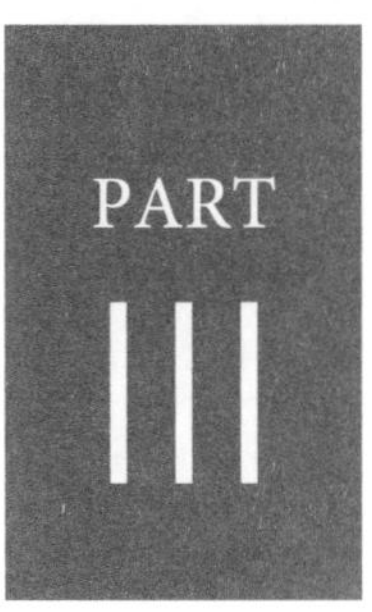

RAISING CAPITAL

PRESENTING TO INVESTORS

It is often said that great entrepreneurs need to be great storytellers. If you think about it, founders are always creating a narrative around bringing their vision to reality. They are charged with convincing employees to join the company, convincing partners and companies to do business with them, fighting against incumbent thinking to innovate, and changing the status quo. The cannabis economy is one in which that narrative matters. For example, when voters start grassroots movements to legalize cannabis, local business owners have to work with regulators to explain the upside and potential of the cannabis economy. Selling is all about storytelling, and selling your investment to an investor requires the same approaches. And as with any complex sale, there are layers and nuances that you need to be aware of and manage through so you can produce a successful result—even when you are up against steep statistical odds.

Telling that story starts with perspective. Your role as a masterful presenter is to acknowledge the other person's point of view and speak to their unique perspective. It is not about convincing the investor to accept your view of the world, but rather to identify how they view the world and demonstrate how your business fits that view. The most off-putting characteristic that many presenters revert to is their belief that the investor is wrong and there needs to be an argument to bring them around to the presenter's way of thinking. Many times, I will challenge an entrepreneur's assumptions or business model in their presentation to identify potential risks and lack of fit for the investment to see how the entrepreneur reacts when challenged. This brings forward two key character traits:

- A willingness to listen to feedback
- Thoughtfulness in the business planning stage

Your success in the pitch room is as much a representation of the business acumen and detail that went into the plan as it is about being "right." When dealing with predicting the future (which all projections and business plans do), the actual results will be different from what was planned. How you otherwise react to challenges in the presentation will say a lot about you and your team's management capabilities. These evaluations begin from the very first interactions between investors and founders and will inform how far the process progresses and how the negotiations will go.

The quickest way to get to a rejection is to be defensive and inflexible in your presentations and the discussions that ensue in those meetings. It is perfectly fine to say that you may not know something. If there are questions that you don't know the answer to, you should say that you will confirm the facts and get back to the investor—but take the moment to identify that you have thought about the issues and they may be complex or that you require more information. Doing so shows that you are personally invested in the relationship—not just trying to skate your way through the presentation. Investors really want to work with management teams that are compatible, and that goes for both parties. You are entering into a long-term financial and business-management marriage, and no one wants to work with people who will constantly be fighting with each other. So how you communicate from Day One should all be calculated into both your written and in-person communication.

For example, many investors talk most affectionately about entrepreneurs, in particular younger founders in the early stage of venture-backed companies, who are, in their words, "coachable." Likewise, a starting assumption for an investor/entrepreneur dynamic is that the inventors are in the position of managing significant capital and much of it can be their own. This is an indication of some track record of success. Capital seekers love to talk about looking for "value-added" capital, meaning that the investor has capabilities, relationships, and other value that they bring to the investment beyond just writing a check. It's wise to consider that these investors typically have a lot of business experience that you can really benefit from if you are a good listener, take constructive criticism well, and are willing to adapt your thinking—in other words, if you are "coachable."

In the end, your success is determined by your preparation before the pitch and communication during the pitch. The right pitch is like a gourmet dinner. It starts with a recipe, is constructed in a specific way, and takes a well-trained chef to react, modify, and add just the right elements to produce an extraordinary result to wow your ultimate critics—potential investors. Figure 9.1 on page 166 is a matrix of the elements that go into a pitch recipe.

In this chapter, I will walk you through the recipe you need to develop an approach for your investor outreach and presentations that will make your pitch succeed. First, you will read about five strategies for raising capital. Just like a master chef, there are ingredients and factors you need

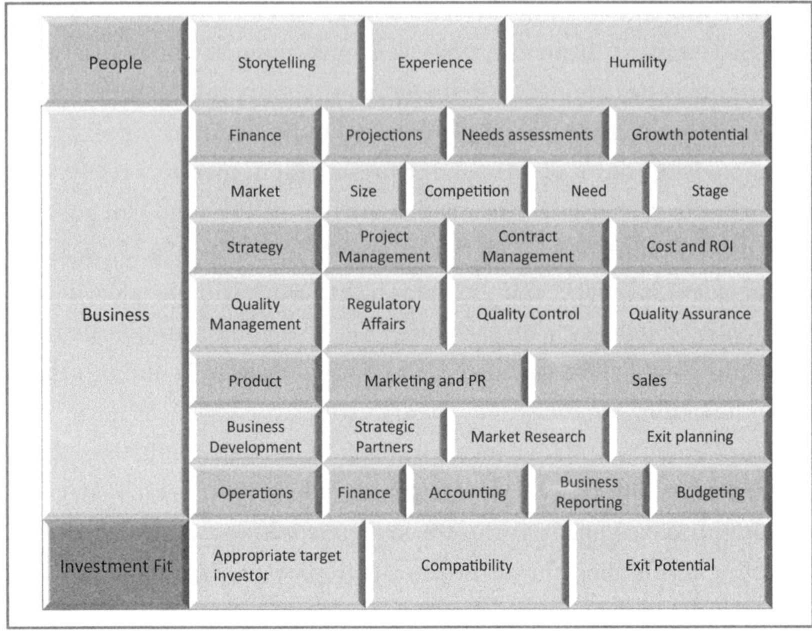

FIGURE 9.1—Pitch Recipe

to consider before you jump right in and start pitching investors. Then, we'll dive into the mechanics and communication tactics for developing and presenting a winning investment presentation.

THE FIVE Rs FOR RAISING CAPITAL

Raising capital is one of the most difficult, complex, frustrating, and time-consuming challenges facing founders in any industry. It is also one of the most critical and nuanced functions of a high-performing leadership team made even more challenging given the complicated and dynamic regulatory considerations in the cannabis industry. There is no one guaranteed way to succeed in soliciting investment, but after doing private transactions for more than a decade, it has become clear to me that success is in part a result of a cohesive strategy and a sustained, multifaceted approach that can be summarized in the following five principles, the "The Five Rs of Raising Capital":

1. Relationships

2. Relevance
3. Resilience
4. Right Ask (offering/structure)
5. Returns

Let's take a closer look at each one of these principles you need to have a handle on when pitching.

Relationships

People have always been at the core of every business and industry. The same is true with raising capital, as you read at the top of this chapter. Do you have an unfair advantage of personal differentiation with the key investors who will back you and your venture? Investing in private companies all comes down to the people involved, and the ideal situation would be that you have a group of investors with whom you are a known person with a track record of success. Although this is one of these things that takes time to develop, we all have to start somewhere. Expanding your network should be a constant activity, and you should always be ready to ask anyone you meet if they are an investor or know an investor to whom they can introduce you. Cultivating these key relationships on a sustained basis will have a direct correlation to your success in raising capital. And remember, it is not always about the "ask," so seek authentic ways to deepen your relationships over time. As the saying goes, "Ask for money and you get advice; ask for advice and you get money."

You should be activating your entire network of business relationships from the moment you start planning your pitch. Ask your attorneys, accountants, and other service providers if they know any cannabis investors who may be interested in your story. Many law firms and accountants are making early inroads in cannabis and are developing a lot of strategic relationships. There are contact lists developing that you can access of lists of investors, and most venture capital investors will be easily searchable online. Family offices and angel investors are most difficult to get access to as they typically don't advertise their interest in investing or have websites. So, seeking out the emerging group of accelerators and incubators is a good way to find investors in your region. Attending events like the Cannabis Dealmakers Summits is a great way to network and find speaking or presentation opportunities.

If you are making a new relationship and reaching out to an investor for the first time, you may be sending an email as the first point of contact. When you are doing this, it's best to spend a lot of time drafting your standard email. Are you being concise and clear? Are you giving enough information so the recipient can take action? Please don't send an email that says something to the effect of "Please let me know how to apply or submit for funding." It is redundant to say you are looking for funding, and that approach does nothing more than create more work for the investor. Any time you are asking someone to do something for you, that's adding items to their to-do list—not advancing your cause. Remember that investors are by default looking to find a way to say "no" as quickly as possible. Asking them to do the work for you is the quickest way to get passed over. Figure 9.2 is a sample email that Betsy prepared. Based on the fictional example of the Happy CBD company. Each company is unique and will have its own style of messaging.

From: Betsy Mekema

To: Ross O'Brien

Title: Leading Cannabis Company Seeking Growth Equity Investment

Dear Ross,

I know you are very busy and likely reviewing countless requests for investment. This will only take a minute of your time. Our mutual contact Joe recommended I forward the attached executive summary for your consideration. Following are the company's headlines, and I am available anytime to submit more detailed information and present to your investment team.

We believe that The Happy CBD Company LLC appears to meet your investment criteria based on your portfolio of leading CBD investments

FIGURE 9.2—Sample Investment Outreach Email

and have included some brief information below. I will reach out directly to your office to confirm you are in receipt of this email and would be happy to submit further detailed information. I can be reached anytime at 123-456-7899 or at betsy@happycbd.com.

Investment Highlights:

- HCC is a leading direct to consumer CBD company, is seeking a $3 million Series A investment to scale resources, expand sales, and bring additional products to market.
- Since launching operations in 2019, the business has generated over $900K in revenue in the last 12 months and is currently projecting $1.95 million in calendar year 2021 and reaching over $10 million within three years of securing this round of financing.
- The founders and management team have over ten years with several successful exits and have personally funded the business to date.
- The company has significant intellectual property and a novel brand and products that is ahead of the market. We adhere to real time regulatory updates allowing retailers to ensure compliance while increasing revenue.
- Management believes that the CBD industry will go through a consolidation with low-quality products being eliminated and high-quality brands such as ours will be attractive acquisition targets.

Warmest Regards,

Betsy Mekema

<Number>

<Email>

FIGURE 9.2—Sample Investment Outreach Email, continued

If I am receiving that email, I can quickly evaluate if the company is representative of the types of investments we look for. I know if the company is raising an amount of capital that fits our investment strategy, if the business is at a stage that we typically invest in, if the management team has relevant experience, if they invested personally in the company, and if there is some thought to an exit strategy. Did you notice that Betsy highlighted that we have a mutual contact who suggested she reach out? Relationship building is the foundation for networking into venture capitalists. Investors see so many deals that looking for a reason to say "no" as quickly as possible is just simply being pragmatic and essential for time management. It takes time to develop rapport and experience with new introductions. When you are looking for partners to invest significant capital in your business and take that risk with you, you can only assume that they will want to get to know you, which takes time. If someone I know and respect suggests an introduction, it's just human nature that that introduction will get my attention.

If you are using references or other contacts, you MUST get their permission first. It is nice to have mutual contacts, but the other side of that strategy is that my first call after receiving an email like this is to call the person to get some background on you before responding. If they say they don't know you at all, or it becomes clear they aren't actually endorsing your candidacy for an investment that is an easy decline. So, keep your facts straight and assume as with anything in due diligence (more on this in Chapter 10) if an investor can confirm the information for themselves independently, they will. Relationships are built on reputations over a long period of time. Raising capital always has a sense of urgency so there are ways to accelerate your credibility: networking and connecting with the key people you want to do business with, having a quality reputation that proceeds you, and dealing in facts and truths. You might be surprised how much this straightforward approach can help you stand out.

Relevance

From the investor's perspective, are you presenting something that is relevant to their worldview? In other words, do you know what types of companies they invest in, how much they invest, and what other portfolio investments they have? All too often, investors are presented deals that are clearly not a fit. You wouldn't present a health-care investment to a real estate fund, so you must do your homework and know that your opportunity fits the investment parameters of the investor. The only way to learn this is to research and have a targeted, thoughtful approach to your investor outreach.

For a company to be a relevant investment opportunity, all the proverbial stars need to be in alignment. If any of the parameters are misaligned, the potential for securing an investment decreases exponentially. This is a continuation of the fictional point-of-sale software company example from the cover email in Figure 9.2.

There is another element to this "R," which is the "right time." This can mean industry timing, the stage of the company (the right time to raise capital), or the right time (relevance) for the investor. This might be the most difficult data point to ascertain outside of a direct discussion with the investor, but you need to find out if they are making investments or have capital to deploy within the time frame that you have set out to raise your financing in. Venture funds will often put out press releases announcing that they have secured sufficient commitments to make investments through their fund. Venture funds will raise multiple funds, so if you are contacting them either before they have the commitments or at the end of the most recent fund, they may not be investing at that time. For private investors such as angels and family offices, they don't have the same restrictions and governance that a fund would, but they also don't always deploy capital in perpetuity. Once you are in early discussions, it is also advisable to ask to clarify your understanding of their investment parameters to ensure alignment.

Resilience

Raising capital requires a thick skin, a balance between adapting and learning, and the ability to stay convicted to your core principles and strategy. For example, I heard of an entrepreneur who celebrated each decline she received because she knew she could move on to the next investor who may say "yes." Resilience was a core value for her, as it should be for you. Always listen and take into consideration how an investor explains why they won't invest. There is much to learn from that kind of feedback. After each decline, you should debrief with your team to help you improve on the process you are running and the offering and presentation materials. If there are core business deficiencies, you may need to stop raising capital and revisit your business plan. On the other hand, success also requires being able to take an almost unlimited amount of rejection and not waver from your core business thesis. Be prepared for a lot of rejection and resilience in this process. It is as much about learning and adaptation as it is committing to keep on raising capital until you succeed.

One fact about venture capital investors is that it is almost impossible to turn a "no" into a "yes" once they have formally declined your investment. Even angel investors have informal committees around them to help them make investment decisions. This is more often than not a spouse and family members along with close attorneys and advisors. For venture funds, they are required to have a formal investment committee. To get any answer, there will be some additional people involved in the decision. If an investor tells you no, that is likely an informed decision that was made with others participating. So, if you go back and try to convince them that they are wrong in their decision, you are essentially asking the investor to go back and disagree with the other people involved. With all the deals they are likely looking at, there is little upside in them taking on this fight.

Resilience in this situation does not mean that you should try to convert a "no" to a "yes," but rather, that you are courteous of the investor's time and you try to glean as much information as you can from your discussions with them. Asking for feedback is not unusual, but it is not always something that the investor will have the time or inclination to do. If you did, however, strike up a great rapport and professional line of communication with the investor, they may know other investors who might be a better fit for your investment. It is common that cannabis investors will take a stand if they invest in plant-touching businesses. An investor who has decided to not invest in cultivation may know other investors who do and might be able to refer you to them.

Being rejected day in and day out when you are raising capital can be demoralizing, exhausting, and seem like a constant uphill battle. The best advice for developing resilience is far more nuanced than "not taking no for an answer." This is the one time when taking "no" for an answer is the only option you may have. It's what you do with those rejections that matter. What can you learn from each pitch meeting and each interaction with investors? Are you actually listening to the feedback and using it to get better? The last thing you want to do is harass an investor to try and convert them to your cause if they are not the right fit. But what you can do is accept the feedback and build such a rock-solid foundation for your investment proposal that it becomes the best use of your time to quickly move on to engaging with an investor who still has an opportunity to say "yes."

Right Ask

Many times, entrepreneurs spend an unnecessary amount of effort negotiating with themselves to concoct a transaction structure or investment terms. In the spirit of selling an investment into the market, many entrepreneurs will try and come up with creative structures and think they are pre-empting key hurdles that investors need to overcome.

This also goes for the amount of capital that you are raising. The amount of capital you are raising should be based on the needs of the business, and if that need is $5 million but the investor you are pitching only invests a minimum of $10 million in any transaction, you unfortunately don't fit their criteria. If the investor you are pitching only invests in control, or majority ownership, and you are only willing to sell a monitory stake in your company, then the probability that there is an investment between the two of you is very unlikely. With a well-thought-out ask and research on the investor you are contacting, you can identify for yourself if the ask is aligned.

Returns

Investors have the ability to allocate capital that they have influence or control over and are making investments for the sole purpose of generating a return on that investment. Capital is a resource, and investors are in the business of allocating that resource to generate a desired profit. Just like any resource, capital can be allocated in all kinds of strategies so the decision that investors make is based on comparing the probability of generating a return, how much risk is involved, and how great the return will be. Your exit strategy and the structure you are prepared to present should align with their investment approach. You should know that because you have done your homework and researched each investor before you present to them.

When you are presenting to an investor, have you clearly identified how they will generate a return on their investment? Let's take for example the desire to structure an investment as debt. This might seem like a good way to ensure that the investor gets repaid, but if you take into consideration how risk and value are correlated, and that investors are looking for a risk-adjusted rate of return to accept that risk, simply structuring some theory on how an investor gets repaid will not excite equity investors. They are not looking to simply be repaid, but achieve a multiplier effect on the investment. Going to an equity investor with a debt offering isn't going to present them with a return profile that they are seeking.

Do you know the desired ownership parameters of the investors you are talking with? And what is your expectation for how much equity in your business you are willing to sell? A deal can be negotiated if those terms are within a reasonable range to start with. If you are only willing to sell a small minority interest in your company, you don't want to find yourself presenting to an investor who only wants to own companies outright or in a super majority.

INVESTMENT PITCH MATERIALS

There is a standard package of information that entrepreneurs need to prepare to submit to interested investors. These specific documents and reports are all necessary for an investor to evaluate the company and the proposed transaction. As the discussions mature, the investor will ask for more information, which you should have ready to submit in the format they are used to seeing. The following is the standard "investment package" of documents that you will need to prepare:

1. Executive Summary (see Chapter 5)
2. Business Plan (see Chapter 5)
3. Financial Projections (see Chapter 6)
4. Management Presentation
5. Investment Terms and Proposed Structure

When you start assembling these materials, it is important to understand that they are intertwined and have to work together as a cohesive story about your business. To effectively accomplish this, it is a good idea to start developing the documents in reverse order from how they will be presented. Each element of the process and what is shared at each step becomes part of an overall narrative that you are trying to create to give investors the confidence that you have an operational plan that produces the financial results you are projecting. These are documents that you should be developing as management and operational tools in running your day-to-day operations, independent of investor presentations. In short, you need these documents no matter what so you can tell your company's story. *Remember*: The best plans and presentations are the ones that are heavily based in the "how" an entrepreneur is executing and plans to build their company for the future.

You've already read about the business plan and the role the executive summary plays in it. However, the executive summary can also live independently of the business plan and is a useful tool for potential investors as a standalone document. Because it pulls double duty, I'd like to unpack it a bit more here, and then walk you through the other two investment package elements we haven't explored yet: the management presentation and the investment terms and proposed structure.

Executive Summary

You will hear investors talk about an executive summary, teaser, or fact sheet, and when they do, they are referring to a one- to five-page document that summarizes all the key elements of the business plan. A practical approach is to write the first version of this document as the final (but first) section of the business plan. Then, you can use this document and modify it for the purposes of specific audiences so you can use it as a standalone document as well. The structure is essentially the same and should be a high-level summary of the business plan, deeply focused on the facts and core business foundational elements. Be succinct and focused, and avoid statements that over-embellish. This is a document that needs to sell the investor on wanting to learn more and engage in a dialog. That said, they won't be making an investment decision solely on an executive summary, so don't try and do too much here. If you say, "We are the leading company that does XYZ," you should actually be the "leading" company, which means you have to prove things like:

- $ You have more sales than all your competitors.
- $ You have the largest global portfolio of intellectual property.
- $ You are the largest supplier in your market.
- $ You operate more retail locations than anyone.

If an investor can otherwise research this and see that there are other companies that are more established or further along in terms of funding, revenues, or overall size and scale, then you really aren't the "leader." You may be innovating in some ways, but that is a different proposition. Be careful to be honest with yourself and create an executive summary that is fact based.

When you are finalizing the business plan, you can write up a more text-heavy executive summary for that document. Think of this like the abstract that explains what anyone reading the business plan would need to know about the company. A strategic process for approaching the development of the business plan is to edit and revisit it at the beginning, during the midpoint of drafting, and then at the end of the process. This allows you to use the executive summary as a guideline that will direct the core elements and objectives of the business (and the related plan), then adjust and modify as you answer the core questions through the process that were addressed in the sections of the full plan. Then, with all the data and information in hand, you can make final edits and be confident that it is the optimal representation of the company. This process creates a circular approach where the executive summary is the central document that all the other elements of the plan flow through as visualized in Figure 9.3 on page 177.

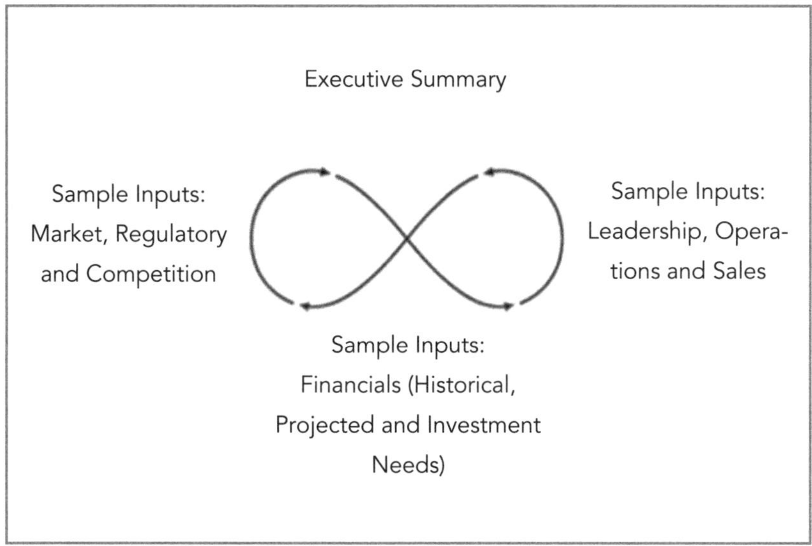

FIGURE 9.3—Executive Summary Development Process

Now you can extract the elements of the executive summary and prepare to present it to investors. It is always advisable to follow a format or outline that investors are used to seeing, but remember that none of the documents or investment packages that you prepare as outlined at the beginning of this chapter are one-size-fits-all.

Chapter 5 walked you through how to create a playbook for your business, and in the investment process you will need to present to investors a business plan built on those inputs. In Chapter 6 we reviewed how to build a set of financials. These are documents 2 (business plan) and 3 (financial model) from the list of materials you need to present. If you have not completed these items, you can go back through Chapters 5 and 6 now to draft them. Once you are finished with creating the business and financial models, you can move on to the management presentation, a key part of any raising capital process that is built from your business plan and financials.

The Management Presentation

The management presentation, or "deck," is your opportunity to summarize your business for investors and tell your story. And like a story, the management presentation should follow a narrative that speaks to the elements investors will be most interested in and clearly conveys what your business does and how you will make it a success. Remember that investors have specific desires and outcomes, and businesses that most closely represent what they want to invest in will appeal to them the most. It may be helpful at this point to revisit Chapter 2 to define for yourself an audience of investors who you think will be most interested in your company and what their motivations are.

When you are telling the story of your company, there are several elements to consider. First, there are the aspects of the business that investors need to clearly understand before they can evaluate if the investment is a good fit for them. Figure 9.4, which is a sample presentation outline, starts to build that foundational narrative and aligns with the narrative elements in the matrix.

I. Cover Page
II. Disclaimer and Confidentiality
III. Executive Summary
IV. Management Team
V. The Opportunity
VI. Product or Service
VII. Business Model
VIII. Sales and Marketing
IX. Operations
X. Regulatory and Compliance
XI. Financials
XII. Transaction Overview
XIII. Appendix

FIGURE 9.4—Sample Presentation Table of Contents

Then, the matrix in Table 9.1 outlines each core element that is consistent in well-constructed management presentations. The best way to think about preparing the presentation is to view each section as a part of the foundation of the story. Each section listed in the table of contents can be multiple pages in length and should frame the narrative for the elements of the presentation section matrix.

The cover page (item I) for your presentation should contain the date and your logo and be simple without much fanfare. Your attorneys are the best resource to provide you with the disclaimers and confidentiality disclosures (item II) that are necessary when you are presenting to investors. The following outlines the remaining meaty sections of the management presentation, from the Executive Summary forward.

Section	Objectives	Investor Perspectives
Executive Summary	To provide an overview of what the business does, key highlights indicating the stage of the business and progress, and value drivers such as IP or certain unique and defensible aspects of the business. The executive summary should conclude with the "ask," how much money you are seeking, for what purpose, and what the company will look like in a few years after the investment.	Before anything further can be understood in the presentation, the basic knowledge of what the business is and what the ask is will frame the narrative from this point forward.

TABLE 9.1—Elements of the Management Presentation

Section	Objectives	Investor Perspectives
Management Team	To show depth of talent and relevant experience, including the advisory board.	It's a cliché, but investors will prioritize a talented team with a track record of successfully building and exiting venture backed companies over an interesting idea. Is this an individual who can manage a company successfully and a team that can execute? Will this be a team that can take feedback and coaching? Has the team done the research and prepared to deliver on the forecast they are presenting?
The Opportunity	By the time you get to presenting to a CVC investor, you should be able to defend the business strategy you are executing and have a clear handle on the opportunity for your business to successes. This is more detailed that just a market analysis, so quickly check the box that you are in a large market and that your company is addressing a real need for customers.	Does the management team have a good handle on the market they are going after? What direct and indirect competition exists, and is the management team aware of the marketplace they plan to compete in?

TABLE 9.1—Elements of the Management Presentation, continued

Section	Objectives	Investor Perspectives
The Opportunity	Understanding the competitive landscape should also speak to the opportunity you are presenting and highlight that you really understand the sector you are operating and competing in.	How large is the addressable market, and what are the anticipated growth rates in the near term?
Product or Service and Business Model	What is the product or service that will be generating revenue for your business? What is specific to your business and your particular offering? How are you designing the business to account for the products and services you are selling, and have you identified the systems and people you need to produce results? How are you planning to keep up with changing market conditions, and what are your core assumptions for how you predict your company will need to function, sell, and compete?	Do I know what products or services the company is selling or planning to sell? What is the probability that the company will achieve its targets? Are the critical assumptions tested and defensible in the context of a dynamic business environment?

TABLE 9.1—Elements of the Management Presentation, continued

Section	Objectives	Investor Perspectives
Sales and Marketing	What research, processes, and systems are the company implementing to generate and grow revenues? Describe your sales team, your target customer, and the research behind who your customer is and why. What marketing and sales programs are you planning to implement? What is the pricing strategy?	Can the company sell? Are the people, systems, and research in place such that the probability that the company will reach its goals is high? Does the management team know their product cost, margins, and sales metrics?
Operations	How will the company deliver on the business model? This includes the systems needed but also requires an overview of what infrastructure is required, in place, or needs to be developed. What controls are in place for financial management, and what is the required supply chain. You should also describe the third parties you do business with if you have any joint ventures or service providers.	Can the team manage the company with sufficient checks and balances in place and scale in a cost-effective way?

TABLE 9.1—Elements of the Management Presentation, continued

Section	Objectives	Investor Perspectives
Regulatory and Compliance	Explain the relevant regulatory and compliance operating requirements you are managing around. What are the specific and most relevant regulations, and how are you adapting and monitoring what changes may be impacting your business in the foreseeable future?	Is the company managing the regulatory risk in the business effectively? Do they know the regulations that are most impacting their business and have a view as to how to manage through a turbulent marketplace?
Financials	Present high-level summaries of any historical financials (if you have them) and a pro-forma projection. Focusing on a P&L statement is sufficient for the management presentation as the data points that are most important to start a more detailed analysis of the financials are revenues, expenses and EBITDA. Also include in this section a summary of the use of proceeds.	Does the team have a good handle on a realistic set of financials? Does the amount of capital they are raising seem logical to achieving the outcomes that are being presented? Is there a good understanding of how the investment will be deployed?

TABLE 9.1—Elements of the Management Presentation, continued

Section	Objectives	Investor Perspectives
Transaction Overview	Provide an overview of the key terms of what the transaction is that you are looking to secure. You can also include your exit strategy either at the end or in the financial section.	Does the transaction fit my investment parameters? Is there a realistic exit strategy that will achieve my return expectations?

TABLE 9.1—Elements of the Management Presentation, continued

To start drafting the management presentation, outline it at a high level using the table of contents above. If you then use the business plan to identify the core elements that need to be communicated and why, you can line up which elements fit in each section of the presentation. They key to a great presentation is that it tells a story starting with the foundational elements and building from there. This is your chance to control the narrative and put yourself and the company in the best light if you start foundational concepts and build from there. For example, it is important to have the management team and people involved up front in the presentation. If you don't establish credibility and some background about the team quickly, whatever comes next in the story won't have as much impact or be believable. Remember that CVC investors are very focused on investing in the people who are managing the company, so if you clarify who is presenting and why your team is best suited to successfully build the company, when you move into discussions about the market, product, or service and ultimately the financials, knowing who is presenting this information adds the necessary context for how believable the assumptions, strategy, and probably of successfully executing the plan are.

Scrutinizing the information you are presenting on a continual basis should be part of your process. Rehearsing and practicing with your team is essential and creating the management presentation takes a village. Submit your presentation to as much scrutiny and critiquing as possible with as many people you can ask to help you with it. When you are developing and iterating the presentation and receiving feedback, take the time to test the aliment with what you are saying and what investors will be evaluating.

Investment Terms and Proposed Structure

Once the investor is ready to discuss terms and a proposed transaction, a hearty negotiation of the terms and structure will ensue between you. Prior to that stage, you do, however, need to communicate to investors what you are looking for. You should have a clear line of sight to the amount of capital you need with respect to the business plan and a proposed set of outcomes. For the investor package, you should have a set of basic terms that you are anticipating and an outline of those in a draft term sheet that you can provide. A detailed outline of terms and structure is provided in Chapter 11.

When discussing valuation, investors want to know what your valuation expectations are in terms of equity. This is, however, a double-edged sword. Valuation and risk assessment are discussed in greater detail in Chapter 7, but as a general rule, when you get to the valuation discussions with investors, refrain from stretching too aggressively. If a company presents a valuation that is way beyond a reasonable assessment, this is the quickest way for an investor to say "no" and move onto other opportunities. So, one approach is to suggest a range that you would accept dependent on the entirety of the terms. What you are most interested in conveying to investors through this investment package is that you are knowledgeable about the structural elements they will seek in the terms of the transaction.

You should generally outline the key financial needs and how you are prepared to structure that financing in terms of the type of equity and what governance will be part of the financing. For example, minority investors (less than 51 percent) will want board representation so they can influence decisions that will affect their investment. Demonstrating that you are anticipating the terms and conditions of the financing will go a long way in facilitating the negotiation of an investment. When an investor starts asking for terms to better understand the valuation, they would only be asking those questions when they are considering an investment. So be transparent, clear in your approach and expectations and, most of all, be prepared!

PREPARING TO PITCH

If an investor reviews your executive summary and wants to learn more, they will ask for a management presentation that will be held either in person or via conference call. If you are meeting in person, bring physical copies of the presentation to provide to everyone in attendance. You should always ask who will be in the meeting ahead of time so you can do some research on the backgrounds of the people to whom you will be pitching. What happens many times is that the physical (or digital) copy of your presentation will be passed along internally to other members of the investment team, so it is very important that the document can be understood without you there to talk someone through it. This is a real art in figuring out how to present your story in a way that does not require all kinds of text as word-heavy presentations are not very effective. So you need to present the core facts and essentials in a way that would make sense to someone who is not in the meeting.

If you are presenting via conference call, the best approach is to send the presentation to everyone in the meeting about an hour before so they have enough time to quickly review it but not enough time to go into detail and ask questions without your direct response. Investors have a tendency to immediately start skipping around the presentation to quickly pick out the sections that are most top of mind for them.

Most presentations should be able to be presented in no more than 30 minutes. If you are unable to communicate the key tenets of your business in under 30 minutes, your presentation is far too detailed and likely full of irrelevant anecdotes that will ultimately confuse or distract from the foundational merits of your venture. You should practice presenting your deck with colleagues or friends until you can you get through it effectively in this time frame. The number of slides doesn't necessarily matter as long as the time frame is workable. One tactic is to take sections that are too detailed or secondary to the core story you are presenting and put them in the appendix. This is similar to the approach to the business plan appendix you read about earlier.

Once you are presenting to a group of investors, be prepared for questions—a LOT of questions. If the meeting is scheduled for one hour and the first 30 minutes are set aside for you to present, the second 30 minutes should be for Q&A. In reality, investors don't hold off asking questions until you are ready and will likely start firing off questions as you are presenting. Don't get rattled. Investors are a highly curious group, and I can speak personally that I will interrupt right away if I don't understand something, want a further explanation, or wish to challenge the assumptions being presented.

They key to a good presentation is clearly explaining the business and encouraging further investigation by the investor. An investment decision is never made in the management presentation. The presentation, if successful, should answer any initial questions that the investor has and demonstrate that you and your team have a well-thought-out plan and can execute against it at the highest level.

Tahira Rehmatullah, managing partner of T3 Ventures, has some great advice for entrepreneurs on pitching their company: "One of the things I like to see is several people from the management team presenting. This shows that all the information isn't with just one person, and there are people who can step in and run aspects of the company."

Tahira also recommends that when you prepare your presentations, you are ready to answer questions and in doing so that you should come across as collaborative in your responses. She says, "It's OK to not necessarily have an answer for every question. It's perfectly fine to say that you have not considered the question but that you will come back with more information."

CANNABIS CAPITAL TAKEAWAYS AND ACTION ITEMS

Preparing to pitch is a multilevel process. First, you have to consider all of the factors surrounding the process, particularly the "Five R's of Raising Capital":

1. Relationships
2. Relevance
3. Resilience
4. Right Ask (offering/structure)
5. Returns

Get familiar with the investors to whom you are pitching, their place in the cannabis economy, and what drives their decision making process. Then, think about where your company intersects with those values and relationships.

Once you research the climate you're walking into, it's time to prepare your investment package, which includes the executive summary, business plan, projections, the presentation itself, and terms and structure.

Finally, be prepared to be in the pitch room. Making sure that you have covered yourself by bringing copies (either physical or digital) of your materials and right-sizing your presentation to 30 minutes followed by a Q&A will help you navigate your talking points and control the room.

Action Item: Stress Testing Your Pitch

You can ask yourself the following questions at any stage, and if you answer honestly, you can use these self-assessments to manage a successful process:

- $ Are you prepared for the endurance sport that is raising capital?
- $ Are you willing to accept significant rejection?
- $ Can you use rejection to extract constructive feedback and adjust and improve?
- $ Despite the challenges, can you tell the story repeatedly with enthusiasm and confidence?
- $ Have you done your research on the investor and identified alignment with their investment strategies?

By now, you should have a framework for developing a fact-based management presentation that will be put under review with and without you to accompany the narrative. Ask yourself questions to help:

- $ If you missed your revenue projections by 50 percent, what would happen to the business?

- $ For every piece of information or data you include in your presentation, what are you trying to convey?
- $ What are you trying to communicate with the information you are providing? Why does it matter?
- $ How do you think investors will interpret what you are presenting? What adverse revelations might you unknowingly be evoking?
- $ What does the presentation say about me?

Action Item: Investor Alignment Checklist

When you are preparing your approach to investors, its good idea to revisit the suitability of your investment proposal with what they invest in. Table 9.2 can be combined with the Chapter 2 takeaways and action items Investor Suitability template and will start to form the investor dossier you will prepare in Chapter 10.

Alignment Questions	Yes	No
Does the investor invest in companies in my sector and industry?		
Does the amount of capital I'm raising fit the amount of investments they make?		
Is the investor currently making investments (has capital to deploy currently)?		
Have they made investments in similar companies that we could work with?		
Do they have an investment in a competitor that would preclude investing in my company?		
Do they invest in companies at a similar stage as my company?		
Does my exit strategy fit their criteria for the return on investment they are looking for?		

TABLE 9.2—Investor Alignment Checklist

THE INVESTMENT PROCESS AND DUE DILIGENCE

With the right preparation completed and your management presentation in hand, you and your team are ready to actively pursue investors for your business. Both investors and companies each have distinct action items and steps to take when you are securing funding, so it is beneficial to articulate a key process that you can manage. By taking on the role of the process quarterback, you can help facilitate advancing the discussions so that formalized business agreements can be produced. Alternatively, the process can produce a decline in which case discussions should be ceased. The only thing better than a "yes" is a quick "no." Sometimes not asking the hard questions can land you and the investors in protracted discussions where neither party wants to move forward but you are having a hard time saying no.

The investment process for raising private capital can be broken into three phases that capture both the company's and investors' steps:

- Phase I—Outreach
- Phase II—Investigation
- Phase III—Commitment

To illustrate how this might work, let's use the fictional example of Betsy and her team again. They are in the final stages of completing all the documents, financial models, and presentations and starting to feel anxious to meet with some investors and share their exciting growth story. Betsy's friend reaches back out to her and asks when they can have a presentation. Apparently, the investment team at his fund is really interested in talking with Betsy and her team. When she shares this information to the group, they want to meet with the fund the very next day, but Betsy suggests that they all stop for a moment and think about managing their capital raising efforts as a process, and not just a one-off discussion. Her main concern is that if one investor moves so far ahead of any other discussions, they will be inefficient with their time and efforts and may lose the opportunity to have multiple offers. So Betsy and the team decide to take the time to outline the phases they will need to manage, and learn how to identify and present to multiple investors to make sure they have a good read on the investment market before making any final decisions. As you'll see in Figure 10.1 on page 193, the overall process can then be broken down further into three steps within each phase. There are three checkpoints (A, B, and C) that represent the investor's process of getting to a decision.

Your job is not to sell the investor in the first meeting but provide just enough information to solicit interest in learning more and moving to the next step in the process. At each checkpoint, the investor will be reviewing

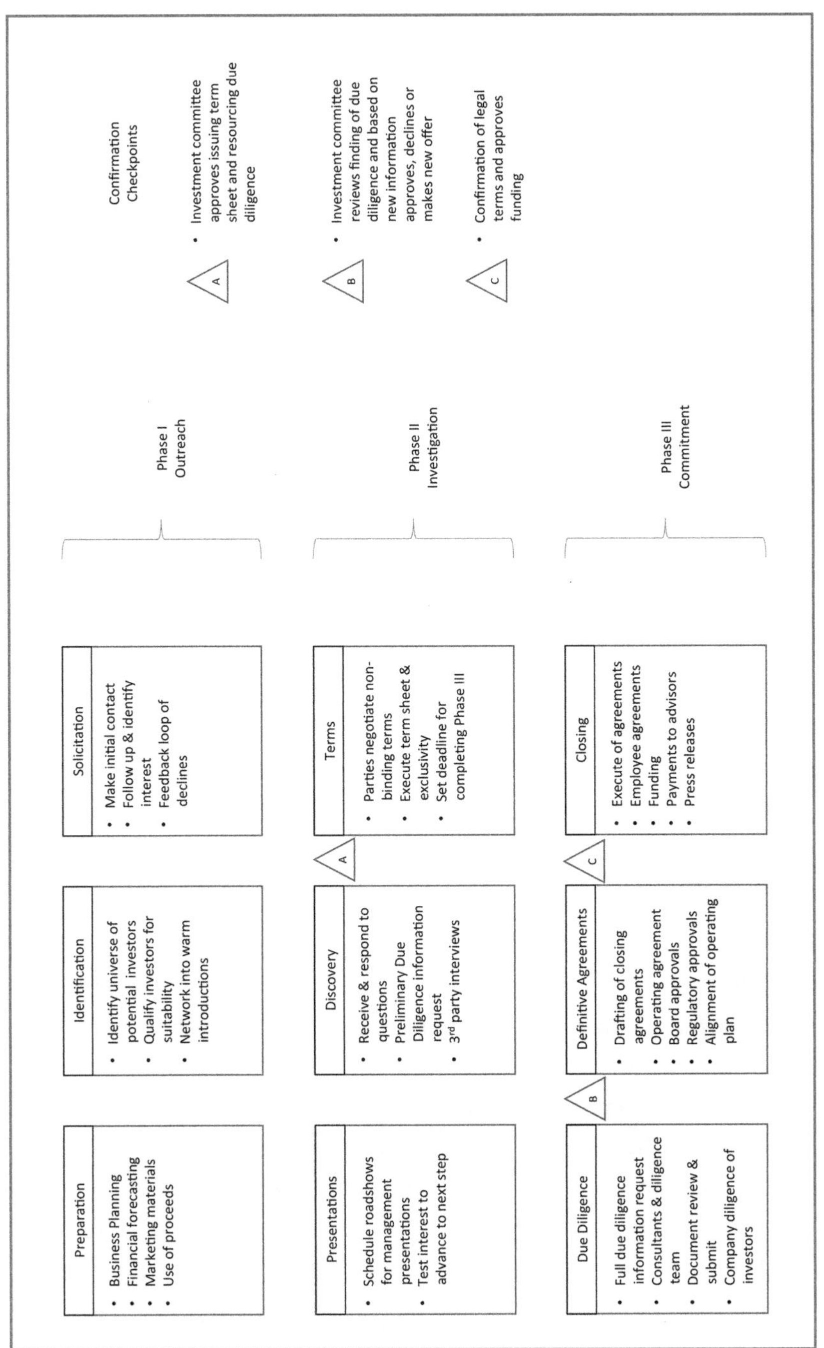

FIGURE 10.1—The Investment Process

your investment proposal with their team and deciding on the merits of either moving forward or declining and moving on, or proposing an alternate structure or approach from what you had previously discussed. You can build in checkpoints in your process that align with those investor decision points. In this chapter, I will take you through all three phases so you know what to expect.

PHASE I: OUTREACH

Phase I is the time when entrepreneurs and investors are first connected. It is incumbent on the company that is seeking capital to identify suitable investors and find ways to contact them. This phase is initiated after you complete the activities in Chapters 5 and 6 where you have identified your needs, created a strategy and plan, prepared your financials and your "ask" completed, and your supporting materials and presentation per Chapter 9. If those items are not yet concluded, you can go back to those chapters now before moving on. It is important to do all this work up front as you don't want to be in a situation where you contact an investor and can't provide a completed business plan when they ask for it. Not only does that make you look wildly unprepared, but by the time you follow up, the investor will have moved on to other deals.

Making Inroads

During the outreach phase, the key is to have a warm introduction. On one hand the cannabis eco-system is still emerging, and as Brett Finkelstein of Phyto Partners (one of the very early investors in cannabis) points out: "at this time we are connected, or no less than one degree of connectivity, from the key entrepreneurs, advisors and investors. The ideal way we get introduced to the founders we invest in is through a warm introduction. It shows initiative and that the entrepreneur is willing to do the work to stand out from the crowd and that's the type of founder we like to back." In other words, conducting a successful campaign is about both who you know and how you connect.

The outreach period requires sustained focus. Once you have identified the investors you want to connect with and the suitability of those investors,

NON-DISCLOSURE AGREEMENTS

As an entrepreneur you have likely put everything into your business, so it is common to have a reluctance to share information for fear of someone co-opting all you have worked on. Many entrepreneurs view NDAs as a matter of process and something to just check off the list before sharing information. NDAs are legal agreements and require more attention, so asking for an NDA prematurely is a sign of inexperience when raising capital. The hard truth is that the ideas that a company is based on are never as unique as you think. There are likely many companies doing something similar, and anything that is otherwise proprietary about your company would fall into the categories of trade secrets or intellectual property, which can be protected through patent filings. None of this information is necessary for an investor to review to assess if they have an interest in the company or not, especially at the beginning of the process.

There are a number of reasons that investors can't, and won't, sign NDAs until the right point in the process. First, investors need to be unencumbered to look at deals that they may want to invest in. Secondly, when you ask an investor to sign an NDA, you are asking them to review and sign a legal document that will require time and effort up front and to monitor going forward. Thirdly, NDAs are rarely enforceable with the exception of M&A transactions.

It does not make sense to focus on an NDA early in the process, especially if neither party knows if they have interest in a deal together. As a general guideline, investors won't steal ideas and have no interest in competing with you; their core business is investing. When it does make sense to protect yourself is at the time that the process moves into the full scope of due diligence. At that time, the investor will want to see your "secret sauce," which can be code, trade secrets such as client

NON-DISCLOSURE AGREEMENTS, continued

lists, or other information that underpins your competitive advantage. None of that information needs to be disclosed to accurately describe the business initially, so be careful to not ask too soon for an NDA or expect it.

your job becomes finding the right way to connect with them. This is a nuanced activity where you need to be persistent but courteous, respectful but assertive, opportunistic but not unknown. By curating a list of investors you are targeting, you can manage this database by doing your background research on the firm and the people, looking for overlap in relationships, and then highlighting next steps. For example, if there is an investor you want to connect with, but you don't have a direct contact who can introduce you, you can see if they are speaking at any conferences or events. You could then plan to attend this event and network your way into meeting them. How this impacts your process is that you will be able to put a date on the calendar when that event is and an action item to make initial contact. If this event is ten months away but you need to secure your investment in six months, then this specific strategy won't work for your timing.

A successfully run process serves as an interactive and evolving roadmap with defined checkpoints to deliver an outcome. In raising capital, there are two outcomes—a "yes" or a "no"—and there is great value in soliciting a thoughtful decline quickly so you can move on to other potential investors. Your process roadmap will deliver an outcome either way. Each outcome will then inform your next activities. If an investor says "yes," you move on to the next step in the process and continue to provide information and work towards documentation and memorializing the investment. If an investor says "no," were you able to gain some insights into your offering? Are you seeing patterns in the declines you are receiving (and to be clear, the bulk of outcomes are going to be declines), and is that feedback helping you and your team get better? If so, great. You should be internalizing that feedback so you can update your presentation and materials on a daily basis when you are deep in the process and receiving actionable feedback.

Relying on Your Team for Support

Raising capital is not a project to take on alone. Many CEOs make the mistake of thinking that it is their job alone to deliver, and this could not be further from the truth. The whole senior management team should be involved in raising capital. Each person should be able to provide insights in the plan and how it is presented and also be able to synthesize the investor feedback. Investors also want to invest in a management team (not just you), so they will want to evaluate all the key players. The other added benefit is that the management team can close the feedback loop with the extended operational team and make any changes in how the business operates in real time.

Your advisory board can also play a key role in your fundraising process. They should not only provide great access and relationships to your defined industry, but also have relationships that can bring you directly to qualified investors.

Make your accountants aware that you are raising capital. They can advise you on any tax issues that arise in the process and help you prepare and validate your historical and projected financial statements. As with all advisor/client relationships, they can also be a great resource for identifying potential investors. In short, involve your primary internal stakeholders as well as your trusted advisors.

Running the Roadshow

When you are managing an efficient process, ideally you will reach a point where several investors are identified and have an interest in meeting you. With several investors identified, it is common to organize presentations for investors during the same window, which is called running a "roadshow." These roadshows typically involve arranging multiple investor meetings over the same time frame, usually in one or two locations. The company takes meetings back-to-back with investors, which helps you clearly define a set start and finish date for presenting to those investors. This leverages the companies' travel and time and also keeps a group of investors at virtually the same stage of the process. Doing so means that you will have a lot of plates spinning all at once, but they are, for the most part, spinning in relative tandem. However, you might experience difficulty if you are raising money in a scattered fashion in which you are meeting one investor on Monday for the first time while another investor may be talking with your customers as part of their final confirmatory due diligence. The new investor, even if they were really enthusiastic about an investment in your company, will be months behind the existing investor. Now you have a situation where you may want the new investor to be part of the deal but won't have time to get them far enough along to participate, and your lead investor may sense you don't have additional capital available and push harder on better terms for them. Managing capital raising as a process addresses scenarios like this.

The ideal presentation format is to present to each investor directly one-on-one. Presenting at group meetings is a great way to identify investors, but be careful about having too many different investors in the room at the same time. Many investors will invite other investors with whom they will invest together in transactions. But when several groups start asking different questions, they can start to convince each other that they should not make an investment. Your role as quarterback of the process means that you are responsible for managing these meetings. The more you can control the story and respond professionally with informed answers, the more you can remain in control of the process and narrative.

The checkpoints in Figure 10.1 represent inflection points for an investor where they are getting to a "go or no-go" point in order to decide if they want to move to the next step with you. At each of these points, the investor will have reviewed where they are in evaluating your company with their internal team and investment committee and will make a decision based on the information they have at that time and how they have interpreted it. Each one of these checkpoints also kicks off the next set of activities to move the process forward. You are also using these checkpoints to manage the process of each of your investor leads and solicit their interest in moving forward so you can eliminate the investors who are not interested and focus on the ones who are. When they decide to move ahead to the next phase, there will be additional requests as they dig deeper and deeper into the opportunity.

PHASE II: INVESTIGATION

As the process matures, the investor is diving deeper and deeper into your business. If the initial management presentation goes well and the investor wants to start evaluating you, your company, and the merits of the investment, you are only the first point in forging a working relationship. The partnership that you will agree to will require much more than just getting the investor to express interest in your pitch deck. That's the point when everyone agrees that there is an *opportunity* for your company and vision, not the point of approving an investment. Before a potential investor gets to "yes," they have to do a lot of legwork and take a deep dive into your company.

Investor interest leads to more questioning and a deeper evaluation of every aspect of you and your company. The is referred to as *due diligence.* The term refers to all the investigation and discovery the investor performs to ensure they have adequately confirmed all the facts you are presenting. They investigate operational elements, financial results and projections, legal and regulatory matters, the people involved in the company, and if there are liens or lawsuits. They will also want to talk to your key vendors, customers, suppliers, and board of directors. Make no mistake—this is an intensive exploration into all aspects of you and your company. Be ready.

Why do investors do this? Despite the commonly held view that investing in cannabis is still a little fast and loose, investors are emerging as more and more sophisticated, or "intuitional" in their activities. They have a responsibility to make informed investment decisions, in particular for CVC funds who have a fiduciary responsibility to their investors that they are making good investment decisions. In the CVC fund structure outlined in Chapter 2, the investment managers, who are the individuals you are working directly with, are paid by their investors (limited partners in their fund) in part because of their ability to evaluate good opportunities and avoid investment in high-risk situations. This requires leaving no stone unturned in verifying what you are presenting, including performing background checks on the individuals running the business. Investors will only invest in a business when they have total assurances that the investment has been sufficiently audited in all respects.

As such, due diligence is an intensive process that can feel highly intrusive. It is necessary, though, and well-run companies welcome being scrutinized and understand that professional investors cannot approve or structure an investment without performing due diligence. One company commented that although they didn't complete an investment with a fund that went through due diligence with them, they know more about their business after the process and were better at managing the company as a result of going through the process despite not closing the investment.

The Components of Due Diligence

Investor due diligence can be broken down into two parts: preliminary due diligence and confirmatory due diligence. Due diligence can be very expensive and time consuming, so neither the investor nor the company wants to submit to the deep investigations until they know there is a transaction that could otherwise get to the finish line if everything goes positively. Investors will:

- Hire third-party consultants and experts;
- Expect to speak to all your customers and employees;
- Find other personal references;
- Perform background checks; and
- Hire attorneys and accountants to structure and audit the transaction.

This is even more complicated when multiple entities are involved as in mergers and for publicly traded companies.

The full process of due diligence can take 45 to 90 days. It is common for investors to ask for some level of exclusivity if they go into this phase in earnest. This not always a bad thing and each situation is unique, but investors want to know that if they spend time and money you won't back out of the deal. This is actually an affirmation of their commitment to getting to the finish line, so be prepared for this to come up. Your attorneys should be in a good position to advise you so don't sign anything without first reviewing it with your legal team.

Due diligence can be broken down into the period before a term sheet is issued and then after it is executed. Pre-term sheet diligence is preliminary. What investors are really looking for is enough detail to make an informed decision. For example, potential investors will want to know if you have stated that you have any key customers, contracts, or agreements critical to your company performing. If an investigation of those came back as untrue or negative, investors would likely not wish to move forward in the process. If all the due diligence confirms the facts you present, they will be more likely to complete the investment. The information needed at this point is largely financial in nature and is used to structure a term sheet.

Due diligence is a process unto itself and can be broken into the step before a term sheet is issued and the step after as "Preliminary Due Diligence" and "Confirmatory Due Diligence," as outlined in Figure 10.2.

Following in Figure 10.3 on page 202 is a generic initial information request. This is just the start of a comprehensive evaluation but indicative of the categories that will be investigated quickly and will be different for each company.

Once an investor starts making information requests, it is expected that you will set up a data room. A *data room* is a virtual folder that contains all the information about your company on a shared drive. You will give the investor access so they and their team can review and evaluate the information and collect it in one consolidated location. If the investors follow the format of the information request in Figure 10.3, then the best

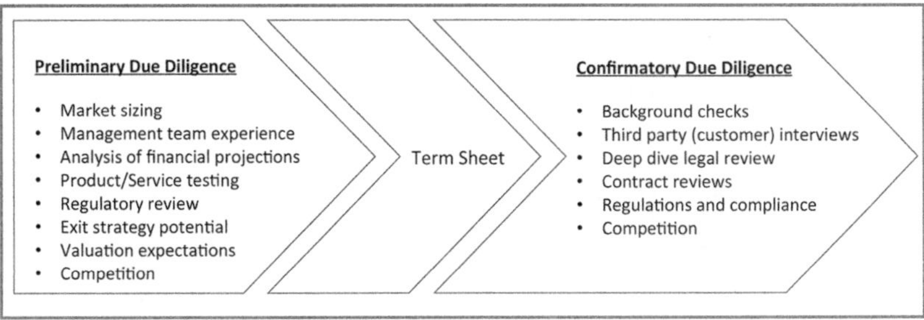

FIGURE 10.2—Due Diligence Steps

1. Organization and Structure
    - Corporate organizational chart
    - Board of directors meeting minutes
    - Management bios
2. Financial Information
    - Audited financial statements
    - Financial model
    - Capitalization table
3. Operational Overview
    - Contracts and agreements
    - Machinery and equipment leases (if applicable)
4. Research and Development
    - List of current programs
    - List of completed programs
5. Suppliers
    - Top ten suppliers
    - Supplier agreements
6. Products and Markets
    - Top ten competitors
    - Market and consulting reports
7. Sales and Marketing
    - Top ten customers
    - Customer agreements
    - Competitors
8. Intellectual Property
    - List of patents, trademarks, and copyrights
    - Software license agreements
9. Management and Employee Matters
    - Employment agreements/benefits

FIGURE 10.3—Initial Due Diligence Information Request

- Employee option details
- Background checks

10. Regulatory Review (company specific)

11. Property or Other Asset

FIGURE 10.3—Initial Due Diligence Information Request, continued

approach is to create folders for each of the 11 categories in the data room and organize the files under each sub section within those folders.

Every company has to manage a variety of issues and complexities unique to their inception and growth story. This usually means that there are elements of the company or about the people involved that the entrepreneur has some degree of anxiety about sharing with investors. Due diligence is exactly intended to uncover these elements so that the investment can be made with total transparency. The best approach is to be upfront and direct the investor right away to the things that you have the most concern about. The investors will find out, so it's better that they find out from you and not discover it on their own. And with transparency, it may not mean that the investment is outright declined but might instead be adapted to the terms of the investment to take those situations into consideration.

Any claims you make at any point in your contact with investors will be dissected. For example, if you claim to have an exclusive contract with a customer and this contact is the cornerstone of your business plan, financials, and valuation, you can expect the investor to contact the customer and ask about the agreement. If it turns out that the contract is not actually signed yet, being negotiated, or not exclusive after all, this would be a major red flag for any investor. Inaccurately characterizing or overstating the elements you think investors will have the most excitement about will bring into question your business acumen. Anyone with deep business experience knows the difference between a contract negotiation and a signed agreement, so you should act accordingly. It also brings into question your credibility and honesty, and that alone is a difficult description to reverse or come back from.

Being prepared for the forthcoming investigative process is essential. Figure 10.4 is a consolidation of advice collected from the dozens of investor interviews conducted for this book. You can review these and think about how they apply to your specific situation, making notes in the journal worksheet as you go.

Look at each piece of due diligence advice below and think about how it applies to your own company. Use the advice as a jumping-off point for how you plan to handle your own due diligence process.

When charts are presented, they don't speak for themselves and bring on more questions than answers. Everything you present should have a purpose and be verifiable and easily understood without you there to provide additional context or interpretations.

____

____

Facts, figures, and numbers all need to be cited as defensible figures from credible sources.

____

____

Make sure your math is correct. Any calculations must stand up to independent verification. There is nothing worse than an investor checking a net income calculation in a meeting only to find out your financial model had an error in it.

____

____

Keep the tone professional. Pitch decks with offensive or unprofessional images or language are a turn off. In particular, using terms like

FIGURE 10.4—Due Diligence Pitfalls Journal Worksheet

"bud," "dope," or "spliff" are pejorative and don't reflect the kind of professional company culture investors want to back.

Time is valuable, so don't share more information than needed or include unnecessary slides. You really don't need to spend any time on the market. Any investor will be talking with you because they are enthusiastic about cannabis, and every investor interviewed for this book had the same advice: "Just get to what the business does right away."

Being courteous of time also relates to the amount of information and emails you send. Investors' time is valuable, so anything you ask them to read is asking them to put you on their to-do list.

Know your company's strengths, but also share the weaknesses—many investors were once entrepreneurs and they love to add value in addition to capital. Give them a roadmap to do so and demonstrate that you have the humility to know you won't have all the answers. Otherwise, why would you be raising money?

Ensure you make the ask: How much do you need, how much are you selling or paying in interest, and what will you do with it?

FIGURE 10.4—Due Diligence Pitfalls Journal Worksheet, continued

Be able to provide vetted financials and be able to explain and defend the balance sheet, P&L statement, and cash flow statement.

___

___

Be able to provide employment agreements for key personnel. Knowing who the key people are, how they are compensated, and the terms for termination and restrictive covenants such as non-competes and confidentiality agreements.

___

___

Understand and identify how you make money and what agreements or historical facts are going to give certainty to your ability to generate sales and profits.

___

___

Real estate (if your business requires it) is an asset and can be a safety net. Make sure yours is locked up via a lease of appropriate length or owned outright and the properly titled.

___

___

Confirm the status of related entities. Investors want to make sure they're buying into all affiliated enterprises because they want your efforts focused on building value for the entity they are investing in. If you have affiliated or co-owned businesses, disclose them and pre-emptively explain why you need multiple entitles. In the age of vertical integration, it's common for companies to have multiple legal entities. What investors have no interest in is backing a management

FIGURE 10.4—Due Diligence Pitfalls Journal Worksheet, continued team that is only spending part of its time on the business they are raising the capital for if the investor doesn't have equal exposure to the value being created by their activities.

Know your affiliates, joint ventures, and commercial partners. Be prepared to offer a list of all the key companies you do business with and provide a point of contact. Affiliates are dangerous for investors because they can be or may have been used to remove money from the operating company that investors have an interest in. Be aware of this when asking an investor to put money into a company that does business with other companies you hold a stake in.

Be able to defend your expenses. If you are spending $60,000 on a website or $350,000 per year on marketing, be able to tell an investor why those amounts are necessary.

Know your competitors, and remember there is no such thing as "no competition." Identify who your competitors are, or you run the risk of looking like you don't know your marketplace. Clearly show how you have identified the competition and how you compare. Remember that competing on "customer service" is not differentiated in business today. All companies need to provide good customer service or die.

FIGURE 10.4—**Due Diligence Pitfalls Journal Worksheet**, continued

Be prepared to explain the exit plan. Know what the investor is looking for and seek alignment.

Understand what intellectual property is, what you actually have (awarded patents are very different from patent pending), and how it equates to value or benefit for your business.

Know and show your corporate structure. Org charts are helpful (both for ownership and management).

Management is key; it's all about the people. Do you know your current board structure? Are you offering a board seat with the investment? Multiple seats? Veto rights?

FIGURE 10.4—Due Diligence Pitfalls Journal Worksheet, continued

Confirmatory due diligence refers to the diligence that an investor undertakes when the decision has been made to fund an investment once details are confirmed in the first round of due diligence. This part of due diligence begins with a signed term sheet. As stated above, this is a very exhaustive activity, and both parties can suffer from deal fatigue if the process drags on for an extended period. It's your job to ensure that you are responding in a timely and thorough manner. As an investment banker once told me: "Deals aren't like a fine wine; they don't get better with age." Before going into this deep-dive step, it's best for both parties to have the investment structure negotiated and accepted to avoid spending a lot of time, effort, and money only to find that the terms both parties would endorse are too far apart to consummate the transaction. This why it is advisable that the term sheet is executed before moving into full diligence.

Entrepreneur Due Diligence

The discussion of due diligence to this point explains how to be on the reciprocal end of an investor's process. Due diligence is, however, a two-way process and this sometimes gets lost. It's appropriate and advisable for entrepreneurs to also conduct an inquiry into the investor. This is to ensure that the fund and people involved are suitable partners. The main thing that entrepreneurs can and should ask for is an introduction to other founders or management teams that the investor has been involved with. It's important to talk to others who are in the position that you are looking to be in. You want to make sure the investor is your capital partner and you are both in a long-term business relationship, even though you will likely encounter conflicts and a difference of opinion. You are both exploring how you will handle those situations during the due diligence process, so talking to other entrepreneurs who have been backed by the investor will give you some insight into their management style, how active they are in the companies they invest in, and what additional value they can bring to the company beyond just capital.

Both parties are interviewing each other for a working relationship during this time. The analogies to getting married are accurate in that it's a long-term commitment, but it's better to think about the partnership less emotionally. To find out how each party will perform on the promise of success after the transaction is largely informed by the clues they leave in their past. So the arrangement the parties enter into is more like a very thorough and thought-out prenuptial agreement than an outright marriage. You can rush into marriage and do it quickly and emotionally. This is not so with transactions, so you need to do your homework. Neither party can negotiate in an informed manner without deeply understanding each other.

PHASE III: COMMITMENTS

In every transaction, there is a tipping point where both parties can see that the momentum is moving towards a successful closing. Commitments need to be made and memorialized in the definitive agreements (all the documentation specific to the investment needed to close the terms of the deal) so you can clear a path for memorializing terms. The investor will be going through their final investment committee approvals, and the company will be seeking their board approvals to issue the new shares or security for the investment. The attorneys will begin working on the documentation as outlined further in Chapter 11.

This is a nuanced part of the process in that the deal isn't technically closed, but it does require that each party be comfortable with investing in completing any remaining due diligence, negotiating terms and drafting agreements, and scheduling closing dates to include the funding of the investment.

Term Sheet Negotiations

Negotiation of the term sheet is a central point for the transaction. This is the point where the investor is making you an offer contingent on completing due diligence successfully. Specific terms will be agreed upon, finalized, and drafted into an agreement. Every deal is different, so there is no one term sheet template that applies to every deal. I'll walk you through some common terms of private investment transactions in Chapter 11. You can also find standard venture capital term sheets at the National Venture Capital Association website (www.nvca.org).

During this entire process, you are being reviewed and evaluated by the investors. As Emily Paxhia, co-founder of one the earliest cannabis investment funds, Poseidon Asset Management, points out:

> *Negotiation around the term sheet is a harbinger for how the working relationship will be going forward. Start the process of defining terms early to align expectations; it is akin to an interview process for the entrepreneur. They run into the most problems when they don't have clarity on their financials or don't contemplate*

the structure and what it would do for a follow-on round. But a prepared founder can explain why they are going to say "no" to certain terms.

This cuts both ways, as in due diligence you are evaluating the investor as well. This is just an example of how through the process of working on an investment together, you will get a good indication of how your collaboration will develop in the future.

The Closing

Closing a transaction is the task of collecting the final executed agreements and documentation. It is also the final checkpoint in the investment process and the main driver of the activities, and in particular the timing, of all the prior steps. The closing date is negotiated in the term sheet, and both parties will look to hold each other to the timeline set forth to complete due diligence. The following is a sample of a generic list of closing items for an investment in a private company.

For an LLC:

- $ Articles of Organization
- $ Operating Agreement and Business Plan
- $ Shareholder and Definitive Agreements
- $ Resolutions Authorizing Investment

For a Corporation:

- $ Shareholders Agreement
- $ Share Purchase Agreement
- $ Schedules to Share Purchase Agreement:
  - No Conflicts
  - Capitalization
  - Required Consents and Approvals
  - Litigation
  - Permits, Products and Regulatory Compliance
  - Financial Statements
  - Intellectual Property
  - Employees

- Benefit Plans
- Agreements
- Affiliate Arrangements
- Employment Contracts
- Stock Certificates
- Business Plan

Closing is a shared task between the direct investor and the company or management team. Both parties will look to manage each other to complete the transaction on time. Delays by either party are not a good sign. Many times, as items come up in due diligence, the investor may discover something that is an impasse to closing and will need to delay the date or back out of the deal altogether. This is ultimately the investor's prerogative, and at no time should the investor or the entrepreneur be pushed to close without being absolutely ready.

Closing is the final action taken by both parties, and although it is a conclusion to this process, it is also the starting point of a partnership between the existing management team and the investor who are now bound together to move forward as financial and operational partners.

CANNABIS CAPITAL TAKEAWAYS AND ACTION ITEMS

Investors will approach any investment with a structured process and disciplined approach to how they evaluate, perform due diligence, and structure a transaction to clear the way to the financing. As the entrepreneur raising capital, you need to manage a detailed process. Understanding inflection points from the perspective of the investor will help you manage your time and resources efficiently to produce the desired outcome, a funded investment. In the ideal situation that you have multiple investors interested in your business, your informed process will be both respectful of what information they need at each stage and how to mature the transaction. Or at times decide quickly to abandon the transaction and move on to other more fruitful activities.

Action Item: Prepare a Dossier of Identified Investors

While you are doing your research on potential investors, when firms come up as potential candidates, it is a good use of your time to do some deeper research in to the people involved. You can create a one- or two-page dossier for each member of the investment team. Start with what you can find online through sources like LinkedIn and then do a deeper dive and answer question such as:

- Where did they grow up?
- What schools and universities did they attend?
- Are they married? Do they have children?
- What investments have they made that they are personally on the board of?
- What jobs have they had throughout their career?
- Do they have any hobbies you can identify through social media?
- Are they active in philanthropy or any not-for profits?

This is not meant to be a background check but rather a task that forces you to understand who the people are that you will be presenting to and potentially working with. Relationships—even business relationships—are built on trust, performance, and rapport. Any opportunity to align yourself with personal interests of investors and highlight compatibility in how you will successfully manage the business together will help both parties move to the right deal.

Action Item: Prepare Your Process Roadmap

Figure 10.5 on page 214 is an example of a simple roadmap tracking form that you can use to manage your team and resources through the capital-raising process. Each category is broken down into the elements that the other steps are depending on being completed in order to keep moving the process forward. Note that there are accountabilities with people on the management team who are responsible for managing that activity. This type of template can be used as a dashboard to communicate internally with the team and keep timelines on track.

Capital Raising Roadmap - Process Timeline and Responsibility Calendar

Anticipated Timeline

Activity	Resp.	Week Beginning Week 1 - dd/mm/yy	Week 2 - dd/mm/yy	Week 3 - dd/mm/yy	Week 4 - dd/mm/yy	Week 5 - dd/mm/yy	Week 6 - dd/mm/yy	Week 7 - dd/mm/yy	Week 8 - dd/mm/yy	Week 9 - dd/mm/yy	Week 10 - dd/mm/yy	Week 11 - dd/mm/yy	Week 12 - dd/mm/yy	Week 13 - dd/mm/yy	Week 14 - dd/mm/yy	Week 15 - dd/mm/yy	Week 16 - dd/mm/yy	Week 17 - dd/mm/yy	Week 18 - dd/mm/yy
Phase I - Outreach																			
Preparation																			
Business Plan Sign Off		x																	
Financial Forecast Sign Off		x																	
Use of Proceeds Completed		x																	
Management Presentation & Marketing Material Sign Off		x	x																
Transaction Objectives Defined		x																	
Legal & Finance Review		x	x																
Practice Run Presentations		x	x																
Valuation Review & Expectations		x																	
Identification																			
Database of Potential Investors			x																
Investor Research and Dossiers			x	x	x														
Solicitation																			
Launch Date of Outreach to Database			x																
Follow Up & Interest Confirmed				x	x														
Collected Feedback Internal Review					x	x													
Questions & Answers Submitted to Investors						x	x												
Phase II - Investigation																			
Presentations																			
Schedule Roadshow Dates					x														
Management Presentations						x	x	x											
Discovery																			
Initial Due Diligence Information Request						x	x	x											
Set up Dataroom					x	x	x	x	x										
Legal Review & Responses to Investor Questions						x	x	x	x										
Provide Third Party Contacts for Investor								x											
Company Side Due Diligence																			
Request References from Investors Portfolio of CEOs								x	x	x									
Terms																			
Receive Initial Term Sheets									x	x									
Review & Respond										x	x								
Re-issue Agreed Final Term Sheet											x								
Execute Non-Binding Term Sheet											x	x							
Phase III - Commitment																			
Due Diligence																			
Provide Full Investor Access to Due Diligence Dataroom													x	x					
Respond to All Due Diligence Requests													x	x	x	x	x	x	
Completed Full due Diligence Process																		x	
Definitive Agreements																			
Select Final Investor Group																	x	x	
Prepare Definitive Agreements																		x	
Closing																			✓
Closing Scheduled			<------------First ~45 Day Checkpoint------------>						<------------Second ~45 Day Checkpoint------------>										

FIGURE 10.5—Process Roadmap Plan

As with any negotiated business objective, both parties need to perform discovery (due diligence) and agree to the terms and conditions precedent to consummating the deal. The next chapters will explore more fully the terms and elements of structing the investment and what happens after you close the transaction (no, you don't go on vacation for a month to celebrate). Now that the uncertainly is manageable through your process, you can think about what happens in the next phase of growing your company.

DEAL TERMS

by Michael Schwamm, partner, Duane Morris LLP
with Justin Santarosa and Neeraj Kumar

There are several key terms (deal points) and agreements that are typically negotiated in an investment transaction. Understanding those terms will equip you to negotiage better on behalf of your company and ultimately have a successful capital raise. As discussed elsewhere in this book, the valuation of the company is one of the key terms that must be decided early on in the capital-raising process. With a valuation set, the company can then determine the amount of stock that will be sold in the offering. In this chapter, we'll walk through the major terms and potential agreements you need to know to successfully secure an investor. First, let's talk about who owns your company and why that is important.

OWNERSHIP CONSIDERATIONS

The cannabis industry is highly regulated and, as such, the ownership of a cannabis business is regulated as well. These regulations can come in many forms such as a restriction on ownership by public companies, out-of-state investors, or other license holders. While the rules and regulations in each state vary, typically an owner of a licensed cannabis business will need to have the ownership approved by a state regulator. An owner generally includes the officers, directors, managers (in the case of an LLC), and controlling shareholders (the thresholds for controlling shareholders range from 5 to 20 percent). Ownership approval generally requires an owner to submit detailed personal information, and fingerprints, and submit to a criminal background check. Additionally, a list of the owners of a licensed entity are typically publicly available.

Further, certain states, such as California, require the disclosure of any individual investor who owns an interest in a licensed entity, regardless of the size of the investment. These individuals do not need to submit fingerprints or undergo background checks, but the information provided is subject to Freedom of Information Act (FOIA) laws and may become public.

As a result of these requirements, investors may be wary to invest because of perceived or actual reputational risks of being associated with a cannabis business. It is important from the outset to inform investors of these potential disclosure requirements to avoid having investors pull out at the last minute or refuse to provide the required information to have their ownership approved.

To alleviate concerns, it is possible to limit the size of an investment or to have an investor invest through a different investment vehicle. However, the trend among regulators in the industry is to have more disclosure of all owners of a licensed entity, including those that do not hold a controlling interest. As discussed below, it will be important for the documents to clearly outline any disclosure and approval requirements related to ownership of the company.

It is important to note that even if the company receiving the investment is a holding company of the licensed operating company, the investors in the holding company will be subject to the disclosure requirements even though they only have an indirect ownership interest in the licensed entity.

REPURCHASE RIGHT

In some cases, acts of certain equity holders (such as a criminal record) could compromise a company's ability to obtain or maintain its license. In such instances, the company would need the ability to cut ties with the holder in order to preserve its license.

As such, a company should consider including something called a repurchase right. A *repurchase right* gives the company the right to purchase the shares from the shareholders at a particular price in the event that a holder, as a result of its equity ownership, either fails to have such ownership approved by the applicable cannabis regulator or a disqualification event occurs that compromises the company's ability to qualify as a license holder as a result of actions taken by the individual after their ownership had been approved (e.g., a felony conviction).

The price at which the company may exercise the repurchase right will likely be subject to heavy negotiation. The investor is going to want the price to be the fair market value of the company at the time of the disqualification event. However, the company will want to fix the price at the price paid for the shares. Setting the price at the original purchase price can work as negative incentive for stockholders to avoid actions that could jeopardize the company's license.

DIVIDENDS

A *dividend* is the distribution of a portion of a company's earnings paid to a company's shareholders, which can be structured as a cash dividend or stock dividend. Dividends are one of the rights that often make a company's equity securities "preferred" (relative to common), and, depending on the terms, are typically paid to preferred stockholders before being paid to the common stockholders.

Dividends are often stated as a percentage of the price paid for the preferred stock by the investors. In the cannabis industry, and especially in venture deals, the dividend rate will tend to be higher to reflect the risk that the investor is taking in investing in an early-state company but are often deferred or paid in stock to avoid a cash drain.

In negotiating a venture deal, a company should understand the various ways dividends can be structured, and consider the likelihood that cash flow will be available to pay dividends currently and the dividend structure's impact on its common stockholders. There are at least three common ways dividends are structured in venture capital deals:

- Cumulative dividends
- Non-cumulative dividends
- Dividends on preferred stock only when paid on the common stock

Cumulative Dividends

Cumulative dividends, which are the most common, are the most beneficial to the preferred stockholders and the least favorable to the common stockholders. Cumulative dividends are calculated for each fiscal year, and the right to receive the dividend is carried forward until the dividend is either paid or until the right is terminated. Even if the company suspends dividend payments, the unpaid dividends owed (known as "dividends in arrears") will continue to accrue and will be paid to the preferred holders in a lump sum when the company liquidates or redeems the preferred stock. As a result, the accruing dividends represent a future obligation of the company to the preferred stockholders and reduces funds available for common stockholders. Cumulative dividends may be structured on a simple basis or on a compound basis, where all prior accrued and unpaid dividends are taken into account in determining future dividends.

Non-Cumulative Dividends

Non-cumulative dividends refer to a stock that does not pay the investor any dividends that are omitted or unpaid. If the board of directors of the company does not declare a dividend during a particular fiscal year, the right to receive the dividend extinguishes for that year. So even though a preferred stock carries a 7 percent dividend, if the board of directors does not declare dividends in a given year, the investor will not have the right to claim any of the unpaid dividends in the future.

Dividends Paid on an As-Converted Basis

The third method of structuring dividends is to have a dividend paid on the preferred stock only if paid on the common stock. The preferred stock is treated as if it had been converted into common at the time the dividend is declared, and the preferred and common stock share in the dividend as if all shares were converted to common. This dividend structure is the least beneficial to the preferred stock and the most beneficial to the common stock.

LIQUIDATION PREFERENCE

The *liquidation preference* dictates the payout order in the event a company liquidates itself or in certain circumstances such as a sale (a "deemed liquidation event"). Typically, the preferred stockholders will get their money back first, ahead of other kinds of stockholders, in the event that the company must be liquidated, sold, or goes bankrupt. Liquidation preferences are typically expressed as a multiple of the price paid by the investor. For example, if the liquidation preference on the preferred stock is one time (1x) the original price paid by the investor, the preferred stockholder will be paid back 100 percent of their investment before any other equity holders.

There are three common ways liquidation preferences are structured:

- Participating Liquidation Preference
- Non-Participating Liquidation Preference
- Capped Liquidation Preference

Participating Liquidation Preference

The participating liquidation preference (also known as double-dip preferred) is most favorable to investors. Under a participating liquidation preference, the preferred stockholders will receive their liquidation preference and then will share in any additional proceeds in proportion to its equity ownership.

Non-Participating Liquidation Preference

Non-participating liquidation preference (also known as straight preferences) are the most commonly used. Under a non-participating liquidation preference, preferred stockholders can choose to either 1) receive their liquidation preference or 2) share in the proceeds in proportion to their equity ownership after converting their preferred shares into common stock.

Capped Participating Liquidation Preference

Capped participating liquidation preference (also known as partially participating preferred) are considered equally favorable to investors and the company. Under a capped liquidation preference, preferred stockholders will be paid back their liquidation preference and then will share in any additional proceeds in proportion to their equity ownership, subject to a cap.

For example, preferred stockholders with a 1x initial preference and a 3x cap on participation will receive the aggregate of: 1) a distribution equal to their initial 1x liquidation preference and 2) a pro-rata distribution along with common stock, in an amount equal to 3x the original issue price.

CONVERSION RIGHT

A *conversion right* is the right to convert shares of preferred stock into shares of common stock. There are two types of conversion rights: optional conversion and mandatory conversion.

Optional Conversion

An *optional conversion* right permits the preferred stockholder to convert its shares of preferred stock into shares of common stock, initially on a one-to-one basis.

For example, let's assume that the preferred stockholder has a $5 million, 2x non-participating liquidation preference, representing 30 percent of the outstanding shares of the company, and the company is sold for $100 million. The investor would thus be entitled to the first $10 million pursuant to its liquidation preference, and the remaining $90 million would be distributed ratably to the common stockholders. If the preferred stockholder, however, elects to convert its shares to common stock pursuant to its optional conversion rights (thereby giving up the liquidation preference), it would receive $30 million.

Mandatory Conversion

A mandatory conversion requires the preferred stockholder to convert its shares of preferred stock into shares of common stock upon a triggering event, such as an initial public offering (IPO) of a pre-determined value and/or a multiple of the original price of the stock. This is typically referred to as a Qualified IPO.

ANTI-DILUTION PROVISION

When a company issues additional shares of equity securities, the additional issuance has a "dilutive" effect on the ownership percentages of all the company's existing stockholders. An anti-dilution provision protects a preferred stockholder and if shares are issued or sold below the price they paid by issuing the holder additional shares.

An anti-dilution provision protects a preferred stockholder from equity dilution resulting from later issues of stock at a lower price than the price paid by the investor. Total shares outstanding may increase because of new shares being issued due to a round of equity financing or perhaps because existing option owners exercise their options.

The two common types of anti-dilution clauses are known as "full ratchet" and "weighted average." The company will prefer to use "weighted average," and an investor would prefer to use "full ratchet." Here's why.

In a *full ratchet anti-dilution provision*, the conversion price of the preferred shares is adjusted downward to the price at which new shares are issued in later rounds. For example, an investor who paid $2 per share for a 10 percent equity ownership in a company would get more shares in order to maintain that stake if a subsequent round of financing were to come through at $1 per share. The investor would have the right to convert its shares at the $1 price, doubling their number of shares.

The weighted average anti-dilution provision is a little more complex. Under *weighted average anti-dilution*, the conversion price is determined using the following equation:

$$C2 = C1 \times (A + B) / (A + C)$$

In this equation, the variables equal the following:

C2 = new conversion price
C1 = old conversion price
A = number of outstanding shares before new issue
B = total consideration received by the company for the new issue
C = number of new shares issued

The weighted average anti-dilution formula adjusts the rate at which preferred stockholders convert into common stock based upon two things:

- The amount of money previously raised by the company and the price per share at which it was raised, and
- the amount of money being raised by the company in the subsequent dilutive financing, and the price per share at which such new money is being raised.

Thus, a new reduced conversion price for the preferred stock is obtained, which results in an increased conversion rate for the preferred stock when converting to common stock.

PROTECTIVE PROVISIONS

Protective provisions are typical in venture deals and provide the preferred stockholders the right to approve certain decisions made by, or with respect to, the company. These approval rights are of critical importance to a company and its investors and often involve significant negotiation. Protective provisions will address key issues such as:

- $ A liquidation, dissolution, or wind-up of the company's affairs; or the effect of any merger or consolidation or any other deemed liquidation event;
- $ Amending the company's certificate of incorporation or bylaws so as to alter or change the powers, preferences, or special rights of the shares of preferred stock so as to affect the holders adversely;
- $ Increasing or decreasing (other than by conversion) the total number of authorized shares of preferred stock or common stock;
- $ Authorizing or issuing of any equity security with a preference over, or on a parity with, any series of preferred stock with respect to dividends, liquidation, or redemption;
- $ Redeeming or purchasing shares of preferred stock or common stock (subject to certain exceptions);
- $ Any declaration or payment of any dividends or any other distribution on account of any shares of preferred stock or common stock; and
- $ Any change in the authorized number of directors of the company.

TRANSFER RESTRICTIONS

When an investor owns shares in a private company, there are restrictions for the company and the investor that govern how they can sell their shares to third parties or transfer ownership through a transaction.

DRAG ALONG RIGHTS

A *drag along rights* gives majority investors the ability to sell a company to a third party without consent from minority shareholders. In a sale of the company, the minority shareholders agree to sell the entirety of the stock they own. In a merger, the minority shareholder agrees to vote in favor of the merger.

TAG ALONG RIGHTS

Tag along rights, also known as "co-sale rights," are similar to drag along rights, except they guarantee minority shareholders the right to sell their shares in the company at the same time and under the same conditions as the majority shareholders. In sum, tag-along rights require the majority shareholder to include the holdings of the minority shareholders and gives such shareholders the ability to capitalize on a deal that a larger shareholder is able to identify and negotiate.

RIGHT OF FIRST REFUSAL

Under the *right of first refusal* (ROFR), in the event that a founder wants to sell any of their shares to a third party, the ROFR requires them to first give the company the right to purchase the shares on the terms and conditions offered by the third party. If the company elects not to exercise its ROFR, the preferred shareholder then has the right to purchase the shares on the same terms and conditions offered by the third party. If neither the company nor preferred shareholders exercise the right, then the founders may proceed to sell their shares to the third party.

REGISTRATION RIGHTS

In a venture deal, the shares that are purchased by investors are considered restricted shares. In other words, they cannot be transferred or sold by the shareholder without being registered with the SEC or pursuant to an applicable exemption from registration. A *registration right* is a right that entitles an investor who owns the ability to require a company to list the shares publicly so that the investor can sell them. There are two types of registration rights: demand registration and "piggyback" registration.

Demand registration rights allow the holders of a certain percentage of registrable securities to require that the company register its shares after a certain period of time, typically three to five years after the investment or six months after an IPO. The number of times the investors can make this demand can be negotiated; one or two is usual.

Piggyback registration rights, as the name implies, enable holders of registrable shares to participate in the registration of any other class of shares by the company.

BOARD SEAT

Depending on the size of the investment, certain investors may ask to have a board seat with the company. The company would agree to nominate a director proposed by the investors each year. The right to the board seat will usually terminate upon certain events, such as the investor holding less than a specified percentage of stock (common or preferred) in the company, the completion of an IPO, or the mutual agreement of the parties. As discussed above, the board member is likely to be subject to regulatory approval. Therefore, any right to a board seat should include provisions that require the investor to nominate only individuals who will not be disqualified from being a board member of a licensed cannabis company.

INFORMATION RIGHTS

Information rights are rights that a preferred stockholder has to demand to receive regular updates from the private company about its financials and operations, such as:

- the right to receive quarterly financial statements;
- the right to receive annual audited financial statements;
- the right to receive any periodic reports required by securities laws;
- the right to receive documents, reports, financial data, and other information as reasonably requested;
- the right to visit and inspect the company's properties, including books of account;
- the right to discuss company's affairs, finances, and accounts with the officers; and
- the right to consult with and advise management on all matters relating to the company's operation.

DOCUMENTATION

The terms discussed above are going to be included in several definitive documents that will set forth all the rights and obligations of the parties. These documents will likely include a stock purchase agreement, the certificate of incorporation, investor rights agreement, right of first refusal, and co-sale agreement and voting agreement.

Stock Purchase Agreement

The *stock purchase agreement* is the document by which the investors agree to pay the purchase price for, and the company agrees to sell, the preferred stock. The stock purchase agreement will contain representations and warranties of the company and the investors. The investors will make representations that include, among other things, they are accredited investors and have the ability to purchase the shares under applicable securities laws, and that they will not be disqualified from owning an interest in a cannabis company. It will also contain the closing conditions for the investment.

The stock purchase agreement should also contain an exhibit that an investor can complete that will ask for the relevant information needed to provide to the cannabis regulators for approval of such ownership interest by the investor. The agreement will also contain a corresponding closing condition that the exhibit must be completed prior to closing.

The company can include additional covenants that require the investor to cooperate in good faith with the company's cannabis regulators both in connection with the approval of the investor's investment, with periodic reports, and with any license renewals.

Certificate of Incorporation

Immediately prior to the closing of the investment, the company will need to amend its certificate of incorporation to include several of the key terms discussed above, including the liquidation preference, the dividend, the mechanics of conversion, if any, the anti-dilution provisions and certain voting matters such as protective provisions and director seats.

Investor Rights Agreement

The *investor rights agreement* is an agreement between the company and the investors that typically governs the registration rights, lock-ups, and information rights. If there is a lead investor, the investor rights agreement may also contain additional provisions regarding matters requiring the lead investor director's approval and board observation rights.

Right of First Refusal and Co-Sale Agreement

This agreement will contain the rights of first refusal, drag-along rights, and co-sale rights, if any.

Voting Agreement

The voting agreement is an agreement to be entered into by the company, the investors and all pre-existing stockholders of the company. This agreement requires all the parties to vote their shares in accordance with the agreement and generally includes obligations regarding the size of the board and voting for director designees.

CANNABIS CAPITAL TAKEAWAYS AND ACTION ITEMS

Now that you have a basic knowledge of the deal terms for raising capital through private investors, you can start to formulate the range of terms that you would like to see in any transaction that you close. It's a good idea to start reviewing with your attorneys and current shareholders the terms you will offer to investors. Term sheets are negotiated and therefore you should prepare the ideal terms and set the limits for what you would accept. The first term is valuation, and it's a good idea to go into any negotiation with a range you would accept. This allows you to work within a range and adjust other terms to accommodate where you end up on your valuation range.

Action Item: Standard Term Sheet Review

The National Venture Capital Association (www.nvca.org) provides a standard venture capital term sheet template on their website. This is an excellent place to start reviewing what is considered standard for the venture capital industry, and they make this template (along with other great resources) available to help entrepreneurs be more informed around structing deals with venture capitalists.

CHAPTER 12

WHAT COMES AFTER CLOSING

During the investment period, the investors and the entrepreneurs are running an intensive process with one aim in mind: to close the investment. Everyone is heads down closing the deal, the lawyers are working overtime, the founders and the board will be spending late nights approving and structuring the transaction, and employees are on edge waiting for the security of the funding to be in place so they can start scaling the business. Many times, in all this flurry of activity, no one stops to really think about what happens after the deal is closed. It's exciting and euphoric to get to the finish line with the investment, but in a practical sense, this is actually not the finish line, but the starting point. The business can now accelerate, grow, and scale with the financing partners in place, and the operations will adapt and update to support the responsibility of managing a larger company with more investor capital at risk.

It is healthy to take some time to celebrate achieving something very difficult to accomplish, securing investment for your company. Don't wait until the day after to really think about how the business will change and operate tomorrow. The company will be forever changed. There are a number of controls and activities you will be required to comply with now that you have a responsibility to your new investors and exiting investors along with all the stakeholders of the organization. What happens AFTER the investor writes a check?

The agreements you sign to secure the funding will include all the terms that have been negotiated, but those terms (as outlined in Chapter 11) will set your requirements that you need to fulfill as part of your responsibility in continuing to run your business. This is referred to as *governance* and is built around a set of covenants that dictate operating controls, policies, and bylaws. This falls under your communications or investor relations activities and defines the part of your new role as a steward of capital.

GOVERNANCE

Requirements to fulfill your obligations to your shareholders are what governs your company moving forward and how to remain in compliance. When an investor owns less than 50 percent of a company, they are considered a minority investor. This means that they are unable to actively influence the day-to-day activities of the company on which the success of their investment is relying on. Investors will require certain operational decisions to be dealt with as if they were a majority shareholder so they can adequately influence those decisions to protect their investment. These are called negative covenants because they block certain activities and relate to situations when things are not going well but also when things are going really well and key decisions need to be made for the future of the company. Loan agreements also have covenants, and if the company is not in compliance with those restrictions, the loan is considered in default.

Examples of negative covenants include enforcing spending limits, approving the hiring and firing of senior leadership, taking on debt or executing a merger, and acquisition or sale of the company. The definitive agreements for the investment will also dictate reporting requirements. Some investors will want to see monthly reports and updates, and some will only require year-end reports and all the tax filings they require in a timely manner. Each company is different and at different stages, so each situation is unique in that respect.

Investors exhibit influence on these decisions by requiring the management team to seek approval at the board level. This is why board seats are so important and investors will insist on them when they make an investment. Your board should always be an odd number (three, five, or seven) to avoid a tie in any vote. Investors will require that in order to follow through with actions related to these covenants decisions will require either a unanimous vote or require their explicit approval. A family office investor once shared with me that they always like to patriciate on the compensation committee (boards will form committees to manage the elements of their oversight). How the company is compensating the team is usually a good indication of how the company is performing. Overcompensating too early is as problematic to a business as is under-compensating or rewarding the team for success.

Another example of a situation that may require approval by the investor is when the company enters into a merger, wants to make an acquisition, or is considering being acquired or going public through an initial public offering. In these situations, the investor will want to play an active role in what is decided, as the performance of their investment is at risk. The terms of the transaction and probability of success will directly impact all the shareholders who will want to be able to defend their investment in the context of a transaction.

The trick is while you are negotiating these terms before the deal is consummated that you are being collaborative with the investors and recognize the need to have these operating controls in place, while taking into consideration the operational burden when you are running the day to day. An investor might seek to approve all spending over $50,000 for example. This would make sense when cash is tight and the company is bootstrapping, so anything over that amount may seem to be a considerable amount of cash at one time related to the amount of the investment. The investor made the investment, so it can be spent on building value in the company. Therefore, you should expect that they will be collaborative and not hinder the business, as they have an interest in seeing you succeed.

A $50,00 spending limit may represent a large portion of the investment, and therefore the investor will want to have the ability to confirm spending at that level. This may, however, not make sense in the context of how the business operates. You may need to buy $50,000 a month in inventory as a general course of business, and seeking their approval each month for a standard activity might be onerous to manage practically.

You should also be identifying how active the investor wants to be in the management of the company before closing. There are passive investors, active investors, and activist investors. A passive investor is likely to simply ask for the standard reports and not want to get actively involved in running the company. They might be happy to attend one annual review meeting. This is more typical for angel investors, friends and family, and some family offices or ultra-high net worth individuals. Venture capital investors and the majority of family offices are very active and want to be involved at the board level, may refer people to join the management team, and certainly want to be abreast of all the major developments of the company, especially to offer help at difficult times. Activist investors like to be very involved in the company, and many times will be adversarial to affect change when things are not going how they expected.

Activist investors can be extremely destructive in smaller companies so just be aware of what the expectations are going into the investment. The best-run companies understand the football analogy that "owners can't coach and coaches can't play." You won't see Art Rooney II, the owner of the Pittsburgh Steelers, jump on the field and catch a pass in a game or call plays for Coach Tomlin. Everyone in the organization has specific roles to play and when the right controls are in place, each can excel.

INVESTOR RELATIONS

I don't know anything about you or your company, but I can guarantee you there will be a situation in the not-too-distant future when things will go wrong. And when they do, they will probably go wrong in a big way. How you react and manage your organization will largely impact how successful you will be in navigating the inevitable crucibles of entrepreneurship. How you communicate with your investors will have a major impact on your ability to manage successfully through the tough times.

Good investor relations begin immediately after you secure the investment, and you should not wait until you are in a difficult situation to start communicating with your investors. In addition to your required investor reports and board meetings, it is wise to set a cadence and format through which you will proactively communicate with your investors. This can take the form of monthly updates that may include sending an email or a letter, hosting a conference call each quarter, or inviting investors to periodic management team meetings that are outside of the purview of the board. Attending industry conferences together can be a great way to find time in person and share what is happing in your direct markets with customers, suppliers, competitors, and regulators.

The last thing you want to have happen is that your investors are surprised by anything. Creating consistent communication and offering additional ways to interact when things are going according to plan will give you the tools you need to be proactive with your investors when you need to communicate challenges or outright bad news. Facing these tough conversations is just part of running a company. The worst thing you can do is try to mask a major issue or hide the situation in the hopes that you can work through it and not have to share the bad news. Taking accountability for when the performance of the company is not meeting expectations is very difficult but a situation that all entrepreneurs will face.

When you have to address a problem, the best approach is to identify the issue and any underlying issues that led to it. Once you and your team understand the issue, you must communicate it in a timely fashion to investors. It's a good practice to do so not simply to be the bearer of bad news, but to also present solutions to the investors so you can get alignment on how to manage through adversity. Present the issues with two or more options for taking the business forward given this new information. This will impact your strategic and operational plan, and you want your investors to be able to offer support and advice in deciding how to navigate any new approaches. The options may be severe such as laying off people, implementing austerity plans and stopping spending, or closing the business altogether. It is likely that one or more of your options will require more capital. If you are seeking additional investment from your shareholders, keeping them up to date on the events, making sure they are aware of the situation, and actively working with them to assess and implement strategic alternatives will increase your ability to finance through a difficult situation.

During the initial stages of an investor evaluating you and your company, this is the type of situation investors are trying to assess your response of. Emily Paxhia, co-founder of Poseidon Asset Management, describes in detail how she works with her management teams when a company is in trouble:

> *Always present bad news to your investors quickly and clearly. If you try and hide something, it will come out, and that erodes the trust with the investor and you will likely be going to and seeking more money as a result. Active investors have networks and resources that can be helpful in managing through problems, and there will always be problems, so be direct and up front about the issues because things always go wrong.*
>
> *As an investor, when you have to have difficult discussions, I try to be honest, direct, and compassionate. They may not like it but it treats the induvial and companies with respect, and more often than not, the entrepreneurs become empowered and rise to the solution because they can handle fair and direct feedback.*

Investors often describe entrepreneurs who are adept at investor relations and have the potential to handle crisis as being good "stewards of capital," a phrase that is becoming more and more common in the world of entrepreneurship.

STEWARD OF CAPITAL

The term *stewardship* is used broadly to describe when someone has an ethical responsibility to care for and oversee the maintenance of resources and assets that have separate or shared ownership. In the case of entrepreneurship, when you have investors participate in your company you are responsible for successfully deploying their capital in effective and efficient ways. Your stewardship of the investors' capital implies that the decisions you make will be in the best interest of everyone and you will defend the equity of the company and the health of your balance sheet. You are responsible for what happens with that capital and then how it translates to value and the overall health of the company.

As a founder, CEO, or other officer charged with running the company, you have a legal obligation to act in ways that are in the best interest of all the shareholders. This is called your *fiduciary duty*. This responsibility informs all aspects of your corporate governance and terms of the transaction. This is a very serious legal matter that all founders need to consider and can result in major legal issues.

A fiduciary has an obligation to treat all shareholders fairly. This means that the fiduciary cannot unfairly enrich themselves at the expense of other members of the shareholder group, irrespective of their percentage ownership. The fiduciary owes a duty of loyalty and a duty of care. Loyalty means that they act in the group's interest, not their own, and avoid conflicts of interest. Duty of care requires competency in how the individual performs. Were the actions taken similar to how other businesses would operate? Is the individual acting in their own interest above the interest of the shareholders or acting in ways that are not standard in how professional businesses are run?

Post-closing the investment, your board becomes the central resource responsible for corporate governance and has a legal responsibility for oversight of financial, strategy, transactions, and personnel and policy. The management team is responsible for day-to-day decisions within the guidelines set forth by the board. Having a well-run board with strong board members is a necessity in operating as a good steward of the investors capital and within your fiduciary duty to your other shareholders. Figure 12.1 shows the relationships in hierarchy of governance between the board, investors, and management team. The non-legal implications is a duty of trust between you and your stakeholders.

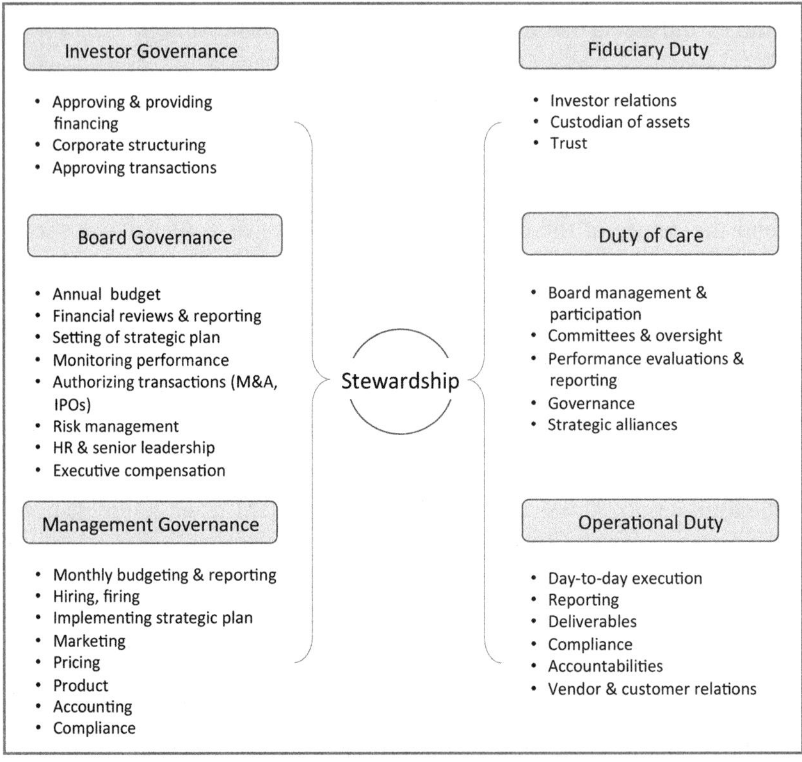

FIGURE 12.1—Corporate Governance

Joe Mimran, a former Dragon on *Dragon's Den* (the Canadian version of *Shark Tank*) is an active private investor in a number of cannabis companies. He looks for investors who "walk the walk." He defines this concept of stewardship quite simply as the "integrity" of the entrepreneur:

Are they being honest with their projections? Entrepreneurs with experience know how to vet their business plans before looking for capital and experienced investors know how to measure their risk tolerance, perform their due diligence, and then move quickly. It's the entrepreneurs who are clearly on a path to building a beautiful business and have a true passion that are the founders I want to be associated with.

He is essentially describing the ultimate multidimensional entrepreneur and sees "beauty" in well-run companies. He looks for "passion, humility, coachability, knowledge of themselves, and the thirst to acquire knowledge" in the founders that he invests in. These elements influence your approach to stewardship. You will be compelled legally to do your best to perform, but at the end of the day, the health of your relationship with your investors is built on trust. Performing and being proactive will create a track record of trust and help you deliver value to your shareholders as a steward of capital.

 CANNABIS CAPITAL POST-CLOSING TAKEAWAYS AND ACTION ITEMS

Go forth and win the day! It's an exciting time to be a cannabis entrepreneur, investor, regulator, or consumer, and I commend you on your initiative in accessing this resource in your endeavors. The keys to your success will in the end be about how you perform in the cannabis economy and access the resources you need to build a "beautiful company." Knowing who your ideal investors are, how to present to them a winning proposition, and manage through a sophisticated process to securing investment are all milestones in the path ahead. Or, they might be in the path you have already taken, and now you find yourself in the wonderful position of managing your company and team going forward.

These final series of Cannabis Capital Action Items should be on your to-do list right away after the investment is closed:

1. Schedule your first board meeting along with the following:
   a. Nominate committees and a corporate secretary
   b. Ratify the business plan for the next 90 days

2. Set dashboards and reporting
3. Schedule a 90-day review meeting

Action Item: Schedule Your First Board Meeting

Your first board meeting is critically important to hold immediately after closing the investment. You need to ratify any new board members and observers who are outlined in the closing agreements. It's a good step to be very proactive in scheduling the first board meeting and then running the meeting professionally. A typical board meeting agenda will include:

1. Call the meeting to order
2. Review and approve meeting agenda
3. Approve the meeting minutes from the prior meeting
4. Business review by the CEO
5. Presentation of financial reports or updates
6. Committee reports
7. Unfinished business
8. New business
9. Adjourn

It's important that you have someone nominated as the secretary for the board to capture the meeting minutes. Each meeting needs to be memorialized and recorded in the corporate records. If your business is more established, you will already be doing this and can now include your new board members. If not you need to start this right away after closing. If you plan to be involved in any transactions in the future, you will need to provide access to the meeting minutes in any due diligence process.

In this first meeting you should review the strategic plan and recommend that board committees be formed. A common committee for a company that just raised money is for hiring and compensation. It is likely that a meaningful part of the investment will be allocated to hiring and recruiting. The committee will oversee this activity, help produce policies, and recommend compensation structures. This committee will also oversee the recruitment process for any senior leadership roles that will report to the board or the CEO.

When you review the business plan with the board, you can set certain milestones and objectives that will outline what you expect to achieve in the next 90 days. It's not common to manage the board with this level of detail, but as an initial board meeting it's probably a good idea to set some achievable milestones and critical goals that you can track and report back in the next board meeting.

Action Item: Set Dashboards and Reporting

You can only manage what is measurable. Now that you have the funding in place to back the plan that you and your investors are expecting, you should review your reporting and make any adjustments or changes. Some companies will have daily dashboards that are submitted to the executive team, weekly status reports, or some schedule of updates that is appropriate. You should have a good idea as to the information (KPIs) you will need to see and in what level of frequency to know if the business is performing.

Action Item: Schedule a 90-Day Review

On the day after you close the investment, you should start preparing for a 90-day review. This is a critical first three months with your new investors and likely new people involved in the company. By setting a checkpoint, you can align the activities and key milestones that you need to meet to confirm that you are on track. And you, of course, will be because you did all the hard work to secure an investment that included a well-thought-out game plan for the company! You know what you need, why you need it, what to track, and what value will be created when you achieve your goals.

By condensing your focus into the first 90-days, you will engage with your team and stay laser focused on transitioning from a startup to a well-funded growing company. This meeting should be held separately from your board meetings. You should engage your management team in the review and then report back to the board the updates from this initial check-in.

EPILOGUE—HAPPY CBD COMPANY, LLC

When we first met Betsy, she and her sister invested $1 million together to start the Happy CBD Company, LLC. They quickly started selling products and found themselves hiring people, purchasing inventory, and building the systems and infrastructure to grow the business further. Once Betsy started analyzing her financial performance, she realized that additional capital would be required to fulfill the potential of the company.

Fast forward three years later, and Betsy not only raised the investment capital she sought, but the business grew so much that some other CBD companies have made offers to buy the business, something she never considered when she started out. She has started interviewing investment bankers to represent her and is meeting the first banker for coffee. When they sit down, the banker asks her how she got into the business in the fist place.

"When I started this, I just thought it was a great way to make money and earn a decent income," Betsy says. "All I really wanted was my independence and to run a small business that allowed me to live a decent lifestyle for me and my family. I struggled with that as we started to grow so quickly. I soon found myself doing things that seemed so administrative, and it took some time to be able to produce data that I could use to manage the business like dashboards and financial reports. But once we did, the potential for HCC was obvious and significant. I never started with a clear business plan, but we knew we had something that could be really big." The banker replies by reaffirming that she has built a great business, but in order to advise her properly, they also needed to understand how she secured her investment capital.

"It wasn't easy," she says. "We got lucky in a few respects in that I had a friend who worked at a cannabis venture capital fund, and he gave me some good advice early on. Ironically when it came time to actually pitch his fund, we knew that we needed to have a well-run process and talk to multiple investors. So we spent a lot of time researching who we should reach out to, if they invested in our type of company, and how we should think about terms. The team had a lot of late nights and internal debates on what the valuation of the company really was. It was just my sister and me who had money at risk. The thing that kept me up at night was that I didn't have the infrastructure to scale the business or keep up with demand. I was concerned that without an investor we would run ourselves out of business and lose everything. People were relying on me to make payroll, and at that time I saw the greatest risk in our company out of anyone."

Betsy knows that she has accomplished a lot but doesn't feel any regret for the deal she did to finance the company and goes on to say, "We received terms from several funds that were all a little different. But you know what is interesting? We accepted the offer from the investor who presented us with the lowest valuation for the company." She sees the banker react to this statement, and before he could ask why, she says, "It was the fund that my friend worked at. So despite talking to several funds, we went with the group we knew the best and who knew us the best. Although they came in with the lowest valuation on day one, they explained to us clearly why they valued the company the way they did, and was the only fund that was willing to provide firm commitments for additional capital should we need it. And we did, so it turned out to be the right thing to do.

"I remember walking into the first board meeting after I closed the venture round three years ago. The month right before we closed was our first month of declining sales since the company started. It was certainly nerve-racking to be holding my first formal board meeting and start with presenting some negative news about financial performance. But because of the relationship, the board member from the fund was a true partner and helped us navigate a rough patch. Looking back on it, the performance was probably due to spending the time raising capital, and we might have lost sight of the day-to-day, even just briefly. But the investors helped us come up with a plan, and we managed through the next year without requiring any additional capital." The banker asked why the took additional capital from the investors if this was the case.

"We came across a small software company that we could buy. It wasn't expensive, and we immediately saw a huge cost savings when we brought it in house. The best part is that in the following year the profitably of the company passed a major threshold that triggered some additional bonuses and equity for me personally. So when I look at the adjustment with those incentives, I was able to benefit from the value I created in the company. So it was almost as if I received a higher valuation when we first did the deal."

The banker thinks to himself that Betsy is one really smart CEO, and he really wants to win the engagement to represent HCC. He's eager to ask why Betsy would want to sell the company now. "Well, that's a good question. Simply put, I have made a lot of money, and my investors have received some nice dividends so far. But it's time to explore a liquidity event that will deliver an exceptional return for my investors. If you can bring us to the right buyers, my smaller piece of a bigger pie will make me wealthy beyond my expectation of what was possible when we started this company."

ABOUT THE AUTHOR

Ross O'Brien is the founder and CEO of cannabis venture capital fund Bonaventure Equity (BVE), and founded the Cannabis Dealmakers Summit (CDS), a series of industry conferences and investment forums. Ross sits on the boards of Green Ignition Ventures (GIV) Florida's first cannabis accelerator, CannaMexico, and is the author of *Cannabis Capital* the first book on cannabis venture capital for Entrepreneur Press.

Ross has a broad spectrum of private company expertise ranging from starting and operating high growth businesses to numerous Venture Capital and private equity transactions, advising portfolio companies on mergers and acquisitions transactions and capital introductions. He has taught entrepreneurship and finance, held board positions and spent his career primarily working with and advising family offices on their self-directed private equity investing activities. He has been an advisor for programs on investing, entrepreneurship and impact investing at MIT and Harvard and was on the steering committee that launched Tech Runway at Florida Atlantic University where they still teach the Entrepreneur Bootcamp program he designed and authored.

Prior to relocating to Florida, Ross worked on Wall Street with a boutique New York investment banking firm and was a manager at Geller & Company and an assistant vice president at JPMorgan Chase. His experience also encompasses many entrepreneurial ventures ranging from being the first employee of a UK based Digital Media Technology firm responsible for launching their North American business to the founder of a digital technology company, which he and his partners exited in 2006. He began his career at Sony BMG and has international experience working in the UK, Europe, Hong Kong, and Canada.

Ross holds an MBA from Fordham University and obtained a bachelor's in business marketing and management from Ferris State University. He also holds his Series 79 and 63 securities licenses.

INDEX

W